THOUGHTS ON RELIGION.

AND OTHER SUBJECTS.

BY BLAISE PASCAL.

A NEW TRANSLATION, AND A MEMOIR OF HIS LIFE,

BY THE REV. EDWARD CRAIG, A.M. OXON.

MEMBER OF THE WERNERIAN SOCIETY.

EDINBURGH:
H. S. BAYNES, 26, GEORGE STREET;
AND W. BAYNES AND SON, LONDON.

M.DCCC.XXV.

Publishing Statement:

This important reprint was made from an old and scarce book.

Therefore, it may have defects such as missing pages, erroneous pagination, blurred pages, missing text, poor pictures, markings, marginalia and other issues beyond our control.

Because this is such an important and rare work, we believe it is best to reproduce this book regardless of its original condition.

Thank you for your understanding and enjoy this unique book!

CONTENTS.

	PAGE.
PREFACE,	vii
MEMOIR OF BLAISE PASCAL,	13
CHAP. I. On Self-Knowledge,	1
II. The Vanity of Man,	8
III. The Weakness of Man,	13
IV. The Misery of Man,	28
V. The wonderful contrarieties which are found in Man with respect to truth, happiness, and many other subjects,	40
VI. On avowed indifference to Religion,	47
VII. That the belief of a God is the true wisdom,	57
VIII. Marks of the True Religion,	64
IX. Proofs of the True Religion, drawn from the contrarieties in Man, and from the doctrine of Original Sin,	74
X. The due subordination and use of Reason,	84
XI. The character of a Man who is wearied with seeking God by reason only, and who begins to read the Scriptures,	87

CONTENTS.

		PAGE.
Chap. XII.	The Jews,	93
XIII.	Of Figures,	104
XIV.	Jesus Christ,	114
XV.	Prophetical proofs of Jesus Christ,	119
XVI.	Other proofs of Jesus Christ,	127
XVII.	The purpose of God to conceal himself from some, and to reveal himself to others,	132
XVIII.	That the Religion of real Christians, and real Jews, is one and the same,	138
XIX.	We cannot know God savingly, but by Jesus Christ,	141
XX.	Thoughts on Miracles,	145
XXI.	Miscellaneous Thoughts on Religion,	153
XXII.	Thoughts on Death, extracted from a Letter of M. Pascal, on the occasion of the Death of his Father,	194
XXIII.	A Prayer for the sanctified use of Affliction by Disease,	205
XXIV.	A comparison of Ancient and Modern Christians,	217
XXV.	On the Conversion of a Sinner,	223
XXVI.	Reasons for some opinions of the People,	228
XXVII.	Detached Moral Thoughts,	236
XXVIII.	Thoughts on Philosophical and Literary Subjects,	254
XXIX.	On Epictetus and Montaigne,	265
XXX.	On the Condition of the Great,	278

PREFACE.

THE original Manuscripts of Mons. PASCAL's Thoughts are deposited in the Royal Library of Paris. They were in the Library of the Abbey of St Germain des Pres, but having been saved from the fire in the year 1794, which consumed that building, they were deposited where they now lie. They are arranged in one large folio volume; and there is with them, a copy made at the time of printing the first edition of the work, most probably by M. Guerrier, a Benedictine Monk, which very materially assists the reading of the original; but even with this aid, the difficulty is not small.

When the MM. de Port Royal published their edition in 1670, they adopted an arrangement of the Thoughts into chapters, which was still very imperfect; and according to this arrangement, many other editions were published both in France and Holland. In the year 1776, Condorcet published an edition with notes, which, though better in the arrangement, was only a selection of about half the original Thoughts, such, in fact, as might answer his nefarious purpose of blunting the edge of Pascal's masterly arguments against infidelity; and by corrupting the text, and exposing it to ridicule in his comments, bringing his authority as a writer on the side of truth, into contempt. With this view, he appended to his edition a series of notes, of the profanity and wickedness of which, there can now be but one opinion. Some of these notes were Voltaire's; but two years afterwards, Voltaire published an edition of his own, with additional notes by himself, equally objectionable. In these editions, many of the Thoughts are mutilated and altered from the original text, to suit the particular purpose of these infidel writers, and almost all of them, on which any remark is made, are attacked by their keen and biting sarcasm.

Up to this period, therefore, no complete edition of the Pensées had appeared; but in the year 1779, an edition of the whole works of Pascal was sent forth, edited by M. Bossut. He had no occasion to leave out those passages, which the earlier editors withheld from fear of the Jesuits; and he had no wish to follow the dishonourable example of the two infidel philosophers. He printed, therefore, every thing which he could find, adding a number of Thoughts from the

Histoire de Literature, of the Pere Desmolets, and collating the whole with the original papers. He adopted, in some measure, the order which Condorcet had chosen, but not without some improvements. Since then, two small editions of the Thoughts, with a few additional gleanings, were issued by M. Renouard, in the years 1803, and 1812; and in the year 1819, a very complete edition of the whole works was printed at Paris, the editor of which, professes to have availed himself of every advantage which the labours of his predecessors set before him. From the text of this last edition, the present Translation is made.

The Translator is only aware of two English translations of the Thoughts being in existence. Neither of these is complete. They are both made from copies of the work, earlier than the edition of Bossut. One of them is a very antiquated version; and the other, is little more than a reprint of it, a little modernized in the style of expression, together with a few additional Thoughts. Many of the passages in both these, are so very ill rendered, as to convey no definite meaning whatever.

A fresh and a complete Translation of the whole of the published Thoughts became desirable, that Pascal might be really known in this country to the English reader, according to his real merits. As far as the moral and religious Thoughts extended, this has been now attempted.

To translate Thoughts so inaccurately and imperfectly expressed as many of these are, and to give a close and literal rendering that would, at the same time, convey the sense, which, in the original, is really in some instances enigmatical and questionable, was a task of serious difficulty. The Translator does not profess to have accomplished this. If he has done something towards the ultimate attainment of such a faithful version of this valuable book, he will feel thankful. And in the mean time, he will readily avail himself of the critical remarks of those who may differ from him, as to his conception of the Author's idea in any place, with a view to reconsider the passage, in case the work should ever reach another edition.—He has certainly not satisfied himself.

The first three chapters of the original work have been left out, as not being connected immediately with its general object. And the Translator does not hesitate to avow, that he has withheld a few passages, which occur occasionally, on the subject of the peculiar tenets of the Romish Church; because he did not feel warranted, by the mere wish to record faithfully in a translation, all the sentiments of an Author, to circulate what he believes to be dangerous error;

and which, from the strength and accuracy of other statements among which it was found, might lead some weak minds astray. Had the task of original publication devolved on him, he would have felt differently: for it is right that every man should have a fair opportunity of giving his opinions to the world. But in making a translation for the benefit of a subsequent age, it is perfectly equitable to select that which common consent has stamped with its approbation, and to leave out the few remains of prejudice and unscriptural opinion, which might borrow, from the sanction of such a name, an influence that they ought not to have.

Finally, the Translator does not hesitate to say, that the intervals of time, which the duties of an active pastoral charge allowed him to give to this work, and to the meditations which its pages suggested, have been among the happiest and most gratifying portions of his life; and, that if this version, though imperfect, shall afford even a moderate share of such gratification to those readers who are shut out from the pages of the original, or shall lead others to seek for that pleasure in the original text, he will have realized an ample reward.

GREAT KING STREET, EDINBURGH,
1st June, 1825.

MEMOIR

OF

BLAISE PASCAL.

ALTHOUGH the facts of PASCAL's Life cannot but be very extensively known, it seems scarcely correct to send forth a fresh translation of his Thoughts to the world, without a brief Memoir of that extraordinary genius.

BLAISE PASCAL was born at Clermont in Auvergne, 19th June, 1623. His father, Stephen Pascal, was first president of the Court of Aids, and had, by his wife, Antoinette Begon, three other children, a son who died in infancy, and two daughters; Gilberte, married to M. Perier, and Jacqueline, who took the veil in the convent of Port Royal in the Fields, and died there of grief, arising from the persecutions under which that community suffered.

Stephen Pascal was a superior and well educated man, and possessed an extensive knowledge of the Law, of Mathematics, and Natural Philosophy; to which he added the advantages of noble birth, and of manners peculiarly simple. Till the year 1626, he shared with an amiable wife, during the intervals of public occupation, the duties of educating his family; but in that year she died, and he then devoted himself exclusively to this object. For this purpose he retired from office; and having continued a few years in the country, in the year 1631, brought his family to Paris to complete their education.

The attention of Stephen Pascal was, of course, chiefly occupied with his son, who gave promise, at a very early age, of superior genius, and readily received the elementary principles of language, and of the sciences in general; but one of the earliest features of those talents which were subsequently developed, was the eagerness, and the nice, and accurate discernment with which, on all subjects, he sought for truth, and which would not allow him to feel satisfied till he had found it.

The circle of his father's acquaintance was of a superior order. He numbered among his friends, Mersenne, Roberval, Carcavi, Le Pailleur, &c. At their occasional meetings, for the discussion of scientific subjects, Blaise Pascal was sometimes allowed to be present, at which times he listened with great attention to what passed, and thus gradually formed the habit of scientific research. To trace effects up to their causes, was one of his chief pleasures; and it is stated, that at eleven years of age, having heard a plate give forth, on its being struck, a musical vibration, which ceased on its being touched again, he applied his mind to the subject which it presented to him, and at length produced a short treatise upon the nature of sounds.

His father, however, fearful that this evidently strong predilection for scientific pursuits would delay his progress in the attainment of classical learning, agreed with his friends that they should refrain from speaking on such topics in his presence; and this opposition to his evidently ruling tendency was, on principle, carried so far, that on his making an application to his father to be permitted to learn Mathematics, the permission was positively withheld, till he should have mastered the Greek and Latin languages. In the mean time, he obtained no other information on the subject, but that Geometry was a science which related to the extension of bodies—that it taught the mode of forming accurate figures, and pointed out the relations which existed between them. But beyond this general information, he was forbidden to inquire; and all books on the subject were positively forbidden to him.

This vague definition, however, was the ray of light which guided him onward in Mathematical study. It became the subject of continued thought. In his play hours, he would shut himself up in an empty room, and draw with chalk on the floor, triangles, parallelograms, and circles, without knowing their scientific names. He would compare these several figures, and would examine the relations that their several lines bore to each other; and in this way, he gradually arrived at the proof of the fact, that the sum of all the angles of a triangle is equal to two right angles, which is the thirty-second proposition of the first book of Euclid. The young geometer had just attained this point, when his father surprized him, deeply occupied in the prohibited study. But he was himself no less astonished than his son, when, on examining into the nature of his occupation, he ascertained the conclusion to which he had come; and on inquiring how he arrived at it, the child pointed out several other principles which he had previously ascertained, and at length stated the first principles which he had gathered for himself in the way of axioms and definitions.

To control, after this, such evident manifestations of superior mathematical genius, was quite out of the question. Every advantage was afforded to him, of which he eagerly availed himself. At twelve years of age, he read through the Elements of Euclid, without feeling the need of any explanation from teachers; and at sixteen, he composed a treatise on Conic Sections, which was considered to possess very extraordinary merit. He attained rapidly to a very high degree of knowledge and of celebrity as a Mathematician; and before the age of nineteen, he invented the famous Arithmetical Machine which bears his name, and by which, through the instrumentality of a mechanical movement, somewhat similar to a watch, any numerical calculation might be performed. The main difficulty in Arithmetic lies in finding the mode of arriving at the desired result. This must ever be a purely mental operation; but the object of this instrument was, that in all those numerical operations where the course to be pursued was fixed and certain, a mechanical process might relieve the mind from the monotonous and wearisome labour of the mere detail of calculation. Pascal's invention succeeded; but it was found too cumbrous for general use.

About this time, Stephen Pascal was appointed the Intendant of Rouen, to which place he removed his family. He remained there seven years; and during that period, his son diligently pursued his studies, although it was quite evident that his severe application had already affected his health, and marked him with the symptoms of decline.

Here his ardent mind, which had been turned during his retirement to the study of Physics, occupied itself with one of the most striking phenomena of the natural world, and did not rest till he had elicited a satisfactory explanation of it. This phenomenon was that in a pump, in which the piston played at a distance of more than thirty-two feet above the reservoir that supplied it, the water rose to the height of thirty-two feet, and no farther. On this question, Galileo had been consulted; and the explanation of this fact which was offered by him was, that the water rose to a certain height in the pipe, because nature abhorred a vacuum; but that the force by which she resisted a vacuum was limited, and that beyond a height of thirty-two feet, it ceased to act. This answer, however, was not even then satisfactory; and within a short period of that time, Torricelli, the disciple of Galileo, ascertained, by a series of experiments, that the cause of this ascent of the water in fountains and pumps, was the pressure of the weight of the atmosphere upon the surface of the reservoir. At this juncture, however, Torricelli died; but Pascal, to whom the result of his experiments had been communicated by Mr Mersenne, through Mr Petit, the Intendant of Fortifications at Rouen, having repeated the experiments of Torricelli, verified their results, and completely refuted the popular notion of the abhorrence of a vacuum. And in the year 1647, in a small tract dedicated to his father, he published the account of these experiments.

It does not however appear, that, at this time, he had arrived at a satisfactory solution of the phenomenon in question,—he had done little more than ascertained that it could not arise from the cause to which it had been attributed, according to the popular doctrine of the day, and that the notion of nature's abhorrence of a vacuum, had no foundation in fact. Pascal therefore followed out his inquiries most perseveringly; and in the year 1653, he wrote two pamphlets, one on the equilibrium of fluids, and another on the weight of the atmosphere; in which, by a series of satisfactory experiments, he completely established that doctrine on the subject, which is now universally received. The most important and original of these experiments were those which shewed that the rise of the water, or the mercury in the tube, varied in proportion to the height above the level of the sea, of the place where the experiment was tried. Many attempts have been made to rob Pascal of the merit of these discoveries, but they have altogether failed. It was however to be regretted, that the two latter tracts were not printed till 1663, the year following his death.

At the time, however, when M. Pascal issued his first tract on this subject, his health had manifestly given way before the severity of his studies; and at the close of the year 1647, he had an attack of paralysis, which deprived him, in a great measure, of the use of his limbs. He returned to Paris, and resided there with his father and sister, and, for some time, relaxed from study, and took several journies by way of recreation. But in the year 1651, he lost his father; and in 1653, his sister Jacqueline, in the fulfilment of a wish which she had long cherished, joined the sisterhood of Port Royal; and being thus left alone at Paris, for his other sister and M. Perier then resided at Clermont, he returned without restraint to those habits of severe and excessive study which must, in a short time, had they not been interrupted, have brought him to the grave. But his friends interfered, and their advice, seconded by the severity of his bodily afflictions, constrained him for a time to lay aside his studies, and to mingle more than he had done with general society. Here he gradually regained his spirits, acquired a fresh relish for the fascinations of life, and began even to think of marriage. But an *event* which occurred about this time, and which we shall have occasion afterwards to mention, dissipated all these thoughts, and gave an entirely new colour to his whole life, and tended especially to induce him to consecrate his splendid talents to the noblest of all employments,—the service of God.

There is reason to suppose, that the paralytic attack that Pascal experienced in the year 1647, first led him to the serious consideration of the subject of religion. He read, at that time, some few devotional books, and the effect which they produced upon his mind, was a clear conviction of the truth of the Christian religion, and of the propriety of its high requirements. He saw that it enjoined upon men the necessity of living for God, and of making Him the supreme object of their attention and love; and so strong was his conviction of this, that he determined about that time to renounce the studies to which, up to that period, he had so eagerly applied himself, and thenceforth, to devote the powers of his mind to that subject of supreme interest, which Jesus Christ has declared to be *the one thing needful*.

It is evident that the resolution then formed, did materially influence M. Pascal's whole character and habits, and that gradually he gave an increased attention to the subject of religion. Still there is reason to suppose, that the state of his mind underwent some material variations in this respect, and that, for several years, he was not altogether so entirely devoted to religious topics, nor so cordially separated from irreligious society, as he afterwards considered to be necessary. His residence at Paris, and his entrance into its society, with a view to recreation, tended, for a time, to dissipate in a degree his religious impressions, and to awaken a desire to return to the ways of that world which he had professed to renounce, and to those pursuits and pleasures, the vanity and fruitlessness of which he had already confessed.

It does not follow necessarily, that a man convinced of the truth, and feeling, in some degree, the power of religion, does at once, from the time of that conviction, give himself unreservedly and entirely to the duties and the pleasures of a religious life. Experience shews that there is a wide difference between the most satisfactory conviction of the understanding in favour of such a course, and the effectual and habitual controul of the strong passions of the heart so as to accomplish it; and too frequently it is found, that even after an individual has really seen and loved the religion of the Bible, and made the path which it points out the object of his decided preference,—the temptation to recur to the thoughtless and irreligious, but fascinating and seductive habits of the majority, again acquires fresh force; and though he may not be led aside sufficiently to allow his religious inconsistency to be seen, and reproved by less devoted men, yet he declines so far, as to exhibit to himself in a stronger light his own weakness, and to induce him to seek, when convinced of the need of recovery, for greater assurance, and more palpable assistance in the grace of the gospel of Christ.

This appears to have been the case with Pascal, during his residence in Paris. His sister, Jacqueline, witnessed with regret, on his occasional visits to her at Port Royal, the deteriorating effect of the promiscuous society with which he associated; and she remonstrated faithfully and earnestly with him on the necessity of greater decision, and the need of a more real and marked separation from those who lived only for this present world.

The mind of Pascal, however, notwithstanding these minor aberrations, had taken a decidedly religious turn; and the power of Scriptural truth gradually gained a permanent influence over his heart, and gave a colour to all his pursuits. His attention was drawn off from matters of merely sublunary importance, and fixed on the phenomena of the moral world, and the principles of that book which unveils to us the glories, and imparts the hope of an eternal existence; and this change gradually exhibited itself with greater distinctness.

The first public incident of his life which indicated this change, was of a controversial and scholastic nature. During his residence at Rouen, he attended a series of lectures on philosophy, in which the lecturer took occasion to advance some positions which tended to call in question the decisions of the church, and which led him to infer that the body of Jesus Christ was not formed of blood of the the Virgin Mary. M. Pascal addressed himself boldly to the suppression of this heresy. He first remonstrated with the lecturer; *but finding* this useless, he denounced him to the

Bishop of Rouen; and being foiled there by an equivocal confession, he carried the matter before the Archbishop, by whom the philosopher was compelled publicly to renounce the dangerous notions which he had advanced; and the whole of this process was conducted with so much temper, that the defeated philosopher never retained the least acrimonious feeling against his youthful antagonist. That Pascal should apply his extraordinary powers to combat and to give importance to such subtleties, is to be attributed to the genius of the times. In those days the grand and simple truths of revelation were much lost sight of, and theological knowledge and religious zeal were shewn in those metaphysical speculations, and those ready powers of logical discussion, which may gratify the pride of the understanding, but do not mend the heart.

Pascal was not, however, to be kept down by the trammels of the schools, and the semi-barbarous theology of the day. He read and thought for himself. It was impossible for a mind like his to do otherwise; and such was the practical influence of his religious studies on his character, that it was felt and acknowledged by all around him. Even his father, previously to his death, did not hesitate to learn at the feet of his son, and gradually reformed his own manner of life, and became more devoted to the subject of religion; and abounding in his later days in Christian virtues, at length died a truly Christian death.

The circumstance, however, which seemed in the

providence of God most effectually to influence M. Pascal's mind in favour of religion—to dissipate all remaining attachment to this world, and to give the especial character to his remaining years, was an accident which happened to him in October 1654. He was taking his usual drive in a coach and four, when, as they passed the bridge of Neuilly, the leaders became unmanageable at a point of the bridge where there was no parapet, and they were precipitated into the Seine. Happily the traces broke suddenly by the weight of the horses, and the carriage remained safely at the very verge of the bridge. Pascal's valuable life was preserved; but the shock which his frail and languishing frame sustained was very great. He fainted, and remained for a long time in a state of insensibility; and the permanent nervous impression which this alarm produced was so strong, that frequently afterwards, in moments of peculiar weakness, or during a sleepless night, he fancied that there was a precipice close to the side of his bed, into which he feared that he should fall.

It was after this event that Pascal's religious impressions regained that strength which they had in a degree lost. His natural amiability of temper,—his ready flow of wit,—the fascinations of the best circles of Parisian society, and the insidious influence of well applied flattery, had, previously to this accident, succeeded in cooling, in some measure, the ardour of his piety, and had given him somewhat more of the air of a man, whose hopes and whose treasures were to be found within the limits of this transitory and imperfect existence. But this providential deliverance from sudden death, led to a very decided and permanent change of character. He regarded it as a message from heaven, which called on him to renounce all secular occupations, and to devote the remainder of his life exclusively to God. From that time, he bade adieu to the world. He entirely gave up his habits of general visiting, and retiring altogether from merely scientific society, retained only the connection which he had formed with a few religious friends of superior intellectual attainments and devotional habits. In order to accomplish this the more effectually, he changed his residence, and lived for some time in the country.

He was now about thirty years of age; and it was at this time that he established that mode of life in which he persevered to the last. He gave up all search for earthly pleasure, and the use of all indulgences and superfluities. He dispensed as far as possible with the service of domestics. He made his own bed, and carried his own dinner to his apartment. Some persons may be disposed to consider this as a needless and ascetic peculiarity. Nor is it attempted here to justify the stress which he laid upon these minor and comparatively unimportant matters; but be that as it may, every one must admire the elevated piety with which these peculiar notions were associated, and the principle on which these acts of self-denial were performed. Prayer, and the study of the Scriptures became the business of his life, in which he found inexpressible delight. He used to say, that the Holy Scriptures were not a science of the understanding, so much as of the heart; and that they were a science, intelligible only to him whose heart was in a right moral state, whilst to all others they were veiled in obscurity. To this sacred study, therefore, Pascal gave himself, with the ardour of entire devotion; and his success in this line of study, was as eminent as it had been in matters of general science. His knowledge of the Scriptures, and his facility in quoting them, became very great. It was quite remarkable in that day. His increasing love for the truth of religion, led him also to exercise readily all the powers of his mind, both by his pen, and by his very great conversational powers, in recommending religion to others, and in demolishing whatever appeared likely to oppose its progress, or to veil and to deform its truth. An opportunity of the very first importance shortly afterwards occurred, which called forth the exercise of his splendid talents and extensive knowledge in that way which he most especially desired.

The sincere religion of M. Pascal, together with the connection of his family with the religious recluses of the Monastery of Port Royal, had gathered round him as his friends, many of the illustrious scholars and Christians who were associated together in that retirement. About the time when Pascal's mind had been led to the formation of his religious principles, and to the more serious adoption of his religious habits, the Monastery of Port Royal had risen into importance and notoriety, which were increased by the difficulties with which it had to contend. Under the superintendance of Angelique Arnauld, sister of M. Arnauld, the celebrated doctor of the Sorbonne, the society of female recluses there, had undergone a very extensive and thorough reform; and many young persons of superior rank and exalted piety had gathered round this renowned leader, and risen under her instructions, and the pastoral guidance of a few excellent men of similar sentiments, the male recluses of the same society, to still loftier attainments in the love of God, and in conformity to his revealed will.

At the same time also, many men of the first talents and acquirements, disgusted with the world, with the fruitlessness of its service, and the falsehood of its promises, and sick of the heartless and dissipated state of society around them, came to dwell together in a retired mansion in the same neighbourhood, and to seek in the solitude of the wilderness, that peace which the world cannot give. Among these were two brothers of the Mere Angelique, her nephews Le Maitre and De Sacy, Nicole, Lancelot, Hermant, and others. Here they devoted themselves to the instruction of youth, both in literature and science, and in religion, and their seminaries soon rose into importance. From this little society of recluses, issued forth many elementary works of learning and science, which became the standard works of the day; and such was their progress and the celebrity of the Port Royal schools, and the Port Royal grammars, and other treatises, that they seriously threatened the Jesuits with ejection from that high station which they had long almost exclusively held as the instructors and spiritual guides and governors of all the young people of condition throughout France.

The true principle of the Romish apostacy from the simplicity of the Christian faith, has ever been a despotic dominion over the consciences of men. That fallen and false church has, in all the varying phases of its condition, ever held this point steadily in view; and if a few words may delineate the essential feature of her enormous and unchristian pretensions, it is the substitution in the stead of true religion, of a system of terror and power, founded upon unwarranted and unscriptural assumptions, altogether contrary to the spirit of the gospel of Christ, which is the rational dominion of Divine influence over the heart, through the medium of the doctrinal truths of Scripture. To veil, in some degree, this presumption, and to render it palatable to men in general, Rome has gathered round her, in the style of her buildings, the formularies of her worship, the splendour of her attire, and the fascinations of her choral music, every thing that is imposing and calculated to seduce the affections through the medium of the senses. But as knowledge spread among the nations, and the art of printing providentially rendered the suppression of knowledge more difficult, it became necessary to adopt a more efficient system of police to guard all the avenues of this widely extended dominion of priestcraft over ignorance. The court of Rome, therefore, eagerly availed itself of the plan of Loyola, and the order of the Jesuits was established for the defence of the Roman Catholic church; and never was any system more admirably organized for such a purpose.

Framed from infancy to intrigue, and hardened to all the evils of the morality of expediency, these emissaries of the Roman power formed a complete system of police spread over the whole extent of Papal Christendom; and thoroughly informed, by means of auricular confession, of the secret history of courts, families, and individuals, and bound to each other in the most solemn manner by the covenant of their order, they were prepared to adopt and to vindicate any measures, however infamous, that might advance the cause of the church with which they were identified. History furnishes an abundance of well-authenticated facts of the darkest dye, to shew the boldness with which, at all risks, they rushed on to their object, and the dangerous errors with which they endeavoured to justify their crimes. There is in the unsanctified heart a fiend-like delight in power. Union is power: and for the sake of feeling that they have that power, men are content to become even subordinate agents, according to their capacities, in a great scheme, that they may thereby realize, by combination, an influence extensive, irresistible, and terrific, which no one could have obtained alone. This is most probably the secret of the efficiency of that system of ecclesiastical *espionage;* and it certainly was carried to such an awful degree of success, that the thrones of Europe, and even the Papal tiara itself, trembled before it. It was not therefore to be wondered at, that this powerful body, whose reign over France, at that time, was almost uncontrolled, should behold, with bitter malice, the growing influence and success of a few retired pietists, who now threatened to invade their chartered rights, and by the simple principles of Scriptural truth, to divide, if not to annihilate their power.

But while the prejudices and hostilities of the Jesuits were thus roused against the Port Royalists, it would not have been a consistent Jesuitical ground of complaint against them, to say that they endangered their craft. It was needful to seek an objection against them in the things concerning their God. And they soon found ample food to nourish and to embitter their venom, and to lay the basis of a plot for their ruin, in the sound doctrinal sentiments, and practical piety of these separatists from the corrupt manners of the time. And though probably the sentiments of these gentlemen might have been left unnoticed, but for their interference with the secular interests of the disciples of Loyola, yet when once these artful men had found real ground of hostility in the success of the Port Royalists in education, they were thankful indeed to find a still more plausible ground of assault against them, in the peculiarity of their religious sentiments. They rejoiced at the opportunity afforded to them of covering that envy, which originated in the success of their opponents in a course of honourable rivalry on the field of science, by the more specious pretext of zeal for the purity of the faith, and the integrity of the pontifical power. On this ostensible ground, therefore, a series of persecutions were commenced, which terminated only by the entire destruction of the brightest ornaments that ever graced the church of France.

In the year 1640, the celebrated work of Jansenius,* Bishop of Ypres, entitled, Augustinus, was published. It was published about two years after the death of the author, and is a very clear and luminous exposition of the doctrine of Scripture on the subject of the fall and redemption of man. It exhibits very prominently the opinions of St Augustine, and as distinctly condemns the Pelagian errors.

The recluses of Port Royal, who were diligent students of the Scriptures, and had derived their opinions from that source only, were led to adopt views precisely similar to those of Augustin and Jansenius; and the more deeply they searched the Scriptures by the mutual aid of superior intellect and sound erudition, the more abundantly were they confirmed in these opinions, and in rooted aversion to the whole system of false and ruinous theology then prevalent in the schools of the Jesuits. These opinions they did not hesitate to avow; and the Jesuits beheld with dread, the progress of a doctrine so fitted for the enlightening and comforting of the human heart, and the

---

* His real name was Otto; but at Louvain he was called first Jansen, or the son of John, and this in the Latinized form became Jansenius.

consequent decline of their popularity and their dominion, before the simple, but powerful statements of Scriptural truth.

It is a well established fact, that however plainly the Scriptures speak on these subjects, the careless multitude who have not religion at heart, and especially those ecclesiastics, whose chief object in the sacred profession has been its emoluments, will not receive the truths which those Scriptures teach; and hence the prevailing opinion, even among the teachers of the Christian church, has always been hostile to the gospel declarations of human corruption, and Divine mercy. So that in those days of ignorance and irreligion, although the doctrine of St Augustin had been formally sanctioned as the doctrine of the church of Rome, the authorities of that church were fully prepared by the corrupt bias of the irreligious mind, to act in direct opposition to dogmas which the church itself had recognized. To those who have not looked closely into ecclesiastical history, this may seem exextraordinary. But the fact is not uncommon. And the present state of religion, both in the English and Scottish Establishments, exhibits a case of a similar kind; the larger portion of the clergy in both churches holding doctrines decidedly opposed to the dogmatical statements of their standard documents, and in the strength of their majority, denouncing, as heretical, those members of the church whose opinions precisely and literally accord with their Articles and Confessions.

The Jesuits, therefore, relying on the preferences and strong prejudices of the great body of the priesthood, boldly assailed the writings of Jansenius, and the opinions of the Port Royalists; and a long and tedious controversy arose, in which M. Arnauld and several other members of the society of Port Royal abundantly distinguished themselves; but which did not appear at all likely to draw to a close, except as it threatened the Port Royalists with ruin, when Pascal was induced to take up his pen in defence of his persecuted friends, and of those Scriptural truths to which he was sincerely attached.

In the year 1656, M. Pascal published the first of his twenty celebrated letters, on the subject of the morality of the Jesuits, and which have been improperly called "The Provincial Letters." They were published first under the title, "Letters Written by Louis de Montalte to a Provincial, and to the Reverend the Fathers of the Jesuits, on their moral and political principles;" and from this they acquired the erroneous title by which they are universally known. Of the merit of these letters, nothing need be said here. They are known to every one. Even Voltaire has said of them, that "Moliere's best comedies are not so pungent in their wit as the earlier letters; and that Bossuet has nothing more sublime than the latter." They are now regarded as the first book which purified and fixed the French language. The effect of them was wonderful. The whole edifice of the *reputation* of the society fell before the power of

Pascal's genius. Their boldest casuists fled from the two edged sword of his manly and honest sarcasm. An universal clamour rose against them. They were on every side regarded as the corrupters of morals; and after having, in one or two pamphlets, most unwisely and vainly endeavoured to justify the system of casuistry which Pascal had exposed, they were compelled for a time to shrink before the scourge with which he had chastised them, and to bear in silence the general indignation of the more virtuous portion of society, which he had effectually roused against their errors.*

Enmity, however, such as theirs did not languish, because for a time, it was repressed. Though the multitude had now seen and abhorred the immoral principles of the Jesuits, they had not the means to overthrow their power. These were men who could resolutely and pertinaciously maintain their position after their character was gone. Their channels to influence over men of power, were too effectually occupied for any one to shake their dominion over the court and the government; and in the mysterious providence of God, a few years gave to this intriguing society a complete and bitter revenge. The history of the persecution, dispersion, and ruin of the saints of Port Royal, is perhaps one of the most interesting points in the annals of the Christian church. It does

---

* No serious attempt was made to answer the Provincial Letters for forty years.

most powerfully establish the truth, that the kingdom of Christ is not of this world, and that the reward of the true servants of God is reserved for another.

The contest of M. Pascal with the Jesuits continued for about three years, during which time, he was very much occupied. To expose their errors, required a very diligent study of their voluminous and useless writings; and though, in this respect, Pascal was much indebted to the labours of Arnauld and Nicole, yet much application on his own part was absolutely necessary. He says, " I have been asked if I had read all the books which I have quoted? I answer, No. To do this, I must have spent a large portion of my life in reading very bad books. But I have twice read the works of Escobar through; the others, my friends read for me. But I have never made use of a single passage, without having read it in the book from which I quoted, and without having studied the ground on which it was brought forward, and examined the context both before and after, that I might not run the risk of citing that as an averment, which was brought forward as an objection."

Application so close, could not but materially affect a constitution already seriously enfeebled by disease; and the evils which were gathering, were doubtless aggravated by the severe mode of life to which he rigidly adhered. His food was of the plainest kind. His apartment cleared of every thing like luxury, or even comfort; and in order to check the risings of *vanity, or any other* evil suggestion, he wore beneath his clothes a girdle of iron, with sharp points affixed to it, the inconvenience of which, must have been at all times great; but whenever he found his mind wandering from the one great subject, or taking delight in the things around him, he struck this girdle with his elbow, and forced the sharp points of the iron more deeply into his side. This fact cannot be recorded with approbation. It is one of the strong evidences of the evil occasioned by the false doctrines of the Church of Rome, that even a genius so elevated and liberal as that of Pascal, could not altogether free itself from the errors of education. What a far more effectual principle of reform is the love of Christ! All the bodily suffering which we can inflict upon ourselves, will not be sufficient alone to inspire one holy, or restrain one unholy thought; but a faithful, affectionate lifting up of the soul to the God of all grace, is blessed by Divine appointment as the means of victory over temptation; and they who have sincerely tried this "more excellent way," have realized its success. They know what is the liberty wherewith Christ has made them free.

But though Christians, in a day of clearer light and richer privilege can discern the error into which Pascal had been led, and can mourn over the bondage in which he was still retained, yet they who know the difficulty of a sincere and uncompromising service of God, will look with reverence at these evidences of serious devotion to the cause of holiness, and admire the resolute self-denial which dictated and endured such extraordinary sufferings. It is surely not becoming in the careless, sensual professor of the Christian faith, who in any degree makes his liberty a cloak for licentiousness, to look with contempt on these striking proofs, that Pascal hated vain thoughts, more than he loved his own flesh. It has been well said, that " a poor mistaken Papist, wounded by a girdle, or bleeding under a scourge, with a broken and a contrite heart, is nearer to the kingdom of God, than a proud, insolent, intolerant professor of religion, who, with a less exceptionable creed, is lamentably deficient in the graces of humility, self-denial, and charity." Happy will that man be, who, if he is working upon sound principles, and has renounced the notion of human merit before God, shall find, in his daily conduct, proofs equally strong with those which the life of Pascal furnishes, of a sincere desire to *mortify the deeds of the body*, and to silence the impure suggestions of carnal inclination.

Worn down, however, by rigid self-denial, and painful devotion to study, the frame of Pascal began to exhibit serious symptoms of decline. The constitutional disease, which had shewn itself in earlier years, gained ground; and after five years of active exertion, his general health completely gave way, and he became, in several respects, a very great sufferer. One part of his affliction was a severe, and almost unceasing pain in the teeth, so that he was unable to sleep, and was compelled to lie whole nights in thought, in order, if possible, to divert his attention from the agony that he endured.

At this time, however, an incident occurred which must not be omitted, because it tends to exhibit, in a striking point of view, the originality and superiority of his mind. During one of his wakeful and painful nights, some propositions respecting the curve, called the Cycloid,* recurred to his recollection. He had, for a long time, given up all mathematical study; but the train of thought to which these recollections led, interested him, and beguiled the pain under which he was suffering. He allowed himself, therefore, to be led on by the beauty of the thoughts which occurred to him, and at length pressed his examination of the subject to such important results, that even now the discoveries which he made that night, are regarded among the greatest efforts of the human mind. Yet so completely had his attention been turned away from such speculations, and occupied with those religious contemplations, which, as relating to God and eternity, he thought far more important, that he did not attempt to commit to paper these interesting and splendid discoveries, till speaking one day of them to the Duke de Roannez, it was suggested to him that they might be made useful in support of the cause of the true religion, at that time persecuted in the persons of the Jansenists; and he then consented to the mode of publication which was subsequently adopted.

* It is the curve, described by a nail upon the felly of a wheel of a carriage in motion.

In June 1658, therefore, Pascal issued a paper, under the signature of Amos Dettonville, which is an anagram of the name of Louis de Montalte, the signature affixed to the Provincial Letters, proposing certain questions for solution, respecting the properties of the Cycloid, and offering two rewards if the questions were solved, and the mode of solution were exhibited, by a given day, to certain judges chosen for the purpose. The proposal gave rise to much discussion, and called forth much mathematical talent. Only two persons, however, claimed the prize, the Jesuit Lallouère, and Dr Wallis the Savilian Professor of Geometry at Oxford; but at the expiry of the given time, they had not satisfied the judges that a proper solution of the questions had been offered, and then immediately Pascal printed his own treatise on the subject, which completely established his claim to the discovery of the right method of solution.

How far this Mathematical discovery could aid the cause of religion, is very questionable. Probably the Duke de Roannez wished it to be inferred, that the highest gifts of superior intellect are bestowed by a kind providence upon the servants of God, as a mark of approbation, and a proof of the nobler gifts of grace; but this is, to say the least of it, a very questionable position, and one not borne out by fact; for generally speaking, the children of this world, are, in their generation, wiser than the children of light. The event, however, has its use in a different way. It tends to confirm our confidence in the superior mind of Pascal as one of those lights that God has graciously vouchsafed to his church, to mark out the path of truth, amidst the mazes of error. And it exhibits, in a very interesting manner, the reality of Pascal's religion, that discoveries so calculated to gratify a mind like his, and to call out the ambitious desire of giving them to the world, should have appeared of little importance to him, compared with the general course of pious meditations, in which his days and nights were spent, and only worthy to occupy him seriously when it could be made to appear to him, however erroneously, that the publication might subserve the interests of that religion which was, of all things, nearest to his heart. There is very little indeed of this practical elevation above the world. There are few who really feel it; and whenever it is seen, it is worthy of reverence; for few proofs of the realizing consciousness of another existence, and of a rational hope of happiness in it, are more satisfactory and impressive than the calm and composure with which some superior minds loose their grasp upon those things of the present scene that are naturally precious to them, and find their highest delight in the promises of holiness and glory, beyond this scene of death. As St Paul says, *Yea doubtless, and I count all things but dung that I may win Christ, and be found in him, not having mine own righteousness, which is of the law, but that which is through the faith of Christ, the righteousness which is of God by faith; that I may know him, and the power of his resurrection, and the fellow-*

ship of his sufferings, being made conformable unto his death ; if by any means I may attain unto the resurrection of the dead.

In Pascal, turning aside from the career of fame to which his acute and active mind almost involuntarily led him, and neglecting those imposing discoveries which spontaneously opened to the energies of his genius, even in the very agonies of disease, to occupy himself with prayer and meditation on the Divine perfections, and with designs for the moral and religious improvement of his fellow-creatures, an instance of true magnanimity presents itself, which nothing but the reality of the great subject of his hopes can at all explain. Sceptics may profess to smile at what they call the superstitions of weaker minds, and they may find ample food for unholy mirth in the errors and imbecilities of many faithful Christians, but when they see the loftiest spirits of the age, men whose comprehensive grasp of intellect makes all their boasted philosophy look mean and meagre, making light of all that the material world can offer to their notice, and eagerly holding forth the torch of revelation, to catch, as their worthiest prospect, a view of the realities of the eternal world, they are compelled to admit that there is, at least, no small probability that the testimony of that book is true, and that it is not folly to carry inquiry farther.

The most interesting and important of the productions of this great mind, remains to be noticed. It has been seen, that the original tendencies of Pascal's mind, aided by the habits of his early education, had peculiarly fitted him for patient and accurate investigation into any subject that came before him. He grappled with the difficulties of his subject, and never was satisfied till he had discovered the truth. Subsequently, the decline of his health, and some other providential circumstances, followed up by the advice of his pious relatives, gave a decidedly religious bias to his mind, and with all his native ardour and acumen, and patience and perseverance in inquiry, he applied himself to the study of the Scriptures, the writings of the Fathers, and every book of importance on the subject, on which he could lay his hand. In this way, following up his reading, according to his usual method, with frequent and mature reflection on the points in question in all the variety of their bearings, he gradually became completely master of the subject of the Christian religion, of the evidence for its truth, the suitability of the remedy to the state of man, the poverty and want of solidity in all the Scriptural objections brought against it, and the true method of confuting each. The abstract which he has given of the opinions of Montaigne and Epictetus, shews how diligent had been his research into the opinions of other men, and how admirably fitted his mind was for unravelling their sophistries, and exposing their errors.

Pascal, feeling no doubt master of his subject, and conscious, in a degree, of the fitness of his powers for it; at all events, tracing in his own mind a clear road *to conviction* of the truth of the Christian religion, determined to write a comprehensive work on the subject. Like most of his subjects of thought, he revolved it repeatedly in his mind, and sometimes spoke of it. On one occasion, he was requested to give in conversation, an outline of his plan, before a number of his friends. He consented; and in an extempore discourse of from two to three hours, developed the plan of his work. He pointed out the subject on which he purposed to treat; he gave a concise abridgement of the mode of reasoning, and a synoptical view of the order in which the different branches of the subject were to be treated; and his friends who were themselves as capable as most men of judging in such a case, declared, that they had never heard any thing more admirable, or more powerfully convincing. It is recorded, that, from the hasty conversational view which he then gave them of the work, they anticipated a splendid performance from that mind, the powers of which they well knew, and whose assiduity they knew to be such, that he never contented himself with his first thoughts, but wrote and re-wrote, even eight or ten times, tracts, which any one but himself, would have thought excellent at first.

For this work, Pascal had been preparing several years; but the circumstances which occurred, in connection with the supposed cure of his niece, Mademoiselle Perier at Port Royal,* and which peculiarly di-

---

* The facts of the case are very curious; and there is no doubt that M. Pascal believed the truth of the miraculous cure; but to go into a minute examination of the circumstances, would far exceed the limits of this Memoir, and must be reserved for a more extensive work in contemplation, but which may perhaps never be accomplished.

rected his attention to the subject of miracles, accelerated his efforts to accomplish it. He gave himself entirely to the work; and for a whole year, previously to the general breaking up of his health, he was occupied in collecting materials, and noting down his thoughts for the purpose. From that time, however, his life was an almost unbroken continuance of suffering, during which, he was able to do little towards the furtherance of his object. Worn down with pain, and oppressed by extreme langour, he could not occupy himself in lengthened meditation, and his utmost effort was, during the short intervals of relief from pain that were granted him, to write down his thoughts on the first morsel of paper that came to hand; and at times, when he could not hold the pen, he dictated to his servant.

In this way Pascal accumulated materials for his work. The whole subject came repeatedly before him in the detail of its different parts; and any thought which it might be needful to work into the general scheme was committed to paper as it arose, and with a degree of accuracy or inaccuracy, according to the state of his mind or body at the time, and the degree of attention that he was enabled to give. Hence some of them were expressed in a manner peculiarly short, imperfect, and enigmatical; while others were evidently laboured, and made out with care.

But in the mysterious providence of God, this work was not to be completed. The health of the Author rapidly declined; and at his death, nothing was found of it but this mass of detached Thoughts, written on separate pieces of paper, which were evidently the raw material, out of which he had purposed to erect the fabric that he had planned.

It may be thought by some surprising, that after several years of study, for the express purpose, nothing more connected was found among his writings; but the habit of his mind explains this. It had always been his custom to reflect much on the subjects on which he wrote, and completely to arrange the matter in his mind before he embodied it on paper, in order that he might ascertain carefully the order in which the different parts should be disposed, so as to produce the effect which he desired; and having a memory so retentive, that as he used to say, no thought which he had once strongly impressed on his mind, ever escaped him, it appears probable, that, confiding to the clear analytic view which he had of his plan, he went on, using the intervals of rest from pain, to collect the specific thoughts, and looking to a period of greater freedom from disease, to bring them forth according to the general arrangement on which he had determined. That period, however, did not arrive; and instead of a luminous and comprehensive defence of the whole Christian scheme, we have in his Thoughts, as published, only some imperfect attempts, expressive of his intentions. These are, however, admirably calculated to suggest subjects of interesting speculation to other minds, on many important points of the great question which he had in view, and from their almost unrivalled excellence as far as they go, must ever give rise to sincere and deep regret, that their Author left his work unfinished.

As to the plan of the work, we are left entirely to conjecture, except so far as he unfolded it in the conversation before mentioned; but of that abridged statement, one of his friends who was present has given from memory the following account:—

"After having shewn them what modes of proof produce the greatest impression on the minds of men, and are most effectual as means of suasion, he undertook to shew that the Christian religion had marks of certainty as decided, and evidence in its favour as strong, as any of those things which are received in the world as unquestionable.

"He began by a delineation of man, in which he omitted nothing which might tend to give him a minute and comprehensive knowledge of himself, both within and without, even to the most secret emotions of his soul. He then supposed the case of a man, who, having lived in that state of ignorance in which men generally live, and in indifference to most things around him, but especially to those which concern himself, comes, at length, to consider himself in the picture which he had previously drawn, and to examine what he really is. He is surprized with the discovery which he makes there of a multitude of things, on which he had never previously thought; and he cannot notice without astonishment, all that Pascal's description causes him to feel of his greatness and his vileness, his power and his weakness, of the little light that lingers with him, and the thick darkness which almost entirely surrounds him, and of all those wonderful contrarieties which are found in his nature. After this, however weak his intellectual powers may be, he can no longer remain in indifference; and however insensible he may have been hitherto to such questions, he cannot but wish, after having ascertained what he is, to know also whence he came, and what is to become of him.

"Pascal having, as he supposed, thus awakened in him the disposition to seek for information on a subject so important, proposed to direct his attention, first to the philosophers of this world; and having unfolded to him all that the wisest philosophers of all the different sects have said on the subject of man, to point out to him so many defects, weaknesses, contradictions, and falsehoods, in all that they have advanced, that it would not be difficult for the individual in question, to determine, that it is not in the schools of human philosophy that he must seek for instruction.

"He then carries his disciple over the universe, and through all the ages of its history, and points out to him the variety of religions which have obtained in it; but he shews him, at the same, by strong and convincing reasons, that all these religions are full of vanity and folly, of errors, extravagance and absurdity, so that here also he finds nothing which can give him satisfaction.

"Then Pascal directs his attention to the Jewish people, and points out a train of circumstances so extraordinary, that they easily rivet his attention. And having called his attention to all the singularities of that nation, he fixes it especially on the one book by which that people are guided, and which comprehends at once their history, their law, and their theology.

"Scarcely has he opened this book, when he learns that the world is the work of God, and that the same God has made man in his own image, and endowed him with all the powers of body and mind, adapted to this state of being. Although he has not yet attained to a conviction of these truths, they are a source of gratification to him; and reason alone is sufficient to discover to him more probability in the supposition, that one God is the creator of men, and of all things in the universe, than in all the wild inventions which tradition offers elsewhere to his notice. He soon perceives, however, that he is far from possessing all the advantages which belonged to man, when he first came from the hands of his Maker. But his doubt in this matter is speedily cleared up; for on reading further, he ascertains, that after man had been created in a state of innocence, and gifted with many perfections, his first act was to rebel against his Maker, and to use his new created powers in offending him.

"Pascal proposed then to shew him, that this crime being one of the most aggravated in all its circumstances, it was punished, not only in the first man, who, having fallen by that sinful act, sunk at once into misery, and weakness, and blindness, and error, but also in all his descendants, in all time following, to whom he transmits, and will transmit, his own corrupt nature.

" His plan was then to point out to him several passages of this book, in which he must discover the averment of this truth. He shews him that it never speaks of man but with reference to this state of weakness and disorder; that it is frequently said there, that all flesh is corrupt; that men are become sensual, and that they have a bias to evil from their birth. He shews him that this first fall is the origin, not only of all that is otherwise incomprehensible in the nature of man, but also of many effects which are external to him, and of which the cause is otherwise unknown. In fact, it would be his object to point out man, as so accurately depicted in this book, that he would appear in no respect different from the character which he had previously traced.

" But merely to teach man the truth of his misery, would not be enough. Pascal proposed to shew him, that in this same book also he might find his consolation. He would point out that it is said there, that the remedy of this evil is with God; that we must go to him for strength; that he will have compassion, and will send a deliverer who will make a satisfaction for guilty man, and be his support in weakness.

" After having set before his disciple a number of important remarks on the sacred book of this peculiar people, he proposed to shew him that this was the only book which had spoken worthily of the Supreme Being, and that had given the idea of an universal religion. He would point out what should be the most evident marks of such a religion; which he would then apply to those which this book inculcated, and would direct his attention especially to the fact, that these Scriptures make the essence of religion to consist in the love of God, which is a feature entirely peculiar to themselves, and distinguishes them from all other religious writings in the world, the falsehood of which appears manifestly detected by the want of this essential characteristic.

"Hitherto, although Pascal might have led his scholar so far onward towards a disposition for the adoption of the Christian religion, he had said nothing to convince him of the truth of the things which he had discovered; he had only induced in him the disposition to receive them with pleasure, if he could be satisfied that it was his duty; he had led him to wish with his whole heart, that these things were substantial and well-founded truths, since he found in them so much that tended to give him repose, and to clear up his serious and distressing doubts. And this, M. Pascal considered, is the state in which every reasonable man should be, who has once seriously entered on that train of considerations that he wished to set before the mind of his disciple; and that there is reason to believe, that a man in such a state of mind, would then easily admit all the proofs which might be brought to confirm the reality of those important truths of which he had spoken.

" Then in the way of proof, having shewn generally that these truths were contained in a book, the genuineness and authenticity of which, could not reasonably be doubted, he proposed to look minutely into the writings of Moses, in which these truths are especially taught, and to shew by an extensive series of unquestionable proofs, that it was equally impossible that Moses had left a written statement of untruths, or that the people to whom he left them, could have been deceived as to the facts, even though Moses himself had been an impostor.

" He would speak also of the miracles recorded there, and he would prove that it was not possible that they could not be true, not only by the authority of the book that relates them, but by the many attendant circumstances which made them, in themselves, unquestionable.

" Then he would proceed to shew, that the whole law of Moses was figurative; that all which happened to the Jews, was but a type of the realities accomplished at the coming of Messiah; and that the veil which covered these types having been withdrawn, it had become easy now to perceive the complete fulfilment of them, in those who had received Jesus Christ as the promised teacher come from God.

" He then undertook to prove the truth of religion by prophecy; and, on this point, he spoke more fully than on some others. Having thought and examined deeply on this subject, and having views which were quite original, he explained them with great accuracy, and set them forth with peculiar force and brilliancy.

52   MEMOIR OF BLAISE PASCAL.

"And then having run through the books of the Old Testament, and made many powerful observations, calculated to serve as convincing proofs of the truths of religion, he proposed to speak of the New Testament, and to draw from it the proofs which it afforded of the truth of the gospel.

"He began with Jesus Christ; and although he had already triumphantly proved his Messiahship by prophecy, and by the types of the law which he shewed to have in him their perfect accomplishment, he adduced further proofs still, drawn from his person, his miracles, his doctrine, and the events of his life.

"He then came down to the Apostles; and in order to shew the truth of that faith which they had so generally preached, he *first* established the notion that they could not be accused of supporting a false system, but upon the supposition, either that they were deceivers, or were themselves deceived; and then in the *second* place, he shewed that the one and the other of these suppositions were equally impossible.

"Finally, he took a very comprehensive view of the evangelic history, making some admirable remarks on the gospel itself,—on the style and character of the evangelists,—on the apostles and their writings,—on the great number of miracles,—on the saints and martyrs of the early church, and on all the various means by which the Christian religion had obtained a footing in the world: and although it was quite impracticable in such a discourse, to treat such an extensive range of material at length, and with the minuteness, accuracy, and collective force which he purposed in his work, he said enough to exhibit most luminously, the conclusion to which he wished to come, that God only could have so conducted the issue of so many different agents and influences, as that they should all concur in supporting the religion which he himself wished to establish among men."

This is the short Abstract which has been handed down of the plan of M. Pascal's work; and short as it is, it gives us some faint view of the comprehensiveness of his genius—of the grasp that he had of his subject, and of the irresistible mass of evidence in existence for the support of the Christian religion, if it could be thus brought to bear upon the question by the energies of one great mind adapted for the purpose. It must remain a matter of wonder to shortsighted mortals, why a work apparently so important, should not have been permitted to reach its completion. Perhaps the explanation of this difficulty may, in some measure, be obtained from one of M. Pascal's Thoughts, in which he says, " So many men make themselves unworthy of God's clemency, that he is willing to leave them ignorant of those blessings for which they do not care to seek. It was not right that he should appear in a mode unequivocally divine, so as to force conviction upon all men. Nor was it right that he should be so entirely concealed, as not to be recognized by those who sincerely seek him. To such he wished to be known; and willing therefore to be discovered by those who seek him with their whole heart, but hidden from those who as heartily avoid him, he has so regulated the discovery of himself, that he has given evidences which will be clear and satisfactory to those who really seek him, but dark, and doubtful, and depressing to those who seek him not." On this ground probably it is, that the evidences for our religion which do exist, have never yet been accumulated with all their force and brilliancy, so as to exhibit one comprehensive and conclusive testimony to the truth.

But though Pascal did not live to complete his work, the fragments that he left behind him were too valuable to be lost. It was necessary that they should be given as a posthumous work to the public. His friends, therefore, who were aware of his design to write such a work, were peculiarly careful after his death, to collect every thing which he had written on the subject; and they found only the Thoughts which are published, with others yet more imperfect and obscure, written, as has been mentioned, on separate pieces of paper, and tied up in several bundles, without any connection or arrangement whatever, but evidently being, in the greater proportion of instances, the mere rough expression of the thought as it first entered his mind. He had been often heard to say, that the work would require ten years of health to complete it; and he had only been able to devote to it the short intervals of comparative ease, or rather of less acute suffering, which he enjoyed during four or *five years* of a complicated mortal disease.

At first, from their confused and imperfect state, it seemed almost impossible to give these papers publicity; but the demand for them, even as they were, was so impatient, that it became necessary to gratify it; and the labour of editing them was committed to his leading confidential friends, the Duc de Roannez, and Messieurs Arnauld, Nicole, De Treville, Dubois, De la Chaise, and the elder Perier.

And here a serious difficulty was to be encountered on the threshold. In what form should these fragments be given to the world? To print them precisely in the state in which they were found, would be worse than useless. They would have been a mass of mere confusion. To complete them, as far as possible, by adding to the imperfect Thoughts, and enlightening the obscure, would have produced a very interesting and useful work; but it would not have been the work of Pascal, even supposing the editors able to enter fully into his original design. Both these methods, therefore, were rejected; and a third plan was adopted, according to which they are now re-printed. The editors selected from a great number of Thoughts, those which appeared the most perfect and intelligible; and these they printed as they found them, without addition or alteration, except that they arranged them as nearly as might be in that order, which, according to the Syllabus that Mr Pascal had formerly given of his plan, they conceived would come nearest to his wishes.

The first editions of the work were comparatively

imperfect; but subsequently, many other v
Thoughts were gleaned from the MSS. and
later editions an accurate collation with the
papers, has secured, as far as possible, the mea
the Author. The first edition was printed in
and was surprisingly successful. Tellemont, in
ing of it, says, " It has even surpassed all the
pected from a mind which I considered the
that had appeared in one century. I see c
Augustin that can be compared with him."
most unquestionably, however imperfect the w
mains, or rather, though it falls entirely short
ing the efficient defence of the Christian religion
Pascal had contemplated; yet even now, this
tion of scattered Thoughts stands forth to cl
meed of praise, as a work of unrivalled excellen
bears the marks of the most extraordinary gen
exhibits a master's hand in touching the difficu
tions of the evidences for our religion, and in
the secrets of the human heart. It exhibit
points of the argument with great originality ar
and contains the germ of many new and valual
culations. Many of these Thoughts, hastily
perfectly expressed as they are, have been the
ore, out of which other students have drawn t
valuable and elaborate treatises on different poir

But one of the finest features of the work, is, the mastery which his mighty mind had over the human heart. Pascal had been a diligent student of his own heart; he knew its tendencies, its weaknesses, its errors. He knew what were its natural resources for comfort, and he knew their vanity; and having gone down into the depths of this question for his own sake, he was able to deal with a resistless power with the children of sin and folly. He could strip their excuses of all vain pretence. He could exhibit their lying vanities in all their poverty and comfortlessness; and he could set forth man in all the reality of his misery, as a dark and cheerless being, without hope or solace, except he find it in the mercy of his God, and in the revealed record of his compassion.

It is this extensive knowledge of human nature which constitutes the peculiar charm of the Pensees. They who read it, feel that the writer gets within their guard; that he has, from experience, the power of entering into the secret chamber of their conscience, and of exhibiting to them the many evils which would otherwise lie there unmolested, but which, seen in the light in which he placed them, must be recognized as their own. The arguments of such a writer must have weight ; and it is almost natural to feel, that he who has so thorough a know-

---

posed of particular prophecies, and prophecies relating to the Messiah; in order that the prophecies of Messiah might not be without collateral proof, and that the prophecies relating to particular cases, might not be useless in the general system."

ledge of the disease, may be followed also in his recommendation of a remedy.

The close, however, of M. Pascal's life, demands our attention. His infirmities and sufferings rapidly increased; and at length unfitted him for any exertion whatever; but they had a most blessed effect upon himself as the means of preparing him more manifestly and entirely for a holier world. It was evidently his wish to detach himself as much as possible from the present material scene; and, with this view, he made it a matter of conscience to check the indulgence of all his appetites and affections. His disease rendered it absolutely necessary that his food should be very delicate, but he was always anxious to take it without occupying his mind with it, or remarking upon its flavour. All this he considered as savouring strongly of sensuality. He objected therefore to the introduction of any kind of sauces, even the juice of an orange into his food, and rigidly regulated the quantity which he thought he ought to take daily for his sustenance; and this he would not exceed. He watched with an anxious jealousy over the still stronger passions, lest the slightest indulgence should be given to them, in himself or others. His views of the necessity of purity in general conversation, were of the highest kind; and he would not even allow his sister to remark on the personal beauty of any one whom she had seen, lest in the minds of his servants, of young people or himself, it should give rise to a questionable thought.

M. Pascal felt it necessary, even to detach himself

still more from the present world, and to restrain within himself those excessive attachments to lawful objects here, to which he was by nature strongly disposed. His most ardent affections for any thing in this life, were given to his sister Jacqueline; yet so effectually had he, by Divine contemplation, become elevated above the common views which men take of separation by death, and so entirely was he absorbed in approbation of the will of God, that when her death was announced to him, an event which occurred about six months anterior to his own, he merely said, " May God give us grace to die as she died ;" and thenceforth, he never spoke of her, but to remark on the grace with which God had blessed her during her life, and the peculiar mercy of her death at that time, in the crisis of the afflictions and persecutions of the Port Royal establishments; concluding always with the passage of Scripture, " *Blessed are the dead that die in the Lord.*"

But this endeavour to break loose from all earthly attachments, did not arise in him, as it does in some stoical minds, from a proud sense of superiority, and a dominant feeling of satisfaction in himself. On the contrary, he powerfully felt his own defects,—he was equally anxious that others should not form any attachment to him. On this point he became so determined, and so conscientiously strict, that his manner seriously grieved his sister, Madame Perier, during his last illness, who complained of the evident coldness and reserve with which he received her tenderest and most assiduous attention to his infirmities. Madame Perier states, that this dryness and reserve were to her very enigmatical, because she saw, notwithstanding the coldness of his general manner, that whenever an opportunity occurred in which he could serve her, he embraced it with all his original ardour; and she mentions, that the difficulty on her mind in this respect, was never cleared up till the day of his death, when he stated his views to a friend, that it was highly criminal, for a human being, full of infirmities, to attempt to occupy the affections of a heart which should be given to God only, and that it was robbing God of the most precious thing that this world afforded.

Nor did Pascal's endeavour to rise superior to earthly attachments, originate in hard-heartedness or misanthropy. On the contrary, in proportion as he separated himself from the ties of affection to relatives, and well known individuals, his affections towards the poor and the afflicted of his fellow-creatures increased. And herein he obtained an eminent degree of assimilation to the Divine mind. When a stone is thrown into the water, the ripple occasioned nearest to the centre of impulse, is the largest; and as the circles widen and recede, it diminishes. This is an emblem of human affection. The nearer the relation of the object to ourselves, the warmer is our love; and as the objects become remote, our love declines, till it is scarcely perceptible. Perfect love, the love of God, is the same to all; and with him, nearness of relation, or position makes no indifference. All

God's creatures are loved by him, with an affection proportioned to their real worth: and the more fully we are assimilated to the Divine Being, the more shall we realize of this reigning principle of love; we shall love, not because we are loved, or because we receive any thing again, or because, in the person of our relatives, we bestow our affection remotely on our own flesh; but we shall love souls for their own sake, for their intrinsic value as the creatures of God, and as sharers with us in the same necessities and distresses.

M. Pascal's regard for the necessities of the poor was so great, that he could not refuse to give alms, even though he was compelled to take from the supply necessary to relieve his own infirmities. And when at times he exceeded his income, and his friends remonstrated with him on account of it, he would answer, " I have invariably found, that however poor a man is, he has something left when he dies." He was often reduced to the necessity of borrowing money at interest, to indulge himself in these charitable donations. And at one time, when there was à prospect of his income being increased, he proposed to borrow a large sum in advance, upon the strength of his expectations, that he might send it to the poor of Blois, whose distresses were then peculiarly severe.

His views on the subject of charity towards the poor, are thus given by Madame Perier. " His regard for the poor had always been great; but it was so far increased towards the close of his life, that I could not please him better than by indulging it. For four years

d

he continued to press upon me the duty of dedicating myself and my children to the service of the poor. And when I replied, That I feared this would interfere with the proper care of my family, he answered, ' That this was only the want of good-will, and that this virtue might be practised without any injury to domestic concerns.' He said that charity was generally the vocation of Christians, and that it needed no particular mark to indicate a call to it, for it was certain, that on that very ground, Christ would judge the world; and that when we consider that the mere omission of this duty will be the cause of the soul's eternal ruin, this one thought, if we have faith, should lead us willingly to suffer the privation of all things. He said also, that the habit of going among the poor, is extremely useful, because we acquire a practical conviction of the miseries under which they suffer; and we cannot see them wanting, in their extremity, the common necessaries and comforts of life, without being willing to part with our own luxurious superfluities.

" Such sentiments led us to adopt some general plan, according to which, the necessities of all might be supplied; but this he did not approve. He said, we were not called to act on general principles, but to meet particular cases; and he believed, that the most pleasing method of serving God, was in serving the poor out of our poverty; that each should relieve the poor around him, according to his several ability, without occupying his mind with those great designs which aim at a fancied and probably unattainable excellence of operation, and leave the practicable good undone; and that instead of intermeddling with great enterprises which are reserved for but few, Christians generally were called to the daily assistance of the poor in the particular cases which occurred within the sphere of their own immediate influence."*

One very interesting instance of Pascal's benevolence occurred about three months before his death. As he returned one day from the Church of St Sulpice, he was accosted by a young person about fifteen years of age, and very beautiful, who asked charity. He felt the danger of her situation, and inquired into her circumstances; and having learned that she came from the country—that her father was dead, and that her mother being ill, had been that day brought to the Hotel Dieu for medical assistance; he regarded himself as sent of God to her relief, in the crisis of her necessity; and he took her, without delay, to a seminary, where he placed her under the care of a pious clergyman, provided for her support, and, through the assistance of a female friend, settled her, at length, in a comfortable situation.

Another instance of the extreme force of the principle of charity in his mind, occurred subsequently to

---

* This thought will recall to the attention, the lessons of a modern school of no little celebrity; and the peculiar, but important and convincing statements of one great mind, from which that school has originated. It is impossible to be well acquainted with the writings of Pascal and of Chalmers, and not to feel in more instances than one, the striking coincidence of thought between them.

this. He had been seized with such a degree of nausea, that his medical attendant had required him to abstain from all solid food; and he was, in consequence, reduced to great weakness. He had in his house at the time, a poor man, with his wife and family, for whose accommodation, he had given up one of his rooms. One of the children had fallen ill of the small-pox; and Pascal, who needed at the time, on account of his great debility, the attendance of his sister, was unwilling that she should come to him, from the risk of infection to her children. It became necessary, therefore, that he and his sick inmate should separate; but considering the probability of danger to the child, if he were removed, he preferred to submit to the inconvenience himself, and consequently, allowing the poor family to retain possession, he left his own house, never to return, and came to die at Madame Perier's. Whether this be viewed in the light of an act of tenderness to the poor, or of self-denial for the comfort and the safety of his relatives, it is equally lovely, and worthy of regard and veneration.

Three days after this circumstance, Pascal was visited by that attack of disease which removed him out of this present world. It began with violent internal pain; the severity of which, he endured with wonderful patience and composure. His medical attendants perceived, that his sufferings were very great; but finding his pulse good, and no appearance of fever, they ventured to assure his friends, that there was not *the least* shadow of danger. Pascal however felt, that owing to the severity of his sufferings, and the exhaustion of constant sleeplessness, he was becoming much enfeebled, and on the fourth day of his illness, sent for the curate of the parish, and confessed. The report of this spread rapidly among his friends; and they gathered round him, overwhelmed with apprehension. The medical men were so surprized by this, that they said, it was an indication of fear on his part, which they did not anticipate from him; and, notwithstanding his suspicions, they persisted in maintaining a favourable opinion of his case. In the mean time, however, he became much more emaciated; and believing, in opposition to all their representations, that he was really in danger, he communicated freely and repeatedly with the curate, on the subject of his religious hope.

At this time also he made his will, on which occasion he stated, that if M. Perier had been at Paris, and would have consented, he would have given all his property to the poor. He said to Madame Perier, "How is it that I have done nothing for the poor, though I have always loved them?" To which she replied, "Your means have not been such as to enable you to do much for them." "But," said he, "if I could not give them money, I might, at least, have given my time and my labour. Here I have come short indeed! And if the physicians are right, and God permits me to recover, I am determined to have no other employment all the rest of my life."

There are multitudes of persons gifted with both

wealth and leisure, who know nothing whatever of the wants and miseries of the poor, and of those scenes of distress and death which occur around them, and which, a little attention on their part, might materially alleviate. To float upon the stream of pleasure,—to indulge a luxurious and selfish listlessness, in the expenditure of all the means that they can command,— to turn away from, and forget that others are miserable, this seems with many the great object of life. Let such persons look at Pascal, at the close of a life of disease, the small intervals of which, he had dedicated to useful and charitable purposes ;—let them consider his sincere and penitential regrets, that he had done so little for his poorer fellow-creatures; and then let them ask themselves, how they will meet the solemn scrutiny of that hour, when God will enter into judgment with them? It is an awful sentence, " In as much as ye *did it not*, to the least of these my brethren, ye did it not to me." The truly Christian view of duty in this respect is, that the gifts of a bounteous Providence are not bestowed on us for personal indulgence; but that while we take a moderate and rational enjoyment of the comforts of life, we should regard ourselves as stewards of the manifold gifts of God, to dispense blessings to those who suffer, and to make the opportunity of relieving temporal distresses, the channel for a gift still more valuable, in the instruction of the soul in righteousness.—To live for this, is duty and happiness.

The Saviour of mankind lived among the poor of

this world, and laboured for their relief and their salvation. Pascal endeavoured to follow in the steps of his blessed Master, and only regretted, that he had done this so imperfectly. And whoever shall strive sincerely to follow the lovely example of Christ's most holy life, will find in it, both here and hereafter, an abundant blessing,—a blessing which no contingency can alter—the present sense of Divine favour on earth, and the approving smile of his gracious and compassionate Lord in heaven.

The patience with which Pascal endured pain, was equally remarkable with his overflowing love to the poor. When some one observed to him the distress which they felt at seeing him suffer, he answered, " It does not grieve me. I only fear to be relieved. I know both the dangers of health, and the benefit of suffering. Do not mourn for me; disease is the natural and proper state for Christians. Then we are, as we ought to be,—in a state of affliction, by which we become alienated from the joys and the pleasures of sense, and delivered from those passions which disturb all other periods of our life; we are freed from ambition and from avarice, and looking perpetually for death. Is not this the life that a Christian should live? Is it not a privilege to be brought into a state that makes it imperative so to live; and that requires only the duty of humble and thankful submission? For this reason, I desire no other blessing now of God, than that he would continue to me the grace of sanctified affliction."

He was so simple and child-like in his spirit, that he would listen to any one who pointed out a fault in him, and yielded implicitly to their advice. The exquisite sensitiveness of his mind, sometimes betrayed him into impatience; but if this was mentioned to him, or if he discovered that he had grieved any one, he instantly addressed himself to the reparation of his fault, by acts of the most unqualified tenderness and kindness. The Curate of St Etienne, who attended him during the whole of his illness, used to say repeatedly, " He is an infant—humble and submissive as an infant." And another ecclesiastic who came to see him, and remained an hour with him, said to Madame Perier when he left him, " Be comforted, Madame; if God calls him, you have good reason to bless him for the grace bestowed on your brother. I have always admired many noble points about his character; but I have never noticed any thing superior to the child-like simplicity which he now exhibits. In a great mind like his, this is incomparably lovely. I would gladly change places with him."

As the time drew on, he earnestly desired to receive the sacrament; but the medical men opposed it, on the ground that they could not justify the administering *the viaticum*, because he was not in immediate danger of death; and because he was too weak to receive it with fasting, according to the customary method of persons not dangerously ill; and that it was preferable, that he should wait till he was able to receive it at the church. His sufferings, however, continued to increase; and though they yielded, in a degree, to the influence of medicine, they were, at length, attended with severe pain and giddiness in the head, which distressed him greatly, and induced him to press on his friends with the greatest earnestness, that they would allow him to partake of the Lord's Supper, and cease to make those objections by which he had hitherto been prevented from receiving it. He said, "They do not feel what I suffer; and they will find themselves mistaken about me. There is something very extraordinary about the pain in my head." When, however, he found that his wish was still opposed, he ceased to importune, but said, "Since they will not grant me this favour, let me, at least, substitute something else in its stead. If I may not communicate with the head, at least, let me have communion with the members. Let a poor person be brought into the house and treated with the same attention as myself, that in the confusion with which I am overwhelmed at the abundance of my mercies, I may, at least, have the gratification of knowing, that one poor creature shares them with me. For when I think of my own comforts, and of the multitude of poor who are in a worse state than I am, and are destitute of the merest necessaries, I feel a distress which I cannot endure." And when he found that this wish could not be granted, he entreated to be carried out to the Hospital of the Incurables, that he might die among the poor. He was told, that the physicians could not consent to his being removed, at which he was much grieved, and made his sister promise, that if he at all revived, this indulgence should be granted to him.

About midnight, however, of the 17th of August, he was seized with violent convulsions, at the termination of which, he appeared to be rapidly sinking; and his friends began to fear, that although Madame Perier had, of her own accord, made arrangements for his partaking of the Lord's Supper on that day, he must, at length, die without the comfort of that sacred ordinance which he had so earnestly requested, and which they, at the instance of the medical advisers, had withheld. But, as if God was willing graciously to indulge his request, his convulsions subsided, and his senses became as perfectly collected, as if he were in health; and just at this moment, the Curate arrived with the sacred elements. As the Curate entered the room, he said, "Now you shall be indulged in your earnest wish." This address completely roused him. He raised himself by his own strength on his elbow, to receive the communion with greater outward reverence. On being questioned previously as to the leading points of the faith, he answered distinctly to each question, "Yes, sir, I believe this with all my heart." He then received the *viaticum*, and *extreme unction*, with sentiments of the tenderest emotion, and with tears. He repeated the several responses; he thanked the Curate for his attention; and when he received his blessing, said, "May my God never forsake me." Excepting a short expression of thanksgiving, these were his last words. Immediately afterward, the convulsions again returned, and continued till his death, about twenty-four hours after, without any returning interval of consciousness. He died on the 19th of August, 1662, at one o'clock in the morning, aged thirty-nine years, and two months.

On examination, his stomach and liver were found very much diseased, and his intestines in a state of mortification.

Thus died a man who was one of the brightest ornaments that the Church of Rome could ever boast. If nothing else were wanting, there is, in the life and death of Pascal ample proof, that notwithstanding all the wretched errors and criminal abominations of that apostate church, and the fearful wickedness, hypocrisy, and pretence of a large portion of its ecclesiastics, there have been some faithful men, sincere servants of God, who have adhered to its communion. In proof of this, it is fashionable and popular now, for the friends of Rome, to make a parade of the virtues and merits of Pascal; but then, it must ever be remembered, that though he remained in the communion of the Romish Church, and cordially submitted to its discipline, and respected what he considered as the unity of the Church, never was any man a more determined enemy of its errors. He was hated as the very scourge of its abominations; and there is good reason for suspicion, that the man of whom now they make their boast, was not permitted by them to continue the exercise of those commanding talents, which would have gone far towards working a reformation in the

Church of France, at least, if not elsewhere. Louis de Montalte could never be forgiven, by that deep designing body of men, whom he had exposed; and who have always regarded poison among the most legitimate modes of silencing an adversary.

Most probably Pascal felt the slow, but certain victim of their enmity. The circumstances of his disease were very peculiar. They were evidently unintelligible to his physicians, who had no conception that he was so near his end; and the extensive decay that had taken place within, can scarcely be referred to any one specific disease, without the symptoms of it having been such, as to render its nature unequivocal. To these grounds of suspicion are to be added, the unquestionable sentiments of the School of the Jesuits, on this method of removing an obnoxious person, and the many well authenticated instances of murder in which they are implicated. It would be cruel indeed to charge the Jesuits, as a body, with more than the enormous load of guilt which lies upon their heads; but knowing as we do historically, their dark machinations, their bitter and unmitigable hate, and their bold admission of the principle, that the end sanctifies the means,—knowing also that no individual ever did more than Pascal did to sting them to the quick, and to bring all their rancour and malice in its deadliest form upon his head, it is impossible to look at the suspicious circumstances of his death-bed, without fear and indignation. This is, however, one of those mysteries which must be referred, with many other scenes of horror and treachery, in which Rome has borne a part, to that day when " the earth shall disclose her blood, and shall no more cover her slain." It is impossible, however, to leave this subject, without recalling to the recollection, that the Society of the Jesuits is revived,—that their principles of morals and of policy are precisely the same as ever,—that they have never disclaimed a single sentiment of all their code of vice; and that at this moment, they have large educational establishments, not only in Ireland, but in the very heart of Britain.

But to return; it does seem strange, that Pascal and his friends should now be made the prominent subject of praise, by the friends of the Papacy, when, in fact, they were treated when living, as its bitterest enemies, and their works proscribed in the Index of prohibited books. And if the History of the MM. de Port Royal were well known, it would be seen that the Jesuits never ceased from their political intrigues, till they had succeeded in expelling this last remnant of pure religion from the Church of France. The Protestants were murdered by thousands. This need not be wondered at. But in proof, that the hostility of the Jesuits was not against names and sects, so much as against principles, we have their inflexible hostility and unrelenting persecution of these great and holy men, who were faithful and regular members of their communion, but who differed from the Jesuits, mainly in this, that instead of making a religious profession a cloak for personal aggrandizements, for the accumulation of wealth, the attainment of power, and the secret command of every sensual indulgence, they were, in the midst of a corrupt church with which they were conscientiously associated, faithful, humble, self-denied followers of the blessed Jesus. The fact is a valuable one. It teaches, that there may be in remote corners, and in private life, and possibly even in the priesthood, some individuals in the communion of Rome, who are the sincere servants of God; yet that wherever they are, they must, in their conscience, protest against and renounce some of the evils by which they are surrounded; but that the grand scheme and system of its hierarchy is a mere pretence—a forcing upon men of a human system of policy and power, garnished with every trick and trapping that art can invent, and blind and childish superstition receive, to conceal its real deformity, infidelity, and cool intentional iniquity from its deluded followers. Through all this mass of mischief, it is just possible, that in the mercy of God, a man may find his way to the Saviour; and repose his soul upon the simple promise of salvation through him; but he who does so, must first renounce those other grounds of confidence which the Romish Church puts far more prominently forward; the merit of his own works and penances,—the blasphemous indulgences of the Pope and his vicars,— the value of money as a coin current at the gate of heaven,—the impious adoration of a woman who has herself entered heaven only as a forgiven sinner, and the idolatrous worship, and the fabled intercession of the whole Kalendar of Saints, many of whom, it is to be feared, are not in heaven, and never will be. Not one of these vital errors stained the creed of Pascal. His great mind threw them all off as utterly inconsistent with the simplicity of the Christian faith. But how few must they be, who have strength for this! How few are likely to discern, through these mists of error, the simple object of worship and confidence in the incarnate Son of God, or to break through all this bondage, to the liberty wherewith Christ has made us free!

The man who is saved in the Romish Church, must be essential *protestant* against its errors; and till the whole body of its hierarchy shall be brought to this, and to lay their unscriptural and unholy honours at the feet of Him whose power they have usurped, and whose truth and purity they have libelled and insulted, this must continue to be the case. And if this be the fact, then it must ever be a subject of mourning, that any portion of our empire is so criminally left to this meagre chance of salvation in her communion. However men may differ as to their opinion of the rights of men, as subjects of a human government, it becomes them to remember what the Church of Rome has ever been, and what in all its avowed sentiments and public documents it still is—the patron of ignorance and debasing superstition in the mass of its bers; and if they see it right to give liberty to with one hand, they should be yet more stregive them light with the other. Nothing can be more awful, and to the British Empire more disgraceful, than that 300 years after the reformation, four millions of its subjects, at our very doors, should be in a state of the most melancholy ignorance of the first principles of the pure word of God, worshipping idols, doing meritorious penances, wearing charms and consecrated amulets, trusting purchased indulgences, vowing allegiance to a foreign potentate, as the representative of their God, and denouncing certain perdition on all those who are not partakers of their folly. When will the spirit of our fathers come upon us again? Where is the mantle of our Elijahs of former days? When will a truly Protestant heart return again to the British people? When will the day come, in which we shall be prepared, as a people, in the simplicity of a Scriptural faith, to leave the message of mercy unfettered by the safeguards of human prudence, to win its own triumphant way to the hearts of men? When will the churches of this favoured land, rise, as with one consent, against the vile and debasing superstitions which the influence of Rome still pours as a poisonous deluge over so fair a portion of the British dominions; when they shall go forth, not to increase or to perpetuate the political rigours of former days,—not to punish, by the privation of civil rights, the errors of an uninformed and misguided conscience; but to visit these sad victims of priestcraft and delusion, with the kindly offices of mercy and love, to remonstrate affectionately, to reason calmly, to open and explain the Scriptures, to preach in their high-ways and hedges the unsearchable riches of the gospel of Christ, and to triumph as the Head and High-priest of our profession triumphed, by *turning them from darkness to light, and from the power of Satan unto God.*

Pascal was a very striking instance of the superiority of a great mind, enlightened by the reading of Scripture, to the errors and superstitions of his age and country. Though he was a layman, yet to him, as a man of learning, those Scriptures were open; from which the common people are, by authority, excluded; and the promised blessing of God attended the obedient study of His word. The progress of his mind was rapid, in the perception of religious truth, and in the discrimination of it from the essential and destructive errors with which it had been mixed up, in the avowed doctrinal sentiments of the Romish Church. His views were clear, perspicuous, and liberal; and, at the same time, he maintained a chastened, childlike, and humble spirit. But there was in him that inflexible rectitude of mind, by which he saw almost intuitively, the prominent and essential features of truth; and grasping these with gigantic firmness, he was prepared, in the seraphic strength which they imparted, to combat for them against the world. Of course, the accuracy and keenness with which he detected error was equally remarkable, and only equalled by the honesty with which he went forth against it. He knew his own principles too well to be inconsis-
He ..... the power and the promises of God
o be   other than undaunted. He was

prepared equally to defend Divine truth against infidelity or superstition, or against that worst, and most frequent of all opponents in the Romish Church, against him who upholds for sinister purposes, the superstitious practices which, in the secret of his heart, he holds in contempt.

To this unbending rectitude of spirit, Pascal united talents, peculiarly adapted to make him a powerful and efficient controversialist. The readiness which brings all his powers up at the moment of necessity; the perspicuity which facilitates the communication of ideas, and the playful wit which adorns them; the habitual humility which is the best safeguard against betraying himself by the indulgence of any evil passion, and the simple, affectionate reliance upon the blessing of a Divine power, which makes a man regardless of consequences, as long as he does his duty,—these were the qualities which fitted him, in an especial manner, to be the champion of Scriptural truth, in the fallen church of the Papacy. Had he been gifted with health and strength, he was the man, of all others, adapted to accomplish a general return to the Christian principles from which that Church had strayed; and if views, simple and Scriptural as his, had spread and become popular,—if the bad parts of the Romish system had, with others, as with him, fallen into dissuetude and contempt; and its ministers, instead of being the fawning supporters of an unchristian tyranny over the consciences of men and the sceptres of the earth, had become like him, the faithful advocates of the leading features of Scriptural truth,—such a change would have gone far to satisfy the Christian world. There can be no wish, on the part of the universal Church of Christ, to unchurch the Church of Rome, or needlessly to interfere with any of its views or non-essential points, which are harmless in their nature, and are, in fact, ground on which charity requires all to be neutral; and though, upon some points, that Church might still be regarded by some as too superstitious, yet had she openly and honestly maintained and preached the doctrine of her Pascals, and Arnaulds, and Quesnels, and Fenelons, the leading features of quarrel with her on the part of the Protestant Churches, would have almost ceased to exist.

But it is not so. These men must now be looked on only as extraordinary exceptions, from the dominant evils of that community. They are not specimens of the brilliant attainments in knowledge and piety of the disciples of the Papacy. They are anomalies to the universality of error. They are only a few scattered lights, that have been permitted occasionally to shine out amidst the surrounding gloom,— to make the palpable thickness of the darkness that covers the multitude more visible. They are only proofs of what the Romish clergy should have been, and might have been, even while they remained conscientiously in communion with that church. But they stand forth as a swift witness against the errors, that have almost universally been sanctioned and encouraged by its authorities; and perhaps, no condemnation more fearful will issue in the last day against the antichristian errors of Rome, than that which marks, with Divine approbation, the solemn protestation of Pascal and his friends, and recognizes the melancholy fact, that sound Scriptural truth was hunted down and persecuted, and condemned in their persons, and the true religion of the Saviour once more sacrificed in them to the worldly policy and intrigue, to the pride and passion of the Jesuits.

With the death of Pascal, and the banishment of his friends, all rational hope of the reformation of the French church ceased. " Darkness covered the people—gross darkness that might be felt." And from that day to this, successive woes have fallen, in almost unmingled bitterness, on that irreligious and careless people. What further evils may yet assail them, time will unfold; but even now, increasing darkness gathers round. The sad lessons of experienced suffering, are already thrown aside; and darker superstition frowns, while she forges for them new and heavier chains. In the prospect of the gloom that lowers upon that melancholy country, and in the belief that the torch of truth in the hand of the Jansenists, and of their great champion, might have dispelled it, the friends of true religion may well take up the friendly lamentation which mourned over the tomb of Pascal, the loss sustained by his country in his untimely fall, and say, *Heu! Heu! Cecidit Pascalis.*

Pascal was buried at Paris, in the parish church of

St Etienne du Mont, behind the main altar, near to, and directly before the pillar on the left hand, entering the Chapel of the Virgin. A Latin epitaph, remarkably quaint and original in its style, written by Aimonius Proust de Chambourg, Professor of Law in the University of Orleans, was laid over the grave; but as it lay in a very frequented part of the Church, it was speedily effaced; and a second inscription, engraved on a marble tablet, was affixed to the pillar immediately adjoining. This second inscription, owing to some repairs in the Church, was afterwards removed, and placed over the side door at the right side of the Church. During the revolution, it was carried away to the Museum of French Monuments; but on the 21st April, 1818, it was restored to its original pillar, in the presence of the Prefect of the department of the Seine, a deputation of the Academy, and many relations of the deceased.

Nobilissimi Scutarii Blasii Pascalis Tumulus.
D. O. M.
BLASIUS PASCALIS SCUTARIUS NOBILIS HIC JACET.
Pietas si non moritur, æternùm vivet;
Vir conjugii nescius,
Religione sanctus, Virtute clarus,
Doctrinâ celebris,
Ingenio acutus,
Sanguine et animo pariter illustris;
Doctus, non Doctor,
Æquitatis amator,
Veritatis defensor,
Viginum ultor,
Christianæ Moralis Corruptorum acerrimus hostis.

Hunc Rhetores amant facundum,
Hunc Scriptores nôrunt elegantem,
Hunc Mathematici stupent profundum,
Hunc Philosophi quærunt Sapientem,
Hunc Doctores laudant Theologum,
Hunc Pii venerantur austerum.
Hunc omnes mirantur, omnibus ignotum,
Omnibus licèt notum.
Quid plura? Viator, quem perdidimus
PASCALEM,
Is Ludovicus erat Montaltius.
Heu!
Satis dixi, urgent lachrymæ,
Sileo.
Ei qui benè precaberis, benè tibi eveniat,
Et vivo et mortuo.
Vixit. An. 39. m. 2. Obiit an. rep. Sal. 1662.
14 Kal. Sept.
ΩΛΕΤΟ ΠΑΣΚΑΛΙΟΣ.
ΦΕΥ! ΦΕΥ! ΠΕΝΘΟΣ ΟΣΟΝ!
Cecidit Pascalis.
Heu! Heu! qualis luctus!
Posuit A. P. D. C. mærens Aurelian. Canonista.

Pro columna superiori,
Sub tumulo marmoreo,

Jacet Blasius Pascal, Claromontanus, Stephani Pascal in Supremâ apud Arvernos Subsidiorum Curiâ Præsidis filius, post aliquot annos in severiori secessu et divinæ legis meditatione transactos, feliciter et religiosè in pace Christi, vitâ functus anno 1662, ætatis 39, die 19 Augusti. Optasset ille quidem præ paupertatis et humilitatis studio, etiam his sepulchri honoribus carere, mortuusque etiamnùm latere, qui vivus semper latere voluerat. Verùm ejus hac in parte votis cùm cedere non posset Florinus Perier in eâdem subsidiorum Curia Consiliarius, ac Gilbertæ Pascal, Blasii Pascal sororis, conjux amantissimus, hanc tabulam posuit, qua et suam in illum significaret, et Christianos ad Christiana prec sibi et defuncto profutura cohortaretur.

THOUGHTS ON RELIGION.

CHAPTER I.

ON SELF-KNOWLEDGE.

WHEN man considers himself, the first thing that claims his notice is his body; that is a certain portion of matter evidently appertaining to himself. But if he would know what this is, he must compare himself with all that is superior or inferior to him; and thus he will ascertain his own just limits.

But he must not rest contented with the examination of the things around him. Let him contemplate universal nature in all the height and fulness of its majesty. Let him consider that glorious luminary, hung as an eternal lamp, to enlighten the universe. Let him consider that this earth is a mere point, compared with the vast circuit which that bright orb describes.* Let him learn with wonder, that this wide orbit itself is but a speck compared with the course of the stars, which roll in the firmament of heaven. And if here our sight is limited,

---

* The Copernican system was not then generally received by the members of the Romish Church.

> OUR GREATEST GIFT IS OUR COGNITIVE ABILITIES ENABLING US TO KNOW ALL OF THIS. WE CAN REASON, THINK, & PERCEIVE OURSELVES EMPTY, FORLORN, & LOST IN SPACE WITHOUT OTHER HUMAN BEINGS AND ESPECIALLY WITHOUT GOD.

ON SELF-KNOWLEDGE.

let the imagination take up the inquiry and venture further. It will weary with conceiving, far sooner than nature in supplying food for thought. All that we see of the universe is but an almost imperceptible spot on the ample bosom of nature. No conception even approaches the limits of its space. Let us labour as we will with our conceptions, we bring forth mere atoms, compared with the immensity of that which really is. It is an infinite sphere, whose centre is every where, and whose circumference is no where. And, in fact, one of the most powerful sensible impressions of the omnipotence of God is, that our imagination is lost in this thought.

Then let man return to himself, and consider what he is, compared with all else that is. Let him consider himself as a wanderer in this remote corner of nature; and then from what he sees of this narrow prison in which he lies—this visible world; let him learn to estimate rightly the earth, its kingdoms, its cities, himself, and his own real value. What is man in this infinity? Who can comprehend him?

But to shew him another prodigy equally astonishing, let him search among the minutest objects round him. Let a mite, for instance, exhibit to him, in the exceeding smallness of its frame, portions yet incomparably smaller; limbs well articulated; veins in those limbs; blood in those veins; humours in that blood; globules in that humour; and gases in those globules;—and then dividing again their smallest objects, let him exhaust the powers of his conception, and then let the lowest particle that he can imagine become the subject of our discourse. He thinks, perhaps, that this is the minutest atom of nature, but I will open to him, within it, a new and fathomless abyss. I can exhibit to him yet, not only the

"It is not good, man should dwell alone."

visible universe, but even all that he is capable of conceiving of the immensity of nature, embosomed in this imperceptible atom. Let him see there an infinity of worlds, each of which has its firmament, its planets, its earth; bearing the same proportion to the other parts as in the visible world: and in this earth, animals, and even mites again, in which he shall trace the same discoveries which the first mites yielded; and then again the same in others without end and without repose. He is lost in these wonders, equally astonishing in their minuteness, as the former by their extent. And who would not wonder to think that this body, which so lately was not perceptible in that universe, which universe was itself an imperceptible spot on the bosom of infinity, should now appear a colossus, a world, a universe, compared with that ultimate atom of minuteness to which we cannot arrive.

He who thus thinks of himself, will doubtless be alarmed to see himself, as it were, suspended in the mass of matter that is allotted to him, between these two abysses of infinity and nothingness, and equally remote from both. He will tremble at the perception of these wonders; and I would think, that his curiosity changing into reverence, he would be more disposed to contemplate them in silence, than to scrutinize them with presumption. For what after all is man, in nature? A nothing compared with infinity,—a universe compared with nothing,—a mean between all and nothing. He is infinitely distant from both extremes. His being is not less remote from the nothing out of which he was formed, than from the infinity in which he is lost.

His mind holds the same rank in the order of intelligent beings, as his body in material nature; and all that it can do, is to discern somewhat of the middle of things,

ON SELF-KNOWLEDGE.

in an endless despair of ever knowing their beginning or their end. All things are called out of nothing, and carried onward to infinity. Who can follow in this endless race? The Author of these wonders comprehends them. No other can.

This state which occupies the mean between two extremes, shews itself in all our powers.

Our senses will not admit any thing extreme. Too much noise confuses us, too much light dazzles, too great distance or nearness prevents vision, too great prolixity or brevity weakens an argument, too much pleasure gives pain, too much accordance annoys. We relish neither extreme heat, nor extreme cold. All excessive qualities are injurious to us, and not perceptible. We do not feel them, we suffer them. Extreme youth and extreme age alike enfeeble the mind; too much or too little nourishment weakens its operations; by too much or too little instruction it becomes stupid. Extreme things are not ours, any more than if they were not; we are not made for them. Either they escape us, or we them.

This is our real condition. It is this which confines our knowledge within certain limits that we cannot pass, being equally incapable of universal knowledge, or of total ignorance; we are placed in a vast medium, ever floating uncertainly between ignorance and knowledge: if we attempt to go farther forward, our object wavers and eludes our grasp—it retires and flies with an eternal flight, and nothing can stay its course.

This is our natural condition; yet it is ever opposed to our inclination. We burn with desire to sound the utmost depth, and to raise a fabric that shall reach infinity. But all we build up crumbles, and the earth opens in a fathomless abyss beneath our deepest foundation.

ON SELF-KNOWLEDGE.   5

2. I can readily conceive of a man without hands or feet; and I could conceive of him without a head, if experience had not taught me that by this he thinks. Thought then is the essence of man, and without this we cannot conceive of him.

What is it in us which feels pleasure? Is it the hand? the arm? the flesh? the blood? It must be something immaterial.

3. Man is so great, that his greatness appears even in the consciousness of his misery. <u>A tree does not know itself to be miserable.</u> It is true that it is misery indeed to know one's self to be miserable; but then it is greatness also. In this way, all man's miseries go to prove his greatness. <u>They are the miseries of a mighty potentate—of a dethroned monarch.</u>

4. What man is unhappy because he is not a king, except a king dethroned. Was Paulus Emilius considered miserable that he was no longer consul. On the contrary every one thought that he was happy in having it over, for it was not his condition to be always consul. But Perseus, whose permanent state should have been royalty, was considered to be so wretched in being no longer a king, that men wondered how he could endure life. Who complains of having only one mouth? Who would not complain of having but one eye? No man mourns that he has not three eyes; yet each would sorrow deeply if he had but one.

5. We have so exalted a notion of the human soul, that we cannot bear to be despised by it, or even not to be esteemed by it. Man, in fact, places all his happiness in this esteem.

[Margin note top: "? WE DON'T LIKE TO BE THOUGHT OF AS A DULLARD OR UNLEARNED PERSON. WE WOULD LIKE "RESPECT", AS RODNEY SAYS. JUST GOT BACK FROM DM CONFERENCE. GAME WAS INTERESTING."]

ON SELF-KNOWLEDGE.

If on the one hand this false glory that men seek after is a mark of their misery and degradation, it is on the other a proof of their excellence. For whatever possessions a man has on the earth, and whatever health or comfort he enjoys, he is not satisfied without the esteem of his fellow-men. He rates so highly the human mind, that whatever be his worldly advantages, if he does not stand, as well also in man's estimation, he counts himself wretched. That position is the loveliest spot in the world. Nothing can eradicate the desire for it. And this quality is the most indelible in the human heart; so that even those who most thoroughly despise men, and consider them equal with the brutes, still wish to be admired by them; their feelings contradict their principles. Their nature which is stronger than their reasonings, convinces them more forcibly of the greatness of man, than their reason can do of his vileness.

6. Man is but a reed; and the weakest in nature; but then he is a reed that thinks. It does not need the universe to crush him: a breath of air, a drop of water will kill him. But even if the material universe should overwhelm him, man would be more noble than that which destroys him; because he knows that he dies, while the universe knows nothing of the advantage which it obtains over him.

Our true dignity then, consists in thought. From thence we must derive our elevation, not from space or duration. Let us endeavour then to think well; this is the principle of morals.

7. It is dangerous to shew man unreservedly how nearly he resembles the brute creation, without pointing

[Margin note: "THINKING REED"]

out, at the same time, his greatness. It is dangerous also to exhibit his greatness exclusively, without his degradation. It is yet more dangerous to leave him ignorant of both, but it is highly profitable to teach him both together.

8. Let man then rightly estimate himself—let him love himself, for he has a nature capable of good; but yet let him not love the evils that he finds there. Let him despise himself, because this capacity is without an object; but let him not on that account despise the natural capacity itself. Let him both love and hate himself. There is in him the power of discerning truth, and of being happy, but he is not in possession of certain and satisfying truth. I would lead man to desire to find truth, to sit loose to his passions, and to be ready to follow truth wherever he may find it; and knowing how sadly his powers of comprehension are clouded by his passions, I would wish him to hate in himself that concupiscence which overrules his judgment, that henceforth it may not blind him in making his choice, nor impede his progress when he has chosen.

9. I blame with equal severity those who elevate man, those who depress him, and those who think it right merely to divert him. I can only approve of those who seek in tears for happiness.

The stoics say, Turn in upon yourselves, and there you will find your repose. This however is not true. Others say, Go forth from yourselves, and seek for happiness in diversion. This is not true either. Disease will come. Alas! happiness is neither within us, nor without us. It is in the union of ourselves with God.

10. There are two ways of regarding human nature, one according to the end of man, and then it is grand and incomprehensible; the other according to his habits, as we judge of the nature of a horse or a dog, by the habit of observing his going, and then man is abject and vile. It is owing to these two different ways that philosophers judge so differently, and dispute so keenly; for one denies what the other assumes. One says, man is not born for this noble end; for all his actions are opposed to it. The other says, when he commits such base and grovelling actions, he wanders from the end of his being. Instinct and experience, taken together, show to man the whole of what he is.

11. I feel that I might not have been; for when I speak of myself, I mean my thinking being; and I, who think, would not have been, if my mother had been killed before I was quickened. Then I am not a necessary being, nor am I eternal, nor infinite; but I see clearly that there is in nature, a being who is necessary, eternal, infinite.

CHAPTER II.

THE VANITY OF MAN.

WE are not satisfied with the life that we have in ourselves—in our own peculiar being. We wish to live also an ideal life in the mind of others; and for this purpose, we constrain ourselves to put on appearances. We labour incessantly to adorn and sustain this ideal being, while we neglect the real one. And if we possess any degree of

> Whom do I seek to admire me? Want my grandkids? Work associates — "appreciate you"? I want God to love, value, want to be with me as a person —— I would like for Him to desire me to be in His company...

THE VANITY OF MAN.

equanimity, generosity, or fidelity, we strive to make it known, that we may clothe with these virtues that being of the imagination. Nay, we would even cast off these virtues in reality, to secure them in the opinion of others; and willingly be cowards, to acquire the reputation of courage. What a proof of the emptiness of our real being, that we are not satisfied with the one without the other, and that we often sacrifice the one to the other; for he is counted infamous who would not die to save his reputation.

Glory is so enchanting, that we love whatever we associate it with, even though it be death.

2. Pride countervails all our miseries, for it either hides them, or if it discloses them, it boasts of acknowledging them. Pride has so thoroughly got possession of us, even in the midst of our miseries and our faults, that we are prepared to sacrifice life with joy, if it may but be talked of.

3. Vanity is so rooted in the heart of man, that the lowest drudge of the camp, the street, or the kitchen, must have his boast and his admirers. It is the same with the philosophers. Those who write to gain fame, would have the reputation of having written well; and those who read it, would have the reputation of having read it; and I who am writing this, feel probably the same wish, and they who read this, feel it also.

> HONEST

4. Notwithstanding the sight of all those miseries which wring us, and threaten our destruction, we have still an instinct that we cannot repress, which elevates us above our sorrows.

> *My honest desire would be that I could make a contribution to the understanding of God*

THE VANITY OF MAN.

5. We are so presumptuous that we wish to be known to all the world, and even to those who come after us; and we are so vain, that the esteem of five or six persons immediately around us, is enough to seduce and satisfy us.

6. Curiosity is but vanity: too frequently we only wish to know more, that we may talk of it. No man would venture to sea, if he were never to speak about what he sees—for the mere pleasure of seeing, without ever speaking of it to others.

7. We do not care to get a name in the towns through which we are travelling: but if we come to sojourn there a short time, we soon become desirous of it, and what time is sufficient for this? a period proportioned to our vain and pitiful duration.

8. The nature of self-love and of human egotism, is to love self only, and to consult only self-interest. But to what a state is man reduced! He cannot prevent this object of his love from being full of defects and miseries. He wishes to be great, but he sees himself little: he wishes to be happy, but he sees himself miserable: he wishes to be perfect, but he sees that he is full of imperfections: he wishes to be the object of men's love and esteem, and he sees that his errors deserve their hatred and contempt. This state of disappointment generates in him the most wretched and criminal passion that can be imagined: he conceives a deadly hatred against that truth which reproves him, and convinces him of his faults: he desires to destroy it, and unable actually to destroy it in its essential nature, he blots it out as far as

possible from his own knowledge and from that of others: that is, he does his utmost to conceal his faults both from others and from himself, and will not suffer others to exhibit them to him, or to examine them themselves.

It is surely an evil to be full of faults; but it is a far greater evil to be unwilling to know them, since that is to add to them the guilt of a voluntary delusion. We do not like others to deceive us; we do not think it right that they should wish to be esteemed by us beyond their deserts: it is not right then that we should deceive them, and that we should wish them to esteem us more than we deserve.

So that when they discover in us nothing but the imperfections and vices which we really possess, it is evident that in this they do us no wrong, because they are not the cause of those errors; and that they even do us good, since they aid us in avoiding a real evil—the ignorance of these our imperfections. We should not be indignant that they discover these errors if they really exist, nor that they should know us to be what we really are, and despise us, if we really are despicable.

These are the thoughts that would rise spontaneously in a heart full of equity and justice: what then shall we say of our own, when we see its disposition to be just the reverse. For is it not true that we hate the truth, and those who tell it us; and that we love men to be deceived in our favour, and wish to be estimated by them very differently from what we really are?

There are different degrees of this aversion for truth; but we may affirm that in some degree it exists in every one, because it is inseparable from self-love. It is this vile sensitiveness to applause, which compels those whose duty it is to reprove another, to soften the severity of

As my life ends, I know of no other man who really should go through life taking it upon himself to "reprove" others. Rare is the person who can "correct" others, because he walks in sin.

THE WEAKNESS OF MAN.

the shock, by so many circuitous and alleviating expressions. They must appear to attenuate the fault; they must seem to excuse what they mean to reprove; they must mix with the correction the language of praise, and the assurances of affection and esteem. Yet still this pill is always bitter to self-love: we take as little of it as we can, always with disgust, and often with a secret grudge against those who presume to administer it.

Hence it is that those who have any interest in securing our regard, shrink from the performance of an office which they know to be disagreeable to us; they treat us as we wish to be treated; we hate the truth, and they conceal it; we wish to be flattered, and they flatter; we love to be deceived, and they deceive us.

And hence it arises that each step of good fortune by which we are elevated in the world, removes us farther from truth; because men fear to annoy others, just in proportion as their good will is likely to be useful, or their dislike dangerous. A prince shall be the talk of all Europe, and he only know it not. I do not wonder at this. To speak the truth is useful to him to whom it is spoken, but sadly the reverse to him who speaks it, for it makes him hated. Now they who live with princes, love their own interests better than that of him whom they serve, and do not therefore care to seek his benefit by telling him the truth to their own injury. This evil is doubtless more serious and more common, in cases of commanding rank and fortune, but the very lowest are not free from it; because there is always some benefit to be obtained by means of man's esteem. So that human life is a perpetual delusion,—nothing goes on but mutual flattery and mutual deceit: no one speaks of us in presence, as he does in our absence. The degree of that there is among men, is founded on this mutual deception; and few friendships would subsist, if each one knew what his friend says of him when he is not present, although at the time he speaks sincerely and without prejudice.

Man, then, is nothing but disguise, falsehood, and hypocrisy, both towards himself and others. He does not wish them to tell him the truth,—he will not tell it to them: and all these dispositions, so far removed from justice and sound reason, have their root naturally in his heart.

CHAPTER III.

THE WEAKNESS OF MAN.

THAT which astonishes me most is, that no man is astonished at his own weakness. Men act seriously; and each one follows his occupation, not because it is actually good to follow it, since that is the custom; but as if each one knew precisely where to find reason and truth. Each one however finds himself deceived repeatedly, and yet by a foolish humility thinks that the failure is in his own conduct, and not in the faculty of discerning truth, of which he continually boasts. It is well that there are so many of these persons in the world, since they serve to show that man is capable of holding the most extravagant opinions; inasmuch as he can believe that he is not naturally and inevitably in a state of moral weakness; but that on the contrary, he has naturally wisdom adequate to his circumstances.

14   THE WEAKNESS OF MAN.

2. The weakness of human reason appears more evidently in those who know it not, than in those who know it.

He who is too young will not judge wisely; no more will he that is too old. If we think too little or too much on a subject, we are equally bewildered, and cannot discover truth. If a man reviews his work directly after he has done it, he is pre-occupied by the lively impression of it: if he reviews it a long time after, he can scarcely get into the spirit of it again.

There is but one indivisible point from which we should look at a picture; all others are too near, too distant, too high, or too low. Perspective fixes this point precisely in the art of painting; but who shall fix it in regard to truth and morals?

3. That queen of error, whom we call fancy and opinion, is the more deceitful because she does not deceive always. She would be the infallible rule of truth if she were the infallible rule of falsehood: but being only most frequently in error, she gives no evidence of her real quality, for she marks with the same character both that which is true and that which is false.

This haughty power, the enemy of reason, and whose delight is to keep reason in subjection, in order to shew what influence she has in all things, has established in man a second nature. She has her happy and her unhappy, her sick and her healthy, her rich and her poor, her fools and her sages; and nothing is more distressing than to see that she fills her guests with a far more ample satisfaction, than reason gives; since those who think themselves wise have a delight in themselves, far beyond that in which the really prudent dare to indulge. They treat other men imperiously; they dispute with fierceness and assurance,—whilst others do so with fear and caution; and this satisfied air often gives them advantage in the opinion of the hearers: so much do the imaginary wise find favour among judges of the same kind. Opinion cannot make fools wise, but she makes them content, to the great disparagement of reason, who can only make her friends wretched. The one covers her votaries with glory, the other with shame.

Who confers reputation? who gives respect and veneration to persons, to books, to great men? Who but opinion? How utterly insufficient are all the riches of the world without her approbation!

Opinion settles every thing. She constitutes beauty, justice, happiness, which is the whole of this world. I would like much to see that Italian work, of which I have only heard the title. It is called " Opinion, the Queen of the World." It is worth many other books. I subscribe to it without knowing it, error excepted.

4. The most important concern in life, is the choice of an occupation; yet chance seems to decide it. Custom makes masons, soldiers, bricklayers, &c. They say, " That's a capital workman," or when speaking of soldiers, " What fools those men are:" others again say, " There is nothing noble but war, all men but soldiers are contemptible." And according as men, during their childhood, have heard those several occupations praised and others vilified, they make their choice; for naturally we love wisdom and hate folly. It is these words that influence us; we err only in the application of them; and the force of custom is such, that in some countries, the whole population are masons; in others, soldiers. Now we do not con-

ceive that nature is so uniform. It is custom which does this, and carries nature with it. There are cases however in which nature prevails, and binds man to his specific object, in defiance of custom, whether bad or good.

5. We think very little of time present; we anticipate the future, as being too slow, and with a view to hasten it onward; we recall the past to stay it as too swiftly gone. We are so thoughtless, that we thus wander through the hours which are not here, regardless only of the moment that is actually our own:—so vain, that we dream of the times which are not, and suffer that only which does exist, to escape us without a thought. This is because, generally, the present gives us pain; we hide it from our sight, because it afflicts us; and even if it ministers pleasure, we grieve to see it flying: and hence we bring up the future to sustain it, and speculate on doing things which are not in our power, at a time which we can have no assurance that we shall ever see.

Let any man examine his thoughts; he will find them ever occupied with the past or the future. We scarcely think at all of the present; or if we do, it is only to borrow the light which it gives, for regulating the future. The present is never our object: the past and the present we use as means; the future only is our object. Thus in fact we never live, we only hope to live; and thus ever doing nothing, but preparing to be happy, it is certain that we never shall be so, unless we seek a higher felicity than this short life can yield.

6. Our imagination so magnifies this present existence, by the power of continual reflection on it; and so attenuates eternity, by not thinking of it at all, that we reduce an

> *Point is well made. As Flew said of Lewis, he did not agree with man knowing innately truly what is right, or easily choices & conduct....*

THE WEAKNESS OF MAN. 17

eternity to nothingness, and expand a mere nothing to an eternity; and this habit is so inveterately rooted in us, that all the force of reason cannot induce us to lay it aside.

7. Cromwell would have laid desolate all Christendom. The royal family was ruined; his own was completely established: but for a small grain of sand, which entered the urethra, even Rome would have trembled before him; but when only this atom of gravel, which elsewhere was as nothing, was placed in that spot, behold he dies, his family is degraded, and the king restored!

8. We see scarcely any thing, just or unjust, that does not change its quality with its climate. Three degrees of latitude upset all the principles of jurisprudence; a meridian determines what is truth, or a few years of settled authority. Fundamental laws may vary. Right has its epochs. Droll justice indeed, that a river or a mountain limits! Truth on one side of the Pyrenees is error on the other.

9. Theft, incest, parricide, infanticide, each has been ranked among virtuous actions. Is there any thing more ridiculous, than that a man has the right to kill me, because he lives across the water, and that his prince has a quarrel with mine, though I have none with him?

There are certainly natural laws, but this corrupted reason has corrupted every thing, *Nihil amplius nostri est; quod nostrum dicimus, artis est; ex senatusconsultis et plebiscitis crimina exercentur, ut olim vitiis sic nunc legibus laboramus.*

From this confusion it arises that one affirms that the

essential principle of justice is the authority of the legislature; another, the convenience of the sovereign; another, present custom; and this is the safest. There is nothing, if we follow the light of reason only, that is in itself, independently just. Time alters every thing; custom makes equity, simply because it is received. That is the mystic basis of its authority, and he who traces it to its origin, annihilates it. Nothing is so faulty as those laws which redress faults. He who obeys them because they are just, obeys that which he has conceived to be justice, but not the essence of the law. Its whole force lies in this, It is law and nothing more. He who looks into the principle will find it so weak and flimsy, that if he is not accustomed to the prodigies of the human imagination, he would wonder how a century could have nourished it with so much pomp and veneration.

The secret for overturning a state, is to shake to their foundation established customs, by going back to their origin, and shewing the defect of the authority or the principle on which they rest. "We must return," say they, "to those fundamental and primitive laws of the state, which corrupt custom has abolished." This is a sure play for losing every thing. In such a balance nothing will appear right: yet the people listen eagerly to such discourses. They throw off the yoke as soon as they perceive it; and the great make their advantage of this to ruin both them and these curious inspectors of established customs. Yet there is an error directly the reverse of this, and there are men who think that any thing can be done justly, which has a precedent in its favour.

Whence one of the wisest legislators said, "That for the welfare of man, he must frequently be deceived;" and another great politician says, *Cum veritatem qua*

THE WEAKNESS OF MAN. 19

liberetur ignoret, expedit quod fallatur. Man should not ascertain the truth of the usurpation; for it was introduced in ancient times, without good reason. But now it must always be held up as authentic and eternal; we must veil its origin, if we wish it to be perpetuated.

10. Set the greatest philosopher in the world upon a plank, even broader than the space he occupies in walking on plain ground, and if there is a precipice below him, though reason convinces him of his safety, his imagination will prevail to alarm him: the very thought of it would make some perspire and turn pale. Who does not know that there are persons so nervous, that the sight of a cat, or a rat, or the crushing of a bit of coal, will almost drive them out of their senses.

11. Would you not say of that venerable magistrate, whose years command the respect of a whole people, that he is under the controul of pure and dignified wisdom, and that he judges of things as they are, without being influenced by those adventitious circumstances which warp the imagination of the weak. But see him enter the very court where he is to administer justice; see him prepare to hear with a gravity the most exemplary; but if an advocate appears to whom nature has given a hoarse voice, or a droll expression of countenance,—if his barber has but half shaved him, or an accidental splash of mud has fallen on him, I'll engage for the loss of the judge's self-possession.

12. The mind of the greatest man on earth, is not so independent of circumstances, as not to feel inconvenienced by the merest buzzing noise about him: it does

THE WEAKNESS OF MAN.

not need the report of a cannon to disturb his thoughts. The creaking of a vane or a pully is quite enough. Do not wonder that he reasons ill just now; a fly is buzzing by his ear; it is quite enough to unfit him for giving good counsel. If you wish him to see the rights of the case, drive away that insect, which suspends his reasoning powers, and frets that mighty mind which governs cities and kingdoms.

13. The will is one of the principal sources of belief; not that it produces belief, but that things appear true or false to us according to the way they are looked at. The will, which inclines to one thing more than another, turns away the mind from considering the qualities of that which it does not approve; and thus the whole mind led by the will or inclination, limits its observation to what it approves, and thus forming its judgment on what it sees: it insensibly regulates its belief by the inclinations of the will, i. e. by its own preferences.

14. Disease is another source of error. It impairs the judgment and the senses: and if serious disorders do visibly produce this effect, doubtless minor ailments do so in proportion.

Self-interest also is a surprising means of inducing a voluntary blindness. Affection or dislike will alter our notions of justice. For instance, when an advocate is well paid before hand, how much more just he thinks the cause which he has to plead. Yet owing to another strange peculiarity of the human mind, I have known men who, lest they should serve their own interest, have been cruelly unjust, through a contrary bias: so that the sure way to lose a good cause, was to get it recommended to them by one of their near relations.

15. The imagination often magnifies the veriest trifle, by a false and romantic preference, till it fills the whole soul; or in its heedless presumption, brings down the most elevated subjects to our own low standard.

16. Justice and truth are two points of such exquisite delicacy, that our coarse and blunted instruments will not touch them accurately. If they do find out the point, so as to rest upon it, they bruise and injure it, and lean at last more on the error that surrounds it, than on the truth itself.

17. It is not only old and early impressions that deceive us: the charms of novelty have the same power. Hence arise all the differences among men, who reproach each other, either with following the false impressions of their infancy, or with hastily running after new ones.

Who keeps the golden mean? Let him stand forth and prove it. There is not a single principle, however simply natural, and existing from childhood, that may not be made to appear a false impression, conveyed by instruction or the senses. Because, say they, you have believed from your infancy that a chest was empty when you saw that there was nothing in it, you have assumed that a vacuum is possible. But this is a strong delusion of your senses, confirmed by habit, which science must correct. Others on the contrary say, Because you have been taught in the schools, that there is no vacuum in nature, your common sense, which previous to this delusive impression, saw the thing clearly enough, has been corrupted, and must be corrected by a recurrence to the dictates of nature. Now, which is the deceiver here, our senses or our education?

22   THE WEAKNESS OF MAN.

18. All the occupations of men have respect to the obtaining of property; and yet the title by which they possess it, is at first only the whim of the original legislator: and after all, no power that they have, will insure possession. A thousand accidents may rob them of it. It is the same with scientific attainment: Disease takes it away.

19. What are our natural principles, but the result of custom? In children, they are those which have resulted from the custom of their parents, as the chace in animals.

A different custom would give different natural principles. Experience proves this. And if there are some that custom cannot eradicate, there are some impressions arising from custom, that nature cannot do away. This depends on disposition.

Parents fear the destruction of natural affection in their children. What is this natural principle so liable to decay? Habit is a second nature, which destroys the first. Why is not custom nature? I suspect that this nature itself, is but a first custom, as custom is a second nature.

20. If we were to dream every night the same thing, it would probably have as much effect upon us, as the objects which we see daily; and if an artisan were sure of dreaming every night for some hours continuance, that he was a king, I think he would be almost as happy as a king, who should dream every night for twelve hours successively, that he was an artisan. If we should dream every night that we are pursued by enemies, and harassed by distressing phantoms, and that we passed all our days in

different occupations, as if we were travelling; we should suffer almost as much as if this were true, and we should dread to sleep just as much as we dread to awake, when we fear to enter really upon such afflictions. In fact these dreams would be almost as serious an evil, as the reality. But because these dreams are all different, what we see in them afflicts us much less than what we see when awake, on account of its continuity;—a continuity however, not so equal and uniform that it undergoes no change, but less violently, as in a voyage; and then we say, "I seem to myself to dream;" for life is a dream a little less variable.

21. We suppose that all men conceive and feel in the same way, the objects that are presented to them: but we suppose this very gratuitously, for we have no proof of it. I see plainly that the same word is used on the same occasion; and that wherever two men see snow, for example, they express their notion of the same object by the same word,—both saying that it is white; and from this agreement of the application of terms, we draw a strong conjecture in favour of a conformity of ideas; but this is not absolutely convincing, though there is good ground for the supposition.

22. When we see an effect regularly recurring, we conclude that there is a natural necessity for it, as that the sun will rise to-morrow, &c. But in many things nature deceives us, and does not yield a perfect submission to its own laws.

23. Many things that are certain are contradicted; many that are false pass without contradiction: contra-

diction is no proof of falsehood, nor universal assent, of truth.

24. The instructed mind discovers that as nature carries the imprint of its author stamped on all things, they all have a certain relation to his two-fold infinity. Thus we see that all the sciences are infinite in the extent to which their researches may be carried. Who doubts, for instance, that geometry involves in it an infinity of infinities of propositions? It is infinite also in the multitude and the delicacy of its principles; for who does not perceive that any which are proposed as the last, must rest upon themselves, which is absurd; and that in fact they are sustained by others, which have others again for their basis, and must thus eternally exclude the idea of an ultimate proposition.

We see at a glance that arithmetic alone furnishes principles without number, and each science the same.

But if the infinitely small is much less discernible than the infinitely great, philosophers have much more readily pretended to have attained to it; and here all have stumbled. This error has given rise to those terms so commonly in use, as "the principles of things,—the principles of philosophy;" and other similar expressions, as conceited, in fact, though not quite so obtrusively so as that insufferably disgusting title, *De omni scibili*.*

Let us not seek then for assurance and stability. Our reason is perpetually deceived by the variableness of appearances, nothing can fix that which is finite, between the two infinites that enclose it, and fly from it; and

---

* The title of a thesis maintained at Rome by Jean Pic de la Miranadole.

when this is well understood, each man will, I believe, remain quietly in the position in which nature has placed him. This medium state, which has fallen to our lot, being always infinitely distant from the extremes, what matters it whether man has, or has not a little more knowledge of the things round him? If he has, why then he traces them a degree or two higher. But is he not always infinitely distant from the extremes, and is not the longest human life infinitely short of eternity?

Compared with these infinities, all finite things are equal; and I see no reason why the imagination should occupy itself with one more than another. Even the least comparison that we institute between ourselves and that which is finite, gives us pain.

25. The sciences have two extremities, which touch each other. The one is that pure natural ignorance in which we are born: the other is that point to which great minds attain, who having gone the whole round of possible human knowledge, find that they know nothing, and that they end in the same ignorance in which they began. But then this is an intelligent ignorance which knows itself. Out of the many however, who have come forth from their native ignorance, there are some who have not reached this other extreme; these are strongly tinged with scientific conceit, and set up a claim to be the learned and the intelligent. These are the men that disturb the world; and they generally judge more falsely than all others. The crowd and the men of talent generally direct the course of the world; the others despise it and are despised.

26. We think ourselves much more capable of reaching the centre of things, than of grasping the circumference. The visible expanse of the world, manifestly surpasses us; but as we visibly surpass little things, we think ourselves on a vantage ground for comprehending them; and yet it does not require less capacity to trace something down to nothing, than up to totality. This capacity, in either case, must be infinite; and it appears to me that he who can discover the ultimate principles of things, might reach also to the knowledge of the infinitely great. The one depends on the other; the one leads to the other. These extremities touch and meet in consequence of their very distance. They meet in God, and in God only.

If man would begin by studying himself, he would soon see how unable he is to go further. How can a part comprehend the whole? He would aspire probably to know, at least, those parts which are similar in proportion to himself. But all parts of creation have such a relation to each other, and are so intertwined, that I think it is impossible to know one without knowing the other, and even the whole.

Man, for instance, has a relation to all that he knows. He needs space to contain him—time for existence—motion that he may live—elements for his substance—warmth and food to nourish him, and air to breath. He sees the light, he feels his material body. In fact, every thing is allied with him.

To understand man, therefore, we must know wherein it is that air is needful for his support; and to understand air, we must trace its relation to human life.

Flame will not live without air; then to comprehend the one, we must comprehend the other also.

"There is nothing more inconceivable than that matter could comprehend itself."

Since, then, all things are either caused or causes, assisting or being assisted, mediately or immediately; and all are related to each other by a natural and imperceptible bond which unites together things the most distant and dissimilar; I hold it impossible to know the parts, without knowing the whole, and equally so to know the whole, without knowing the parts in detail.

And that which completes our inability to know the essential nature of things is, that they are simple, and that we are a compound of two different and opposing natures, body and spirit; for it is impossible that the portion of us which thinks, can be other than spiritual; and as to the pretence, that we are simply corporeal, that would exclude us still more entirely from the knowledge of things; because there is nothing more inconceivable, than that matter could comprehend itself.

It is this compound nature of body and spirit which had led almost all the philosophers to confuse their ideas of things; and to attribute to matter that which belongs only to spirit, and to spirit, that which cannot consist but with matter; for, they say boldly, That bodies tend downwards; that they seek the centre; that they shrink from destruction; that they dread a vacuum; that they have inclinations, sympathies, antipathies, &c. which are all qualities that can only exist in mind. And in speaking of spirits, they consider them as occupying a place, and attribute to them motion from one place to another, &c. which are the qualities of body.

Instead, therefore, of receiving the ideas of things, simply as they are, we tinge, with the qualities of our compound being, all the simple things that we contemplate.

Who would not suppose, when they see us attach to every thing the compound notions of body and spirit,

28   THE MISERY OF MAN.

that this mixture was familiarly comprehensible to us? Yet it is the thing of which we know the least. Man is, to himself, the most astonishing object in nature, for he cannot conceive what body is, still less what spirit is, and less than all, how a body and a spirit can be united. That is the climax of his difficulties, and yet it is his proper being. *Modus quo corporibus adhæret spiritus comprehendi ab hominibus non potest, et hoc tamen homo est.**

27. Man, then, is the subject of a host of errors, that divine grace only can remove. Nothing shews him the truth; every thing misleads him. Reason and the senses, the two means of ascertaining truth, are not only often unfaithful, but mutually deceive each other. Our senses mislead our reason by false impressions; and reason also has its revenge, by retorting the same trick upon our senses. The passions of the soul disturb the senses, and excite evil impressions; and thus our two sources of knowledge mutually lie and deceive each other.

CHAPTER IV.

THE MISERY OF MAN.

NOTHING more directly introduces us to the knowledge of human misery, than an inquiry into the cause of that perpetual restlessness in which men pass their whole lives.

---

* The union of mind with matter, is a subject utterly incomprehensible to man, and yet this is man's essential nature.

The soul is placed in the body to sojourn there for a short time. She knows that this is only the prelude to an eternal progress, to prepare for which, she has but the short period of this present life. Of this the mere necessities of nature engross a large portion, and the remainder which she might use, is small indeed. Yet this little is such a trouble to her, and the source of such strange perplexity, that she only studies how to throw it away. To live with herself, and to think of herself, is a burden quite insupportable. Hence all her care is to forget herself, and to let this period, short and precious as it is, flow on without reflection, whilst she is busied with things that prevent her from thinking of it.

This is the cause of all the bustling occupations of men, and of all that is called diversion or pastime, in which they have really but one object—to let the time glide by without perceiving it, or rather without perceiving self, and to avoid, by the sacrifice of this portion of life, the bitterness and disgust of soul which would result from self-inspection during that time. The soul finds in herself nothing gratifying. She finds nothing but what grieves her when she thinks of it. This compels her to look abroad, and to seek, by a devotion to external things, to drown the consciousness of her real condition. Her joy is in this oblivion; and to compel her to look within, and to be her own companion, is to make her thoroughly wretched.

Men are burdened from their infant years with the care of their honour and their property, and even of the property and the honour of their relations and friends. They are oppressed with the study of languages, sciences, accomplishments, and arts. They are overwhelmed with business, and are taught to believe that they cannot be

"SUCCESS SUICIDE

happy unless they manage, by their industry and attention, that their fortune and reputation, and the fortune and reputation of their friends, be flourishing; and that a failure in any one of these things would make them miserable. And hence they are engaged in duties and businesses which harass them from morning till night. "A strange method this," you would say, "to make men happy; what could we do more effectually to make them miserable?" Do you ask what we could do? Alas! we have but to release them from these cares, for then they would see and consider themselves; and this is unbearable. And in proof of this we see, that with all this mass of cares, if they have yet any interval of relaxation, they hasten to squander it on some amusement that shall completely fill the void, and hide them from themselves.

On this account, when I have set myself to consider the varied turmoil of life; the toil and danger to which men expose themselves at courts, in war, and in the pursuit of their ambitious projects, which give rise to so much quarrelling and passion, and to so many desperate and fatal adventures: I have often said that all the misfortunes of men spring from their not knowing how to live quietly at home, in their own rooms. If a man, who has enough to live on, did but know how to live with himself, he would never go to sea, or to besiege a city, merely for the sake of occupation; and he whose only object is to live, would have no need to seek such dangerous employments.

But when I have looked into the matter more closely, I have found that this aversion to repose, and to the society of self, originates in a very powerful cause, namely, in the natural evils of our weak and mortal state,—a state so completely wretched, that whenever nothing

A DANGEROUS JOURNEY IN HIS MY

THE MISERY OF MAN. 31

hinders us from thinking of it, and we thoroughly survey ourselves, we are utterly inconsolable. Of course, I speak only of those who meditate on themselves without the aid of religion. For most assuredly it is one of the wonders of the Christian religion, that it reconciles man to himself, in reconciling him to his God; that it makes self-examination bearable, and solitude and silence more interesting than the tumults and the busy intercourse of men. But religion does not produce this mighty change by confining man to the survey of himself. It does this only by leading him up to God, and sustaining him, even in the consciousness of his present misery, with the hope of another existence, in which he shall be freed from it for ever.

But as for those who act only according to the impulse of those natural motives, that they find within them, it is impossible that they can live in that tranquillity which favours self-examination, without being instantly the prey of chagrin and melancholy. The man who loves nothing but self, dislikes nothing so much as being with himself only. He seeks nothing but for himself; yet he flies from nothing so eagerly as self; for when he sees himself, he is not what he wishes; and he finds in himself an accumulation of miseries that he cannot shun, and a vacuity of all real and substantial good which he cannot fill.

Let a man choose what condition he will, and let him accumulate around him all the goods and all the gratifications seemingly calculated to make him happy in it; if that man is left at any time without occupation or amusement, and reflects on what he is, the meagre languid felicity of his present lot will not bear him up. He will turn necessarily to gloomy anticipations of the fu-

B 4

ture; and except, therefore, his occupation calls him out of himself, he is inevitably wretched.

But, is not royal dignity sufficient of itself to make its possessor happy, by the mere contemplation of what he is as a king? Must he too be withdrawn from this thought the same as other men? I see plainly that it makes a man happy to turn him away from the thought of his domestic sorrows, and to engage all the energy of his mind in the attaining of some light accomplishments, even such as dancing: but is it so with a king? Would he be happier in a devotion to these vain amusements, than in the thought of his own greatness? What object more satisfying can be given to him? Would it not be thwarting his joy, to degrade his mind to the thought how to regulate his steps by the cadence of a fiddle, or how to strike a billiard ball; instead of leaving him to enjoy in tranquillity, the contemplation of the glory and the majesty with which he is invested? Try it: leave a king to himself without any delight accruing to him through the senses; leave him without any care upon his mind, and without society, to think at his leisure of himself, and you will see that a king who looks within, is a man equally full of miseries, and equally alive to them, with other men. Hence they carefully avoid this; and there is always about the person of kings, a number of menials, whose concern it is to provide diversion when business is done, and who watch for their hours of leisure to supply them with pleasures and sports, that they may never feel vacuity; that is, in fact, they are surrounded by persons who take the most scrupulous care, that the king shall not be left alone to be his own companion, and in a situation to think of himself; because they know that if he does, with all his royalty, he must be wretched.

The principal thing which bears men up under those weighty concerns, which are, in other respects, so oppressive, is that they are thus perpetually kept from thinking of themselves.

For instance: What is the being a governor, a chancellor, a prime minister, but the having a number of attendants flocking on every side to prevent them from having a single hour in the day in which they can think of self? And when such men are out of favour, and are banished to their country-seats, where they have no want of either money or servants to supply their real wants, then indeed they are wretched, because then they have leisure to think of self without hindrance.

Hence it is that so many persons fly to play or to field sports, or to any other amusement which occupies the whole soul. Not that they expect happiness from any thing so acquired, or that they suppose that real bliss centres in the money that they win, or the hare that they catch. They would not have either as a gift. The fact is, they are not seeking for that mild and peaceful course which leaves a man leisure to speculate on his unhappy condition, but for that incessant hurry which renders this impracticable.

Hence it is, that men love so ardently the whirl and the tumult of the world; that imprisonment is so fearful a punishment; and that so few persons can endure solitude.

This, then, is all that men have devised to make themselves happy. And those who amuse themselves by shewing the emptiness and the poverty of such amusements, have certainly a right notion of a part of human misery; for it is no small evil to be capable of finding pleasure in things so low and contemptible; but they do not yet know the full depth of that misery which renders these same miserable and base expedients absolutely necessary to man, so long as he is not cured of that internal natural evil, the not being able to endure the contemplation of himself. The hare that he buys in the market, will not call him off from himself, but the chase of it may. And therefore, when we tell them that what they seek so ardently will not satisfy them, and that nothing can be more mean and profitless, we know that, if they answered as they would do if they thought seriously of it, they would so far agree with us at once; only that they would say also, that they merely seek in these things a violent impetuous occupation, which shall divert them from themselves, and that with this direct intention, they choose some attractive object which engages and occupies them entirely. But then they will not answer in this way, because they do not know themselves. A gentleman believes sincerely that there is something noble and dignified in the chace. He will say it is a royal sport. And it is the same with other things which occupy the great mass of men. They conceive that there is something really and substantially good in the object itself. A man persuades himself that if he obtained this employment, then he would enjoy repose. But he does not perceive the insatiability of his own desires; and while he believes that he is in search of rest, he is actually seeking after additional care.

Men have a secret instinct leading them to seek pleasure and occupation from external sources, which originates in the sense of their continual misery. But they have also another secret instinct, a remnant of the original grandeur of their nature, which intimates to them that happiness is to be found only in repose; and from these opposite instincts, there emanates a confused project, which is hidden from their view in the very depth of the soul, and which prompts them to seek repose by incessant action; and ever to expect that the fulness of enjoyment, which as yet they have not attained, will infallibly be realized, if, by overcoming certain difficulties which immediately oppose them, they might open the way to rest.

And thus the whole of life runs away. We seek repose by the struggle with opposing difficulties, and the instant we have overcome them, that rest becomes insupportable. For generally we are occupied either with the miseries which now we feel, or with those which threaten; and even when we see ourselves sufficiently secure from the approach of either, still fretfulness, though unwarranted by either present or expected affliction, fails not to spring up from the deep recesses of the heart, where its roots naturally grow, and to fill the soul with its poison.

And hence it is plain, that when Cineas said to Pyrrhus, who proposed to himself, after having conquered a large portion of the world, then to sit down and enjoy repose with his friends, that he had better hasten forward his own happiness now, by immediately enjoying repose, than seek it through so much fatigue; he advised a course which involved very serious difficulties, and which was scarcely more rational than the project of this hero's youthful ambition. Both plans assumed that man can be satisfied with himself, and with his present blessings, and not feel a void in his heart, which must be filled with imaginary hopes: and here they were both in error. Pyrrhus could not have been happy either before or after the conquest of the world; and most probably the life of indolent repose which his minister recommended, was less adapted to satisfy him, than the restless hurry of his intended wars and wanderings.

We are compelled then to admit, that man is so wretched, that he will vex himself, independently of any external cause of vexation, from the mere circumstances of his natural condition; and yet with all this he is so vain and full of levity, that in the midst of a thousand causes of real distress, the merest trifle serves to divert him. So that on serious reflection, we see that he is far more to be commiserated that he can find enjoyment in things so frivolous and so contemptible, than that he mourns over his real sorrows. His amusements are infinitely less rational than his lamentations.

2. Whence is it that this man, who lost so lately an only son, and who, under the pressure of legal processes and disputes, was this morning so harassed, now thinks of these things no more? Alas! it is no wonder. He is wholly engrossed in watching the fate of a poor deer, that his dogs have been chasing for six hours. And nothing more than this is necessary for a man, though he is brimful of sorrows! If he can but be induced to apply himself to some source of recreation, he is happy for the time; but then it is with a false and delusive happiness, which comes not from the possession of any real and substantial good, but from a spirit of levity, that drowns the memory of his real griefs, and occupies him with mean and contemptible things, utterly unworthy of his attention, much more of his love. It is a morbid and frantic joy, which flows not from the health of the soul, but from its disorder. It is the laugh of folly and of delusion. It is wonderful also to think what it is which pleases men in their sports and recreations. It is true, that by oc-

cupying the mind, they seduce it from the consciousness of its real sorrows: and so far is a reality. But then they are only capable of occupying the mind at all, because it has created for itself in them, a merely imaginary object of desire, to which it is fondly and passionately devoted.

What think you is the object of those men who are playing at tennis with such intense interest of mind and effort of body? Merely to boast the next day among their friends, that they have played better than another. There is the spring of their devotedness. Others again, in the same way, toil in their closets to shew the *Savans* that they have solved a question in algebra, which was never solved before. Others expose themselves, with at least equal folly, to the greatest dangers, to boast at length of some place that they have taken: and others there are, who wear out life in remarking on those things; not that they themselves may grow wiser, but purely to shew that they see the folly of them. And these seem the silliest of all; because they are conscious of their folly: whilst we may hope of the others, that they would act differently if they knew better.

3. A man will pass his days without weariness, in daily play for a trifling stake, whom you would make directly wretched, by giving to him each morning the probable winnings of the day, on condition of his not playing. You will say "But it is the amusement he wants, and not the gain." Then make him play for nothing, and you will see that for want of a risk, he will lose interest, and become weary. Evidently, then, it is not only amusement that he seeks. An amusement not calculated to excite the passions, is languid and fatiguing. He must get warmth, animation, stimulus, in the thought that he shall

be happy in winning a trifle, that he would not consider worth a straw, if it were offered him without the risk of play. He must have an object of emotion adequate to excite desire, and anger, and hope, and fear.

So that the amusements which constitute mens happiness here, are not only mean,—they are false and deceitful: that is to say, they have for their object a set of phantoms and illusions, which actually could not occupy the human mind, if it had not lost its taste and feeling for that which is really good,—if it were not filled with low and mean propensities, with vanity, and levity, and pride, and a host of other vices. And these diversions only alleviate our present sorrows, by originating a misery more real and more humiliating. For it is they which mainly hinder us from thinking of ourselves, and make us lose our time without perceiving it. Without them, we should be unhappy, and this unhappiness would drive us to seek some more satisfactory way of peace. But amusement allures and deceives us, and leads us down imperceptibly in thoughtlessness to the grave.

Men finding that they had no remedy for death, misery, and ignorance, have imagined that the way to happiness was not to think of these things. This is all that they have been able to invent, to console themselves in the midst of so much evil. But it is wretched comfort; since it does not profess to cure the mischief, but merely to hide it for a short time. And it does so hide it, as to prevent all serious thought of an effectual cure. And thus a man, finds, that by a strange derangement of his nature, *ennui*, which is the evil that he most strongly feels, is in a certain sense his greatest good; and that amusement which he regards as his best blessing, is, in fact, his most serious evil; because it operates more than any thing else to prevent him from seeking a remedy for his miseries; and both of them are a striking proof of the misery and corruption of man, and of his greatness also; since both that weariness which he feels in all things, and that restless search after various and incessant occupation, spring equally from the consciousness of a happiness which he has lost; which happiness, as he does not find it in himself, he seeks fruitlessly through the whole round of visible things; but never finds peace, because it is not in us, nor in the creature at all, but in God only.

Whilst our own nature makes us miserable in whatever state we are, our desires paint to us another condition as being happy, because they join to that in which we are, the pleasures of a condition in which we are not; and whenever we shall attain to those expected pleasures, we shall not be therefore happy, because other desires will then spring up conformed to some other condition, yet new and unattained.

Imagine a number of men in chains, and all condemned to die, and that while some are slaughtered daily in the sight of their companion, those who yet remain see their own sad destiny in that of the slain, and gazing on each other in hopeless sorrow, await their doom. This is a picture of the condition of human nature.

CHAPTER V.

THE WONDERFUL CONTRARIETIES WHICH ARE FOUND IN MAN WITH RESPECT TO TRUTH, HAPPINESS, AND MANY OTHER SUBJECTS.

THERE is nothing more extraordinary in the nature of man, than the contrarieties, which are discovered in it on almost every subject. Man is formed for the knowledge of truth; he ardently desires it; he seeks it; and yet, when he strives to grasp it, he so completely dazzles and confounds himself, that he gives occasion to doubt whether he has attained it or not.

This has given rise to the two sects of the Pyrrhonists and the Dogmatists, of whom the one would deny that men knew any thing of truth; the other professed to shew them that they knew it accurately; but each advanced reasons so improbable, that they only increased that confusion and perplexity in which man must continue, so long as he obtains no other light than that of his own understanding.

The chief reasons of the Pyrrhonists are these, that we have no assurance of the truth of our principles (setting aside faith and revelation) except that we find them intuitively within us. But this intuitive impression is not a convincing proof of their truth; because, as without the aid of faith, we have no certainty whether man was made by a benevolent Deity, or a wicked demon, whether man is from eternity, or the offspring of chance, it must remain doubtful whether these principles are given to us,— are true or false; or like our origin, uncertain. Further, that excepting by faith, a man has no assurance whether

eps or wakes; seeing that in his sleep he does not
is firmly believe that he is awake, than when he
is so. He sees spaces, figures, movements; he is
le of the lapse of time; he measures it; he acts, in
as if he were awake. So that as one half of life is
ted by us to be passed in sleep, in which, however
y appear otherwise, we have no perception of truth,
ll our feelings are delusions; who knows but the
half of life, in which we think we are awake, is a
also, but in some respects different from the other,
om which we wake, when we, as we call it, sleep.
nan dreams often that he is dreaming, crowding
reamy delusion on another.

ave untouched the arguments of the Pyrrhonists
it the impressions of habit, education, manners, and
ial customs, and the crowd of similar influences
carry along the majority of mankind, who build
opinions on no more solid foundation.

> only strong point of the Dogmatists is, that we
t, consistently with honesty and sincerity, doubt our
ituitive principles. We know the truth, they say,
ily by reasoning, but by feeling, and by a quick and
ous power of direct comprehension; and it is by
ist faculty that we discern first principles. It is
in for reasoning, which has no share in discover-
iese principles, to attempt subverting them. The
onists who attempt this, must try in vain. How-
mable we may be by reasoning to prove the fact,
e know that we do not dream. And this inability
prove the feebleness of our reason, but not as they
id, the want of reality and substance in the sub-
f our knowledge. For the knowledge of first prin-
, as the ideas of space, time, motion, number, mat-

ter, is as unequivocally certain, as any that reasoning imparts. And, after all, it is on the perceptions of common sense and feeling, that reason must, at last, sustain itself, and found its own argument. I perceive that space has three dimensions, and that number is infinite, and reason demonstrates from this, that there are not two square numbers, of which one is just double of the other. Principles are perceived, propositions are deduced: each part of the process is certain, though in different ways. And it is as ridiculous that reason should require of feeling and perception, proofs of these first principles, before she assents to them, as it would be that perception should require from reason an intuitive impression of all the propositions at which she arrives. This weakness, therefore, will only serve to abase that reason which would become the judge of all things, but not to invalidate the convictions of common sense, as if reason only could be our guide and teacher. Would to God, on the contrary, that we had no need of reason, but that we knew everything intuitively by instinct and feeling. But this blessing is withheld from us by our nature; our knowledge by intuitive impression is very scanty; and every thing else must be attained by reasoning.

Here then is war openly proclaimed among men. Each one must take a side; must necessarily range himself with the Pyrrhonists or the Dogmatists; for he who would think to remain neuter, is a Pyrrhonist *par excellence*. This neutrality is the very essence of Pyrrhonism. He who is not against them, is completely for them. What then must a man do in this alternative? Shall he doubt of every thing? Shall he doubt that he is awake, or that he is pinched or burned? Shall he doubt that he doubts? Shall he doubt that he is? We cannot get so far as this;

and I hold it to be a fact, that there never has been an absolute and perfect Pyrrhonist. Nature props up the weakness of reason, and prevents her from reaching this point of extravagance. But then on the other side, shall man affirm that he possesses the truth with certainty, who, if you press him ever so little, can bring no proof of the fact, and is forced to loose his hold?

Who shall clear up this perplexity? Common sense confutes the Pyrrhonists, and reason the Dogmatists. What then must become of thee, O man, who searchest out thy true condition, by the aid of natural reason? You cannot avoid adopting one of these opinions; but to maintain either, is impossible.

Such is man in regard to the truth. Consider him now with respect to that happiness, which in all his actions, he seeks with so much avidity; for all men, without exception, desire to be happy. However different the means which they adopt, they aim at the same result. The cause of one man engaging in war, and of another remaining at home, is this same desire of happiness, associated with different predilections. He will never stir a step but towards this desired object. It is the motive of all the actions of all men, even of those who destroy themselves.

And yet, after the lapse of so many years, no one has ever attained to this point at which we are all aiming, but by faith. All are unhappy: princes and their subjects, noble and ignoble, the old and the young, the strong and the weak, the learned and the ignorant, the sick and the healthy of all countries, all times, all ages, and all conditions.

Experience so lengthened, so continual, and so uniform, might well convince us of our inability to be happy by our own efforts. But then here we get no profit from example. It is never so precisely similar, but that there is some slight difference, on the strength of which, we calculate that our hope shall not be disappointed, in this as in former instances. And thus while the present never satisfies us, hope allures us onward, and leads us from misfortune to misfortune, and finally to death and everlasting ruin.

It is remarkable, that in the whole range of nature, there is nothing that has not been accounted fit to become the chief end and happiness of man. The stars, the elements, plants, animals, insects, diseases, wars, vices, crimes, &c. Man having fallen from his original and natural state, there is nothing however mean on which he does not fix his vagrant affections. Since he lost that which is really good, any thing can assume the semblance of it, even self-destruction, though it is so manifestly contrary at once both to reason and to nature.

Some have sought happiness in power; some in science or in curious research; and some in voluptuous pleasure. These three propensities have given rise to three sects; and they who are called philosophers, have merely followed one or other of them. Those who have come nearest to happiness have thought, that *the universal good* which all men desire, and in which all should share, cannot be any one particular thing, which one only can possess, and which if it be divided, ministers more sorrow to its possessor, on account of that which he has not, than pleasure in the enjoyment of that which he has. They conceived that *the true good* must be such that all may enjoy it at once, without imperfection and without envy; and that no one could lose it against his will. They have rightly understood the blessing, but they could not find

nd instead of a solid and practical good, they have
aced its visionary semblance, in an unreal and chi-
al virtue.

tinct tells us, that we must seek our happiness
n ourselves. Our passions drive us forth to seek
things external, even when those things are not ac-
y present to minister excitement. External objects
hemselves also our tempters, and entice us even
we are not aware. The philosophers then will but
y say, "Be occupied with yourselves, for there you
nd your happiness." Few believe them ; and the few
lo, are more empty and foolish than any. For can
hing be more contemptible and silly, than what the
s call happiness? or more false than all their rea-
gs on the subject?
ey affirm that man can do at all times what he has
once; and that since the love of fame prompts its
ssor to do some things well, others may do the same.
hose actions are the result of feverish excitement,
ι health cannot imitate.

The intestine war of reason against the passions,
iven rise, among those who wish for peace, to the
ition of two different sects. The one wished to re-
:e the passions and to be as Gods; the other to re-
:e their reason, and become beasts. But neither
icceeded; and reason still remains, to point out the
ess and moral pravity of the passions, and to disturb
epose of those who yield to them; and the passions
;ill vigorously in action in the hearts of those who
o renounce them.

This then is all that man can do in his own strength
egard to truth and happiness. We have a powerless-

ness for determining truth, which no dogmatism can overcome: we have a vague notion of truth, which no pyrrhonism can destroy. We wish for truth, and find within only uncertainty. We seek for happiness, and find nothing but misery. We cannot but wish for truth and happiness; yet we are incapable of attaining either. The desire is left to us, as much to punish us, as to shew us whence we are fallen.

4. If man was not made for God, why is he never happy but in God? If man is made for God, why is he so contrary to God?

5. Man knows not in what rank of beings to place himself. He is manifestly astray, and perceives in himself the remnant indications of a happy state, from which he has fallen, and which he cannot recover. He is ever seeking it, with restless anxiety, without success, and in impenetrable darkness. This is the source of all the contests of the philosophers. One class has undertaken to elevate man by displaying his greatness; the other to abase him by the exhibition of his wretchedness. And what is most extraordinary is, that each party makes use of the reasonings of the other, to establish its own opinions. For the misery of man is inferrible from his greatness, and his greatness from his misery. And thus the one class has more effectually proved his misery, because they deduced it from his greatness; and the other established much more powerfully the fact of his greatness, because they proved it even from his misery. All that the one could say of his greatness, served but as an argument to the other, to prove his misery; inasmuch as the misery of having fallen, is aggravated in proportion

as the point from which we fell is shewn to be more elevated; and *vice versa.* Thus they have outgone each other successively, in an eternal circle; it being certain, that as men increased in illumination, they would multiply proofs, both of their greatness and their misery. In short, man knows that he is wretched. He is wretched, because he knows it. Yet in this he is evidently great, that he knows himself to be wretched.

What a chimera then is man. What a singular phenomenon! What a chaos! What a scene of contrariety! A judge of all things, yet a feeble worm; the shrine of truth, yet a mass of doubt and uncertainty: at once the glory and the scorn of the universe. If he boasts, I lower him; if he lowers himself, I raise him; either way I contradict him, till he learns that he is a monstrous incomprehensible mystery.

CHAPTER VI.

ON AVOWED INDIFFERENCE TO RELIGION.

IT were to be wished, that the enemies of religion would at least learn what religion is, before they oppose it. If religion boasted of the unclouded vision of God, and of disclosing him without a covering or veil, then it were victory to say that nothing in the world discovers him with such evidence. But since religion, on the contrary, teaches that men are in darkness, and far from God; that he is hidden from them, and that the very name which he gives himself in the Scriptures, is " a God that hideth himself;" and, in fact, since it labours to establish these two maxims, that God has placed in his church, certain characters of himself, by which he will make himself known to those who sincerely seek him; and yet that he has, at the same time, so far covered them, as to render himself imperceptible to those who do not seek him with their whole heart, what advantage do men gain, that, in the midst of their criminal negligence in the search of truth, they complain so frequently that nothing reveals and displays it to them? seeing that this very obscurity under which they labour, and which they thus bring against the Christian church, does but establish one of the two grand points which she maintains, without affecting the other; and instead of ruining, confirms her doctrines.

To contend with any effect, the opposers of religion should be able to urge, that they have applied their utmost endeavours, and have used all the means of information, even those which the Christian church recommends, without obtaining satisfaction. If they could say this, it were indeed to attack one of her main pretensions. But I hope to shew that no rational person can affirm this; nay, I venture to assert that none ever did. We know very well how men of this spirit are wont to act. They conceive that they have made a mighty effort towards the instruction of their minds, when they have spent a few hours in reading the Scriptures, and have put a few questions to a minister on the articles of the faith. And then they boast of having consulted both men and books without success. Really I cannot help telling such men, what I have often told them, that this negligence is insufferable. This is not a question about the petty interests of some stranger. Ourselves and our all are involved in it.

The immortality of the soul is a matter of such main

mportance, so profoundly interesting to us, that we must be utterly dead to every good feeling, if we could be indifferent about it. And all our actions and thoughts would take so different a course, according as we have or have not the hope of eternal blessings, that it is impossible for us to take one step discretely, but as we keep this point ever in view, as our main and ultimate object.

It is, then, both our highest interest, and our first duty, to get light on this subject, on which our whole conduct depends. And here, therefore, in speaking of those who are sceptical on this point, I make a wide distinction between those who labour with all their power to obtain instruction, and those who live on in indolence, without caring to make any inquiry. I do heartily pity those who sincerely mourn over their scepticism, who look upon it as the greatest of misfortunes, and who spare no pains to escape from it, but who make these researches their chief and most serious employ. But as for those who pass their life without reflecting on its close; and who, merely because they find not in themselves a convincing testimony, refuse to seek it elsewhere, and to examine thoroughly, whether the opinion proposed be such as nothing but a credulous simplicity receives, or such as, though obscure in itself, is yet founded on a solid basis, I regard them very differently. The carelessness which they betray in a matter which involves their existence, their eternity, their all, awakes my indignation, rather than my pity. It is astonishing. It is horrifying. It is monstrous. I speak not this from the pious zeal of a blind devotion. On the contrary, I affirm that self-love, that self-interest, that the simplest light of reason, should inspire these sentiments; and, in fact, for this we need but the perceptions of ordinary men.

C

It requires but little elevation of soul to discover, that here there is no substantial delight; that our pleasures are but vanity, that the ills of life are innumerable; and that, after all, death, which threatens us every moment, must, in a few years, perhaps in a few days, place us in the eternal condition of happiness, or misery, or nothingness. Between us and heaven, hell or annihilation, no barrier is interposed but life, which is of all things the most fragile; and as they who doubt the immortality of the soul, can have no hope of heaven, they can have no prospect but hell or nonentity.

Nothing can be more true than this, and nothing more terrible. Brave it how we will, there ends the goodliest life on earth.

It is in vain for men to turn aside from this coming eternity, as if a bold indifference could destroy its being. It subsists notwithstanding. It hastens on; and death, which must soon unveil it, will, in a short time, infallibly reduce them to the dreadful necessity of being annihilated for ever, or for ever wretched.

Here then is a doubt of the most alarming importance; to feel this doubt is already, in itself, a serious evil. But that doubt imposes on us the indispensible duty of inquiry.

He, then, who doubts, and yet neglects inquiry, is both uncandid and unhappy. But if, notwithstanding his doubts, he is calm and contented; if he freely avows his ignorance; nay, if he makes it his boast, and seems to make this very indifference the subject of his joy and triumph, no words can adequately describe his extravagant infatuation.

Where do men get these opinions? What delight is there in expecting misery without end? What ground is there for boasting in the experience of nothing but impenetrable darkness? Or what consolation in despairing for ever of a comforter?

Acquiescence in such ignorance is monstrous, and they who thus linger on through life, should be made sensible of its absurdity and stupidity, by shewing them what passes in their own breasts, so as to confound them by a sight of their own folly. For men who thus choose to remain ignorant of what they are, and who seek no means of illumination, reason in this way:—

"I know not who has sent me into the world, nor what the world is, nor what I am myself. I am awfully ignorant of all things. I know not what my body is, what my senses are, or what my soul is. This very part of me which thinks what I now speak, which reflects upon all other things, and even upon itself, is equally a stranger to itself, and to all around it. I look through the vast and terrific expanse of the universe by which I am encompassed; and I find myself chained to one petty corner of the wide domain; without understanding why I am fixed in this spot, rather than in any other; or why this little hour of life was assigned me at this point, rather than at any other of all that eternity which was before me, or of all that which is to come. On every side I see nothing but infinities, which enfathom me in their abysses as a mere atom, or as a shadow which lingers but a single instant, and is never to return. All that I know is, that I must shortly die; and that of which I know the least, is this very death, from which I cannot fly.

"As I know not whence I came, so I know not whither I go. This only I know, that when I leave this world, I must either fall for ever into nothingness, or into the hands of an incensed God; but I know not to which of these two conditions I shall be eternally doomed.

"Such is my state; full of misery, of imbecility, of darkness. And from all this, I argue that it becomes me to pass all the days of my life, without considering what shall hereafter befal me; and that I have nothing to do, but to follow the bent of my inclinations, without reflection or disquiet, and if there be an eternity of misery, to do my utmost to secure it. Perhaps inquiry might throw some light upon my doubts; but I will not take the pains to make it, nor stir one foot to find the truth. On the contrary, while I shew my contempt for those who annoy themselves by this inquiry, I wish to rush without fear or foresight upon the risk of this dread contingency. I will suffer myself to be led imperceptibly on to death, in utter uncertainty as to the issue of my future lot in eternity."

Verily, religion may glory in having for its enemies, men so irrational as these; their opposition is so little to be dreaded, that it serves, in fact, to illustrate the main truths which our religion teaches. For our religious system aims chiefly to establish these two principles,—the corruption of human nature, and redemption by Jesus Christ. Now, if these opposers are of no use in confirming the truth of redemption, by the sanctity of their lives; yet they admirably prove the corruption of nature, by the maintenance of such unnatural opinions.

Nothing is so important to any man as his own condition; nothing so formidable as eternity. They, therefore, who are indifferent to the loss of their being, and to the risk of endless misery, are in an unnatural state. They act quite differently from this in all other matters; they fear the smallest inconveniences; they anticipate them; they feel them when they arrive; and he who passes days and nights in indignation and despair, at the loss of an employment, or for some fancied blemish on his honour, is the very same man who knows that he must soon lose all by death, and yet continues satisfied, fearless, and unmoved. Such an insensibility to things of the most tremendous consequences, in a heart so keenly alive to the merest trifles, is an astonishing prodigy, an incomprehensible enchantment, a supernatural infatuation.

A man in a dungeon, who knows not if the sentence of death has gone forth against him, who has but one hour to ascertain the fact, and that one hour sufficient, if he knows that it is granted, to secure its revocation, acts contrary to nature and to common sense, if he employs that hour, not in the needful inquiry, but in sport and trifling. Now, this is the condition of the persons whom we are describing; only with this difference, that the evils with which they are every moment threatened, do infinitely surpass the mere loss of this life, and that transient punishment which the prisoner has to dread. Yet they run thoughtlessly onward to the precipice, having only cast a veil over their eyes to hinder them from discerning it; and then, in a dreadful security, they mock at those who warn them of their danger.

Thus, not only does the zeal of those who seek God, demonstrate the truth of religion, but even the blindness of those who seek him not, and who pass their days in this criminal neglect. Human nature must have experienced a dreadful revolution, before men could live contentedly in this state, much more before they could boast of it. For supposing that they were absolutely certain, that there was nothing to fear after death, but annihilation, is not this a cause rather for despair, than for gratulation. But seeing that we have not even this assurance, then is it not inconceivably silly to boast, because we are in doubt?

54   INDIFFERENCE TO RELIGION.

And yet, after all, it is too evident, that man is
nature so debased, as to nourish in his heart a sec
on this account. This brutal insensibility to the
hell or of annihilation, is thought so noble, that ne
do those who really are sceptically inclined make
boast of it, but even those who are not, are pr
counterfeit a doubt. For experience proves, th
greater part of these men are of this latter kind,
pretenders to Infidelity, and hypocrites in Atheism.
have been told that the spirit of high life consists
ing above these vulgar prejudices. They call this
ing off the yoke of bondage; and most men do th
from conviction, but from the mere servile princ
imitation.

Yet if they have but a particle of common se
maining, it will not be difficult to make them e
hend, how miserably they abuse themselves by s
credit in such a course. For this is not the way
tain respect, even with men of the world; for they
accurately, and know that the only sure way to s
in obtaining regard, is to approve ourselves
faithful, prudent, and capable of advancing the i
of our friends; because men naturally love no
those who can contribute to their welfare. But no
can we gain by hearing any man confess that
thrown off the yoke; that he does not believe in
who watches over his conduct; that he considers
as the absolute master of his own actions, and ac
able for them only to himself. Will he imagine t
shall now repose in him a greater degree of con
than before, and that henceforth we shall look to h
comfort, advice or assistance in the vicissitudes o
Does he think that we are delighted to hear t

doubts whether our very soul be any thing more than a breath or a vapour, and that he can tell it us with an air of assurance and self-sufficiency? Is this then the topic for a jest? Should it not rather be told with tears, as the saddest of all sorrowful things?

If they thought seriously, they would see that this conduct is so contrary to sound sense, to virtuous principle, and to good taste, and so widely removed from the reality of that elevation to which they pretend, that nothing can more effectually expose them to the contempt and aversion of mankind, or more evidently mark them for weakness of intellect, and want of judgment. And indeed, should we require of them an account of their sentiments, and of their doubts on the subject of religion, their statements would be found so miserably weak and trifling, as to confirm, rather than shake our confidence. This was once very aptly remarked by one of their own number, in answer to an infidel argument: "Positively if you continue to dispute at this rate, you will actually make me a Christian." And he was right; for who would not tremble to find himself associated in his opinions and his lot, with men so truly despicable?

They also who do no more than pretend to hold these sentiments, are truly pitiable; for by the assumption of an insincere infidelity, they actually controul their better natural tendencies, only to make themselves of all men the most inconsistent. If from their inmost heart they regret that they have not more light, why do they not confess it? Such a confession would be no disgrace; for there is really no shame, but in shamelessness. Nothing more completely betrays a weak mind, than insensibility to the fact of the misery of man, while living without God in the world. Nothing more strongly indicates extreme

degradation of spirit, than not to wish for the tru
God's eternal promises. No man is so base as he
defies his God. Let them therefore leave those imp
to those who are vile and wretched enough to be it
nest. If they cannot be completely Christians, at
let them be honest men; and let them at length
the fact, that there are but two classes of men, who
be called truly rational:—those who serve God wi
their heart, because they know him; and those who
him with all their heart, because as yet they knov
not.

If there are any who sincerely inquire after God
who, being truly sensible of their misery, affectio:
desire to emerge from it; for these we ought to h
that we may lead them to the discovery of that
which they have not yet discovered.

But as for those who live without either knowing
or endeavouring to know him, they count themsel
little worthy of their own care, that they can hard
serve the care of others: and it requires all the c
of the religion which they despise, not to despise th
far as to abandon them to their folly. But since o
ligion obliges us to consider them, while they rem
this life, as still capable of receiving God's enlight
grace, and to believe that in the course of a few
they may possess a more realising faith than ours
and that we, on the other side, may become as bl
they; we ought to do for them what we would wish
to do for us, if we were in their circumstances; we
intreat them to take pity on themselves, and at le
take some steps forward, and try if they may not ye
the light. Let them give to the reading of this w
few of those hours which they would otherwise spend

ON THE BELIEF OF A GOD. 57

unprofitably. Something they may gain: they can lose but little. But if any shall bring to this work, a perfect sincerity, and an unfeigned desire of knowing truth, I would hope that they will find comfort in it, and be convinced by those proofs of our divine religion, which are here accumulated.

CHAPTER VII.

THAT THE BELIEF OF A GOD IS THE TRUE WISDOM.

LET us speak according to the light of nature. If there is a God, he is to us infinitely incomprehensible; because having neither parts nor limits, there is no affinity or resemblance between him and us. We are, then, incapable of comprehending his nature, or even knowing his existence. And under these circumstances, who will dare to undertake the solving of this question? Certainly not we, who have no point of assimilation with him.

2. I will not undertake here to prove by natural reason, either the existence of God, the doctrine of the Trinity, or the immortality of the soul, nor any other point of this kind; not only that I do not feel myself strong enough to bring forth from the resources of weak reason, proofs that would convince a hardened Atheist; but that this knowledge, if gained without the faith of Jesus Christ, were equally barren and useless. Suppose a man to become convinced that the proportions of numbers are

truths immaterial*, and eternal, and dependant on one first truth, on which they subsist, and which is called God : I do not find that man advanced one step further towards his own salvation.

3. It is surprising that no canonical writer has made use of nature to prove the existence of God. They all tend to establish the belief of this truth ; yet they have not said, There is no void, then there is a God; it follows, then, that they were more intelligent than the ablest of those who have come after them, who have all had recourse to this method.

If it is a proof of weakness to prove the existence of God from nature, then do not despise the Scripture ; if it is a proof of wisdom to discern the contradictions of nature, then venerate this in the Scripture.

4. Unity added to infinity does not augment it, any more than another foot does a line of infinite length. What is finite is lost in that which is infinite, and shrinks to nothing. So does our mind in respect of the mind of God, and our righteousness when compared with his. The difference between unity and infinity is not so great, as that between our righteousness and the righteousness of God.

5. We know that there is an infinite, but we know not its nature. For instance, we know that it is false that number is finite. Then it is true that there is an infinity in number; but what that infinity is, we know not. It cannot be equal or unequal, for the addition of unity

---

* Existing independent of matter.

ON THE BELIEF OF A GOD. 59

to infinity does not change its nature; yet it is a number, and every number is equal or unequal; this is the case with all finite numbers. In the same way, we may know that there is a God, without knowing what he is; and we ought not to conclude that God is not, because we cannot perfectly comprehend his nature.

To convince you of the being of a God, I shall make no use of the faith by which we know him assuredly, nor of any other proofs with which we are satisfied, because you will not receive them. I will only treat with you upon your own principles, and I expect to shew you, by the mode in which you reason daily, in matters of small importance, how you should reason in this; and what side you should take in the decision of this important question of the being of a God. You say that we cannot discover whether there be a God or not. This however is certain, either that God is, or that God is not. There is no medium point between these two alternatives. But which side shall we take? Reason, you say, cannot decide at all. There is an infinite chaos between us and the point in question. We play a game at an infinite distance, ignorant whether the coin we throw shall fall cross or pile. How then can we wager? By reasoning we cannot make sure that it is the one or the other. By reasoning we cannot deny that it is the one or the other.

Do not then charge with falsehood those who have taken a side, for you know not that they are wrong, and that they have chosen ill. "No, say you, I do not blame them for having made this choice, but for making any choice whatever. To take a risk on either alternative, is equally wrong: the wise course is not to choose at all." But you must wager; this is not a matter of choice. You are inevitably committed; and not to wager that

That religion, which consists in the belief of man's fall from a state of glory and communication with God, into a state of sorrow, humiliation, and alienation from God; and of his subsequent restoration by a Messiah, has always been in the world. All things else have passed away, but this, for which all other things exist, remains. For God, in his wisdom, designing to form to himself a holy people, whom he would separate from all other nations, deliver from their enemies, and lead to a place of rest, did promise that he would do this, and that he would come himself into the world to do it; and did foretel by his prophets, the very time and manner of his coming. In the mean while, to confirm the hope of his elect through all ages, he continually exhibited this aid to them in types and figures, and never left them without some evident assurances of his power and willingness to save. For immediately after the creation, Adam was made the witness to this truth, and the depository of the promise of a Saviour, to be born of the seed of the woman. And though men at a period so near to their creation, could not have altogether forgotten their origin, their fall, and the divine promise of a Redeemer; yet since the world in its very infancy was overrun with every kind of corruption and violence, God was pleased to raise up holy men, as Enoch, Lamech, and others, who, with faith and patience, waited for that Saviour who had been promised from the beginning of the world. At the last, God sent Noah, who was permitted to experience the malignant wickedness of man in its highest degree; and then God saved him, when he drowned the whole world, by a miracle, which testified, at once, the power of God to save the world, and his willingness to do it, and to raise up to the woman the seed which He had promised. This miracle,

foolishly. It is false that there is an infinite distance between the certainty we hazard, and the uncertainty of winning. Though it is true that there is an infinite distance between the certainty of gaining and the certainty of losing. But the uncertainty of winning is in proportion to the certainty which is hazarded, according to the proportion of the chances of gain or loss. And hence it follows, that if the risks be equal on both sides, then the match to be played is equal against equal; and then the certainty of that which is hazarded, is equal to the uncertainty of winning; so far is it from being infinitely distant. And thus our proposition is of infinite force, since we have but that which is finite to hazard, and that which is infinite to gain, in a play where the chances of gain or loss are equal. This is demonstration, and if men can discern truth at all, they should perceive this.

I admit this: but is there no mode of getting at the principles of the game? Yes, by the Scriptures, and by the other innumerable proofs of religion. They, you will say, who hope for salvation, are happy in that hope. But is it not counterbalanced by the fear of hell? But who has most reason to fear that hell? he who is ignorant that there is a hell, and is certain of damnation if there is; or he who is convinced of its existence, and lives in the hope of escaping it? He who had but eight days to live, and should conceive that the wisest course for him is, to believe that all this is a matter of mere chance, must be totally demented. Now, if we were not enslaved by our passions, eight days, or a hundred years are precisely the same thing.

And what harm will arise from taking this side? you would become faithful, pure, humble, grateful, beneficent, sincere and true. I grant that you would not be given up to polluting pleasures, to false glory, or false joys. But then, have you not other pleasures? I affirm that you would be a gainer, even in this life; and that every step you go forward, you will see so much of the certainty of what you will gain, and so much of the utter insignificance of what you risk, that you will in the end discover, that you ventured for a good, both infinite and certain, and that to get it, you have given nothing.

You say that you are so constituted, that you cannot believe; and you ask, what you should do. Learn, at least, your inaptitude to believe, seeing that reason suggests belief, as your wisdom, and yet you remain unbelieving. Aim, then, to obtain conviction, not by any increase of proof of the existence of God, but by the discipline and controul of your own passions. You wish to obtain faith, but you know not the way to it. You wish to be cured of infidelity, and you ask for the remedy. Learn it, then, from those who have been, what you are, and who now have no doubt. They know the way for which you are seeking, and they are healed of a disease for which you seek a cure. Follow their course, then, from its beginning. Imitate, at least, their outward actions, and if you cannot yet realize their internal feelings, quit, at all events, those vain pursuits in which you have been hitherto entirely engrossed.

Ah, say you, I could soon renounce these pleasures, if I had faith; and I answer, you would soon have faith, if you would renounce those pleasures. It is for you to begin. If I could, I would give you faith, but I cannot; and consequently, I cannot prove the sincerity of your assertion; but you can abandon your pleasures, and thus make experiment of the truth of mine.

You say, this argument delights me. If so, if this argument pleases you, and appears weighty, know also that it comes from a man, who, both before and afterwards, went on his knees before Him who is infinite, and without parts, and to whom he has himself entirely submitted, with prayer, that he would also subject you to himself for your good, and his glory; and that thus Omnipotence might bless his weakness.

6. We ought not to misconceive our own nature. We are body as well as spirit; and hence demonstration is not the only channel of persuasion. How few things are capable of demonstration! Such proof, too, only convinces the understanding: custom gives the most conclusive proof, for it influences the senses, and by them, the judgment is carried along without being aware of it. Who has proved the coming of the morrow, or the fact of our own death? And yet what is more universally believed? It is then custom which persuades us. Custom makes so many Turks and Pagans. Custom makes artisans and soldiers, &c. True, we must not begin here to search for truth, but we may have recourse to it when we have found out where the truth lies, in order to embue ourselves more thoroughly with that belief, which otherwise would fade. For to have the series of proofs incessantly before the mind, is more than we are equal to. We must acquire a more easy method of belief; that of habit, which, without violence, without art, and without argument, inclines all our powers to this belief, so that the mind glides into it naturally. It is not enough to believe only by the strength of rational conviction, while the senses incline us to believe the contrary. Our two powers must go forth together; the understanding, led

by those reasonings which it suffices to have examined thoroughly once; the affections, by habit, which keeps them perpetually from wandering.

CHAPTER VIII.

MARKS OF THE TRUE RELIGION.

TRUE religion should be marked by the obligation to love God. This is essentially right; and yet no religion but the Christian has ever enjoined it.

True religion ought also to recognize the depraved appetite of man, and his utter inability to become virtuous by his own endeavours. It should have pointed out the proper remedies for this evil, of which prayer is the principal. Our religion has done all this; and no other has ever taught to ask of God the power to love and serve him.

2. Another feature of true religion, would be the knowledge of our nature. For the true knowledge of our nature, of its true happiness, of true virtue, and true religion, are things essentially united. It should also recognise both the greatness and the meanness of man; together with their respective causes. What religion, but the Christian, has ever exhibited knowledge such as this?

3. Other religions, as the pagan idolatries, are more popular; their main force lies in external forms: but then they are ill suited to sensible men; whilst a religion, purely intellectual, would be more adapted to men of

sense, but would not do for the multitude. Christianity alone adapts itself to all. It wisely blends outward forms, and inward feelings. It raises the common people to abstract thought; and, at the same time, abases the pride of the most intellectual, to the performance of outward duties; and it is never complete, but in the union of these two results. For it is necessary that the people understand the spirit of the letter, and that the learned submit their spirit to the letter, in the compliance with external forms.

4. Even reason teaches us that we deserve to be hated: yet no religion, but the Christian, requires us to hate ourselves. No other religion, therefore, can be received by those who know themselves to be worthy of nothing but hatred.

No other religion, but the Christian, has admitted that man is the most excellent of all visible creatures, and, at the same time, the most miserable. Some religions which have rightly estimated man's real worth, have censured, as mean and ungrateful, the low opinion which men naturally entertain of their own condition. Others, well knowing the depth of his degradation, have exposed, as ridiculously vain, those notions of grandeur which are natural to men.

No other religion but ours has taught that man is born in sin: no sect of philosophers ever taught this; therefore no sect has ever spoken the truth.

5. God is evidently withdrawn from us, and every religion, therefore, which does not teach this, is false; and every religion which does not teach the reason of this, is wanting in the most important point of instruction. Our religion does both.

That religion, which consists in the belief of man's fall from a state of glory and communication with God, into a state of sorrow, humiliation, and alienation from God, and of his subsequent restoration by a Messiah, has always been in the world. All things else have passed away, but this, for which all other things exist, remains. For God, in his wisdom, designing to form to himself a holy people, whom he would separate from all other nations, deliver from their enemies, and lead to a place of rest, did promise that he would do this, and that he would come himself into the world to do it; and did foretel by his prophets, the very time and manner of his coming. In the mean while, to confirm the hope of his elect through all ages, he continually exhibited this aid to them in types and figures, and never left them without some evident assurances of his power and willingness to save. For immediately after the creation, Adam was made the witness to this truth, and the depository of the promise of a Saviour, to be born of the seed of the woman. And though men at a period so near to their creation, could not have altogether forgotten their origin, their fall, and the divine promise of a Redeemer; yet since the world in its very infancy was overrun with every kind of corruption and violence, God was pleased to raise up holy men, as Enoch, Lamech, and others, who, with faith and patience, waited for that Saviour who had been promised from the beginning of the world. At the last, God sent Noah, who was permitted to experience the malignant wickedness of man in its highest degree; and then God saved him, when he drowned the whole world, by a miracle, which testified, at once, the power of God to save the world, and his willingness to do it, and to raise up to the woman the seed which He had promised. This miracle, then, sufficed to confirm the hopes of mankind: and while the memory of it was still fresh in their minds, God renewed his promises to Abraham, who dwelt in the midst of idolaters, and opened to him the mystery of the Messiah that was to come. In the days of Isaac and Jacob, the idolatrous abomination was spread over the whole earth; yet these holy men lived in faith, and when Jacob, on his death-bed, blest his children, he exclaimed with an extatic joy, that interrupted his prophetic discourse, "I have waited for thy salvation, O Lord."

The Egyptians were a people infected with idolatry and magic; and even the people of God were drawn aside by their example. Yet Moses and others were permitted to see him who was to them invisible, and they adored him, and had respect unto the eternal blessings which he was preparing for them.

The Greeks and Romans have bowed down to fictitious deities. The poets have invented different systems of theology. Philosophers have split into a thousand different sects; yet were there always in one small spot, and that the land of Judea, some chosen men who foretold the coming of that Messiah, whom no one else regarded.

At length, in the fulness of time, that Messiah came; and ever since, in the midst of heresies and schisms, the revolution of empires, and the perpetual change to which all other things are subject, the same church which adores him, who has never been without his chosen worshippers, still subsists without interruption or decay. And, what must be owned to be unparalleled, wonderful, and altogether Divine, this religion, which has ever continued, has subsisted in the face of perpetual opposition. A thousand times has it been on the very verge of total ruin; and as often as it has been so reduced, God has relieved it, by some extraordinary interposition of his power? This is a most wonderful feature of its history, that it should have been so maintained, and that too, even without any unconscientious submission or compromise to the will of tyrannical men.

6. Civil states would infallibly perish, if their laws did not yield sometimes to the controul of necessity. But religion has never submitted to this: yet one step or the other is necessary, either compliances or miracles. It is no wonder that the kingdoms of this world should try to save themselves by yielding to circumstances; but, in point of fact, this is not preservation. It is change. And yet with all these variations, still they utterly perish. There is not one state that has lasted for 1800 years. If, then, this religion has always continued somewhere in existence, and continued firm and inflexible, is it not divine?

7. There would be too much obscurity over this question, if the truth had not some unequivocal marks. This is a valuable one, that it has always been preserved in a visible church. The proof would be too bright, if there were but one opinion in the Christian church. This, then, has not been the case; but in order to discover that which is truth, we have only to ascertain that which has always existed, for that which really is the truth, must have been there always, but that which is false, cannot.*

Now, the belief in the Messiah has been ever maintained in the world. The tradition from Adam was yet

---

* How completely this simple rule condemns all the Romish superstitions.

recent in the days of Noah, and even of Moses. Subsequently the prophets bore testimony to Him; at the same time predicting other things, which, being from day to day fulfilled, in the eyes of the world, established the truth of their mission, and consequently, of their unfulfilled promises concerning the Messiah. They unanimously declared that the law which had been given, was but preparatory to that of the Messiah; that, till then, it must continue; but that the law of Messiah should endure for ever: so that, either the law of Moses, or that of the Messiah, which it prophetically prefigured, should always continue upon earth. And, in fact, there has been that perpetuity. Jesus Christ came agreeably to all the circumstances of their predictions. He wrought miracles; so did his apostles, by whom he converted the Gentile world. And the prophecies being thus fulfilled, the proof of the Messiah's mission is for ever established.

8. I see many opposing religions. Necessarily, these are all false but one. Each seeks to be received on its own authority, and threatens the incredulous. I do not believe them on that account, for any one can say this. Any one may call himself a prophet. But in the Christian religion, I see many accomplished prophecies, and many miracles attested beyond all reasonable doubt; I find this in no other religion in the world.

9. That religion only which is contrary to our nature, in its present estate, which resists our pleasurable inclinations, and which seems, at first, contrary to the general opinion of mankind, that only has perpetually subsisted.

10. The whole course of things should bear upon the establishment and the exaltation of religion; the opinions

and feelings of men should be found conformable to what religion enjoins; and, in a word, religion should be so manifestly the great object and centre towards which all things tend, that whoever understands its principles, should be enabled to account by it for the nature of man in particular, and for the government of the world at large.

Now, it is upon this very ground that wicked and profane men blasphemously revile the Christian religion, because they misunderstand it. They imagine that it consists simply in the adoration of God as great, powerful, and eternal; which is, in fact, merely Deism, and is almost as far removed from Christianity as Atheism, which is directly opposed to it. And then from hence they would infer the falsehood of our religion; because, say they, were it true, God would have manifested himself by proofs so palpable, that no man could remain ignorant of him.

But let them conclude what they will in this way, against Deism; this is no conclusive objection against Christianity; for our religion distinctly states, that, since the fall, God does not manifest himself to us with all the evidence that is possible. It consists properly in the mystery of a Redeemer, who, by uniting in himself the Divine and human natures, has delivered men out of the corruption of sin, and reconciled them to God in his own Divine person.

It inculcates on men these two truths: that there is a God whom they are capable of knowing and enjoying; and that there is a corruption in their nature, which renders them unworthy of the blessing. These truths are equally important; and it is equally dangerous for man, to seek God without the knowledge of his own misery, and to know his own misery without the knowledge of a

Redeemer as his remedy. To apprehend the one without the other, begets either that philosophic pride which some men have had, who knew God, but not their own misery; or that despair which we find in Atheists, who know their own misery, but not their Saviour.

And as the knowledge of these two truths is equally necessary to man, so it is of the mercy of God to afford the means of knowing both. Now, the Christian religion does this, and that is its avowed and specific object.

Look into the order of things in this world, and see if all things do not directly tend to the establishment of these two fundamental principles of our religion.

11. If a man does not know himself to be full of pride, ambition, lust, weakness, misery, and unrighteousness, he is sadly blind. But, if with the knowledge of the evil, he has no wish to be delivered from it, what shall we say of such folly? Ought we not then to esteem highly a religion which so thoroughly understands our defects; and ardently to hope for the truth of a religion which promises so desirable a remedy?

12. It is impossible to meet all the proofs of the Christian religion, combined in one synoptical review, without feeling that they have a force which no reasonable man can resist.

Consider its first establishment. That a religion so contrary to our nature, should have established itself so quietly, without any force or constraint; and yet so effectually that no torments could prevent the martyrs from confessing it; and that this was done, not only without the assistance of any earthly potentate whatever, but in direct opposition to all the kings of earth combined against it.

Consider the holiness, the elevation, and the humility of a Christian spirit. Some of the pagan philosophers have been elevated above the rest of mankind by a better regulated mode of life, and by the influence of sentiments in a measure conformed to those of Christianity; but they have never recognised as a virtue that which Christians call humility; and they would even have believed it incompatible with the other virtues which they proposed to cherish. None but the Christian religion has known how to unite things which previously appeared so much at variance; and has taught mankind, that instead of humility being inconsistent with the other virtues, all other virtues without it are vices and defects.

Consider the boundless wonders of the Holy Scripture; the grandeur, and the super-human sublimity of its statements, and the admirable simplicity of its style, which has nothing affected, nothing laboured or recondite, and which bears upon the face of it, the irresistible stamp of truth.

Consider especially the person of Jesus Christ. Whatever may be thought of him in other respects, it is impossible not to discern that he had a truly noble and highly elevated spirit, of which he gave proof, even in his infancy before the doctors of the law. And yet, instead of applying himself to the cultivation of his talents by study, and by the society of the learned, he passed thirty years of his life in manual labour, and in an entire separation from the world: and during the three years of his ministry, he called and delegated as his apostles, men without knowledge, without study, without repute; and he excited as his enemies, all those who were accounted the wisest and the most learned of his day. This was certainly an extraordinary line of conduct, for one whose purpose it was to establish a new religion.

MARKS OF TRUE RELIGION.

Consider also those chosen apostles of Jesus Christ: men unlettered and without study; yet who found themselves all at once sufficiently learned to confound the most practised philosophers, and sufficiently firm to resist the kings and tyrants who opposed that gospel which they preached.

Consider that extraordinary series of prophets, who have followed each other during a period of two thousand years; and who, in so many different ways, have predicted, even to the most minute circumstances, the life, death, and resurrection of Jesus Christ; the mission of his apostles, the preaching of the gospel, the conversion of the Gentiles, and many other matters which regarded the establishment of the Christian religion, and the abolition of Judaism.

Consider the wonderful fulfilment of these prophecies, which have their accomplishment so accurately in the person of Jesus Christ, that none but he who is determined wilfully to blind himself, can fail to admit the fact.

Consider the state of the Jewish people, both previously and subsequently to the coming of Christ; how flourishing before his coming; how full of misery since they rejected him! Even at this day, they are without any of the peculiar marks of their religion, without a temple, without sacrifices, scattered over the whole world, the contempt and the scoffing of all men.

Consider the perpetuity of the Christian religion, which has even subsisted from the beginning of the world, either in the Old Testament saints, who lived in the expectation of Christ before his coming, or in those who have received and believed on him since. No other religion has been perpetual, and this is the chief characteristic of the true religion.

D

Finally, consider the holiness of this religion. Consider its doctrine, which gives a satisfactory reason for all things; even for the contrarieties which are found in man. And consider all those singular, supernatural, and divine peculiarities which shine forth in it on every side; and then judge from all this evidence, if it is possible fairly to doubt that Christianity is the only true religion; and if any other religion ever possessed any thing which could bear a moment's comparison with it.

CHAPTER IX.

PROOFS OF THE TRUE RELIGION, DRAWN FROM THE CONTRARIETIES IN MAN, AND FROM THE DOCTRINE OF ORIGINAL SIN.

THE greatness and the misery of man are both so manifest, that it is essential to the true religion, to recognise the existence in man, of a certain principle of extraordinary greatness, and also a principle of profound misery. For that religion which is true, must thoroughly know our nature in all its grandeur, and in all its misery, and must comprehend the source of both. It should give also a satisfactory explanation of those astonishing contrarieties which we find within us. If also there be one essence, the beginning and the end of all things, the true religion should teach us to worship and to love him exclusively. But since we find ourselves unable to worship him whom we know not, and to love any thing beyond ourselves, it is essential that the religion which requires of us these duties, should warn us of our weakness, and guide us to its cure.

Again, religion, to make man happy, should teach him that there is a God; that we ought to love him; that it is our happiness to be his, and our only real evil to be separated from him. It should shew us that we are full of gross darkness, which hinders us from knowing and loving him; and that our duty, thus requiring us to love God, and our evil affections alienating us from him, we are manifestly in a sinful state. It ought to discover to us also the cause of this opposition to God, and to our real welfare. It should point out to us the remedy and the means of obtaining it. Examine, then, all the religious systems in the world on these several points, and see if any other than Christianity will satisfy you respecting them.

Shall it be the religion taught by those philosophers, who offer to us as the chief good, our own moral excellence? Is this, then, the supreme good? Have these men discovered the remedy of our evils? Have they found a cure for the presumption of man, who thus make him equal with his God? And they who have levelled us with the brutes, and held up as the chief good the sensual delights of earth; have they found a cure for our corrupt affections? These say to us, "Lift up your eyes to God, behold him whom you resemble, and who has made you for his worship. You may make yourselves altogether like him; and, if you follow the dictates of wisdom, you will become his equals." Those say, "Look to the dust, vile reptiles, and consider the beasts with whom you are associated." What then is to be the lot of man? Is he to be equal with God, or with the beasts that perish? How awful the scope of this alternative. What shall be our destiny? Where is the religion that shall instruct us, at once to correct both our pride and our concupiscence? Where is the religion that shall teach us, at the same time, our happiness and our duty; the weaknesses which cause us to err, the specific for their removal, and the way to obtain it? Hear what the wisdom of God declares on this subject, when it speaks to us in the Christian religion.

It is in vain, O men! that you seek in yourselves the remedy of your miseries. All the light you have can only shew you that you cannot find within yourselves either truth or happiness. The philosophers have promised you both; but they could give you neither. They know not your real happiness, nor even your real state. How could they cure those ills, who did not even know them. Your chief mischiefs are, that pride which alienates you from God, and that concupiscence which fetters you to earth; and they have invariably fostered, at least, one or other of these evils. If they set God before you, it was but to excite your pride, by making you believe that your nature was similar to his. And they who saw the folly of such pretensions, have but led you to an equally dangerous precipice. They have taught you that your nature was on a level with the beasts, and that happiness was only to be found in those lusts which you have in common with them. This was not the way to convince you of your errors. Seek not then from men, either truth or consolation. I made you at the first, and I only can teach you what you are. You are not now in the state in which you were created by me. I made man holy, innocent, and perfect. I filled him with light and understanding. I made known to him my glory, and the wonders of my hand. Then it was that the eye of man beheld the majesty of God. He was not then in the darkness which now blinds him. He knew not then mortality

misery. But he did not long enjoy that glory, with-
declining to presumption. He wished to make him-
the centre of his own happiness, and to live indepen-
itly of my aid. He withdrew from beneath my autho-
y. And when, by the desire to find happiness in him-
f, he aimed to put himself on a level with me; I aban-
ned him to his own guidance; and causing all the crea-
res that I had subjected to him, to revolt from him, I
ade them his enemies: so that now man himself is ac-
ually become similar to the beasts, and he is so far re-
oved from me, that he scarcely retains even a confused
otion of the Author of his being: so much have his ori-
inal impressions been obliterated and obscured. His
uses uncontrolled by reason, and often overruling it,
urry him onward to pleasure and to indulgence. All
e creatures round him, now minister only sorrow or
mptation. They have the dominion over him, either
bduing him by their strength, or seducing him by their
scinations; a tyrannical controul, which is, of all others,
e most cruel and imperious.

Behold then the present state and condition of men.
n the one hand they retain a powerful instinctive im-
ression of the happiness of their primitive nature; on
he other hand, they are plunged in the miseries of their
wn blindness and lust; and this is now become their
econd nature.

2. In the principles which I have here stated, you may
iscern the spring of those wonderful contrarieties which
ave confounded, while they have distracted and divided
ll mankind. Watch attentively all the emotions of great-
ess and glory, which the sense of so many miseries has
ot been able *to extinguish*, and see if they must not have
heir source in another nature.

3. See, then, proud man, what a paradox thou art to thyself. Let impotent reason be humbled; let frail nature be silent. Know that man infinitely surpasses man; and learn from thy Maker, thy real condition....

For, in fact, had man never been corrupted, he would have ever enjoyed truth and happiness, with an assured delight. And had man never been any other than corrupted, he would never have had any idea of truth and blessedness. But wretched as we are, (more wretched than if we had never felt the consciousness of greatness) we do now retain a notion of felicity, though we cannot attain it. We have some faint impression of truth, while all we grasp is falsehood. We are alike incapable of total ignorance and of sure and definite knowledge. So manifest is it, that we were once in a state of perfection, from which we have unhappily fallen. What then do this and of want, and this impotency to obtain, declare to us, but that man originally possessed a real bliss, of which no traces now remain, except that cheerless void within, which he vainly endeavours to fill from the things around him; by seeking from those which are absent, a joy which present things will not yield,—a joy which neither the present nor the absent can bestow on him; because this illimitable chasm, this boundless void, can never be filled by any but an infinite and immutable object.

4. It is an astonishing thought, that of all mysteries, that which seems to be farthest removed from our apprehension, I mean the transmission of original sin, is a fact without the knowledge of which we can never satisfactorily know ourselves. For, undoubtedly, nothing appears so revolting to our reason as to say that the transgression of the first man should impart guilt to those, who, from

extreme distance from the source of the evil, seem
ible of such a participation. This transmission
 to us not only impossible but unjust. For what
s more repugnant to the rules of our despicable jus-
than to condemn eternally an infant, yet irrespon-
 for an offence, in which he appears to have had so
share, that it was committed six thousand years be-
ie came into existence. Certainly nothing wounds
ire cruelly than this doctrine. And yet without this
iry, to us of all others the most incomprehensible,
e utterly incomprehensible to ourselves. The com-
ed knot of our condition, has its mysterious folds in
byss; so that man is more incomprehensible without
nystery, than is this mystery itself to man.
.e notion of original sin, is foolishness to men. But
we should not condemn the want of reasonableness
s doctrine, for in fact it is not assumed to be within
rovince of reason. At the same time, this very fool-
ss is wiser than all the wisdom of men: *(The fool-
s of God, is wiser than men,* 1 Cor. i. 25.) For with-
his, what explanation can we give of man! His
 condition hangs upon this one imperceptible point.
how could he have discovered this by his reason;
y it is a matter above his reason; and that reason,
om discovering the fact, revolts from it, when it is
led.

These two states of original innocence and subse-
; corruption, being once presented to our view, it is
sible not to recognise them, and admit their truth.
s trace our own emotions, and observe ourselves;
it us see whether we do not detect within, the living
cters *of both these* different natures. Could such
rieties exist in the subject of one simple nature?

This two-fold tendency of man is so visible, that
have conceived him to possess two souls: one so
pearing to them incapable of such great and s
changes, from an immeasurable presumption, to th
debasing and abject depravity.

Thus we see that the several contrarieties which
most calculated to alienate men from the knowle
any religion whatever, are the very things which i
most effectually avail to guide them to the true.

For my own part, I avow, that as soon as the (
tian religion discloses this one principle,—that huma
ture is depraved and fallen from God, my eyes of
once to discover the characters of this truth, inscril
every thing around me. All nature, both withi:
without us, most manifestly declares the withdraw
God.

Without this divine communication, what coul
do, but either feed their pride on the inward impr
yet remaining of their former greatness; or abjectl
under the consciousness of their present infirmity
as they do not discern all the truth, they can nev
tain to perfect virtue. Some regarding their nat
hitherto uncorrupted; others, as irrecoverably lost
could not escape one of the two great sources of al
—either pride or recklessness. They must either
don themselves to vice, through negligence; or e
from it by the strength of their pride. If they wer
to the excellency of man, they would be ignorant
corruption: and though, by this means, they would
the guilt of reckless indifference, they would spli
the rock of pride; and if they recognise the wer
of human nature, they would be strangers to it
nity: and thus they would shun the dangers of a

presumption, only to plunge themselves into the vortex of despair.

From this very source sprung all the various sects of the Stoics and Epicureans; of the Dogmatists, and the Academics, &c. The Christian religion only has been able thoroughly to cure these opposite vices; not by using the wisdom of this world to make one expel the other; but by expelling them both, through the means of the simple truth of the gospel. For while it exalts its votaries to be partakers of the divine nature, it teaches that even in this exalted state, they carry with them the source of all corruption, which renders them, during their whole life, liable to error and misery, to death and sin. At the same, it assures the most impious, that even they might yet experience the grace of the Redeemer. Thus administring salutary dread to those whom it justifies, and needful encouragement to those whom it condemns; it so wisely tempers hope and fear, by means of this two-fold capability of sin and of grace, which is common to all mankind, that it humbles man far below what unassisted reason could do, without driving him to despair; and it exalts man far beyond the loftiest height of natural pride, without making him presumptuous. And hereby it is shewn of the Christian religion, that inasmuch as it only is free from defect or error, to it alone belongs the task of instructing and correcting mankind.

6. We have no conception of the glorious state of Adam, nor of the nature of his sin, nor of the transmission of it to ourselves. These things occurred under circumstances widely different from our own; and they exceed the present limits of our comprehension. The comprehension of them would be of no avail for our deli-

verance from evil. All that we need to know is, that through Adam we are become miserable, corrupt, and alienated from God; but that by Jesus Christ, we are redeemed. And of this, even in this world, we have ample proof.

7. Christianity has its wonders. It requires man to acknowledge himself vile and abominable; it requires him also to emulate the likeness of his Maker. Unless these things had been accurately balanced, such an exaltation would have rendered him extravagantly vain; such a debasement, lamentably abject.

Misery leads to despair; aggrandisement to presumption.

8. The mystery of the incarnation, shews to man the depth of his degradation, in the greatness of the necessary remedy.

9. The Christian religion does not recognise in us such a state of abasement, as renders us incapable of good; nor such a purity as is perfectly safe from evil. No doctrine is so well adapted to human nature, as this which declares man's capability of receiving and of forfeiting grace; because of the danger to which, on either hand, he is ever exposed, of despair and of presumption.

10. Philosophers have never furnished men with sentiments suited to these two features of their condition. They either infused notions of unalloyed greatness, which is certainly not man's real state; or they encouraged the idea of man's total depravity, which is equally an error. We want an actual abasement of soul, not by the

indulgence of our own base nature; but by a real penitence: not that we may abide there, but that we may attain thereby to exaltation. We want the stirrings of greatness; not those which originates in human merit; but those which spring from grace, and follow humiliation.

11. No man is really happy, rational, virtuous, amiable, but the true Christian. How free from pride is his consciousness of union with the Deity! How free from meanness, the humility which levels him with the worms of the earth!

Who, then, can withhold from this celestial light, his confidence and veneration? For is it not clearer than the day, that we discover in ourselves the indelible traces of our excellence? And is it not equally clear, that we experience every moment the sad realities of our deplorable condition. And does not, then, this internal chaos, this moral confusion, proclaim with a voice mighty and irresistible, the truth of those two states, to which revelation bears testimony?

12. That which hinders men from believing that they may be united to God, is the conviction of their depraved state. But if they are sincere in this conviction, let them follow out the fact to its bearings as I have; and let them acknowledge that the effect of this degradation is, to render us incapable of judging rightly, whether God can make us fit to enjoy him or not. For I would like to know where this avowedly weak and degraded creature acquired the power of guaging the Divine compassions, and limiting them according to his own fancy. Man knows so little of what God is, that he does not

know what he is himself; and yet, while unable to judge of his own real state, he presumes to affirm, that God cannot fit him for communion with him. But I would ask, Is not the very thing which God requires of him this, that he should know and love him? And why, then, since he is naturally capable of knowing and loving, should he doubt the power of God to make himself the object of this knowledge and love. For it is unquestionable that he knows, at least, that he is, and that he loves something. Then, if in the darkness in which he is, he yet discerns something, and if he finds amidst earthly things some object of love; why if God should impart some rays of his own essence, should he not be capable of knowing him and of loving him, as he is discovered in that mode in which he has been pleased to reveal himself.

There is then an unjustifiable presumption in these reasonings. Though they appear to be founded in humility, yet that humility is neither sincere nor reasonable; but, as it leads us to acknowledge, that as we do not thoroughly know what we are ourselves, we can only learn it from God.

CHAPTER X.

THE DUE SUBORDINATION AND USE OF REASON.

THE highest attainment of reason, is to know that there is an infinity of knowledge beyond its limits. It must be sadly weak if it has not discovered this. We ought to know where we should doubt, where we should be confident, and where we should submit. He who knows not *this*, does not comprehend the true power of reasoning.

There are men who fail severally on each of these points. Some from ignorance of what is demonstration, assume every thing to be demonstrable; others not knowing where it becomes them to submit silently, doubt of every thing; and others again, unconscious of the right field for the exercise of judgment, submit blindly to all.

2. If we subject every thing to reason, our religion would have nothing in it mysterious and supernatural. If we violate the principles of reason, our religion would be absurd and contemptible.

Reason, says St. Augustin, would never submit, if it were not in its nature to judge, that there are occasions when it ought to submit. It is right, then, that reason should yield when it is conscious that it ought, and that it should not yield when it judges deliberately, that it ought not. But we must guard here against self-deceit.

3. Piety differs from superstition. Superstition is the death of piety. The heretics reproach us with this superstitious submission of the understanding. We should deserve their reproach, if we required this surrender in things which do not require it rightly. Nothing is more consistent with reason, than the repression of reasoning in matters of faith. Nothing more contrary to reason, than the repression of reasoning in matters which are not of faith. To exclude reasoning altogether, or to take no other guide, are equally dangerous extremes.

4. Faith affirms many things, respecting which the senses are silent; but nothing that they deny. It is always superior, but never opposed to their testimony.

5. Some men say, If I had seen a miracle, I should have been converted. But they would not so speak if they understood conversion. They imagine that conversion consists in the recognition of a God; and that to serve him, is but to offer him certain addresses, much resembling those which the pagans made to their idols. True conversion, is to feel our nothingness before that Sovereign Being whom we have so often offended; and who might, at any moment, justly destroy us. It is to acknowledge, that without Him we can do nothing, and that we have deserved nothing but his wrath. It consists in the conviction, that between God and us, there is an invincible enmity; and that, without a Mediator, there can be no communion between us.

6. Do not wonder to see some unsophisticated people believe without reasoning. God gives them the love of his righteousness, and the abhorrence of themselves. He inclines their heart to believe. We should never believe with a living and influential faith, if God did not incline the heart; but we do so as soon as he inclines it. This David felt, when he said, *Incline my heart, O Lord, unto thy testimonies.*

7. If any believe truly, without having examined the evidence of religion, it is, that they have received within a holy disposition, and that they find the averments of our religion conformed to it. They feel that God has made them. They wish but to love him, and to hate only themselves. They feel that they are without strength; that they are unable to go to God, and that unless he comes to them, they can have no communication with him. And then they learn from our religion, that they

should love only God, and hate only themselves, but that being utterly corrupt, and alienated from God, God became man, that he might unite himself to us. Nothing more is wanting to convince men, who have this principle of piety in their hearts, and who know also both their duty and their weakness.

8. Those whom we see to be Christians, without the inspection of the prophecies and other evidences, are found equally good judges of the religion itself, as others who have this knowledge. They judge by the heart, as others do by the understanding. God himself has inclined their hearts to believe, and hence they are effectively persuaded.

I grant that a Christian who thus believes without examining evidence, would probably not have the means of convincing an infidel, who could put his own case strongly. But those who know well the evidence for Christianity, can prove, without difficulty, that this belief is truly inspired of God, though the man is not able to prove it himself.

CHAPTER XI.

THE CHARACTER OF A MAN WHO IS WEARIED WITH SEEKING GOD BY REASON ONLY, AND WHO BEGINS TO READ THE SCRIPTURES.

WHEN I look at the blindness and misery of man, and at those appalling contrarieties which are apparent in his nature; and when I survey the universe all silent, and man without instruction, left alone, and, as it were, a lost

wanderer in this corner of creation, without knowing w
placed him here, what he came to do, or what becom
of him at death, I am alarmed as a man is, who has be
carried during his sleep to a desolate and gloomy isla
and who has awaked, and discovered that he knows
where he is, and that he has no means of escape.
wonder how any one can avoid despair, at the conside
tion of this wretched state. I see others round me h
ing the same nature: I ask them if they know more
this subject than I; and they answer, no. And I
that these wretched wanderers, like myself, having loo
around them, and discovered certain pleasurable obje
have given themselves up to them without reserve.
myself, I cannot rest contented with such pleasures
cannot find repose in this society of similar bei
wretched and powerless as I am myself. I see that t
cannot help me to die. I must die alone. It beco
me then to act as if I were alone. Now, if I were a
here, I should not build mansions. I should not enta
myself with tumultuous cares. I should not court
favour of any, but I should strive to the utmost to
cover what is truth. With this disposition, and consid
ing what strong probability there is, that other th
exist beside those which I see; I have inquired if
God of whom all the world speaks, has not given us s
traces of himself I look around, and see nothing
darkness on every side. All that nature presents to
only suggests cause for doubt and distrust. If I saw

am in a pitiable state, in which I have wished an hundred times, that if a God sustains nature, she might declare it unequivocally; and that if the intimations she gives are false, they may be entirely suppressed; that nature would speak conclusively, or not at all, so that I might know distinctly which course to take. Instead of this, in my present state, ignorant of what I am, and of what I ought to do: I know neither my condition nor my duty. My heart yearns to know what is the real good, in order to follow it. And, for this, I would count no sacrifice too dear.

I see many religious systems, in different parts and at different periods of the world. But I am not satisfied, either with the morality which they teach, nor the proofs on which they rest. On this ground, I must have equally refused the religion of Mahomet, of China, of the ancient Romans or the Egyptians, for this one reason, that any one of them, not having more marks of verity than another, and nothing which simply and positively determines the question, reason could never incline to one in preference to the rest.

But, whilst thus considering this varied and strange contrariety of religious customs and creeds at different periods, I find in one small portion of the world, a peculiar people, separated from all the other nations of the earth, and whose historical records are older, by several centuries, than those of the most ancient of other nations. I find this a great and numerous people; who adore one God, and who are governed by a law which they profess to have received from his hand. They maintain, that to them only, of all the world, has God revealed his mysteries: that all mankind are corrupt, and under the *divine displeasure*: that men are all given up

90   THE CLAIM OF REVELATION.

to the guidance of their corrupt affections, and their own understandings; and that hence originate all the strange irregularities and continual changes among men, both in religion and manners, whilst *they* remained as to their rule of conduct unaltered; but that God will not leave even the other nations eternally in darkness; that a deliverer shall come forth for them; that they are in the world to announce him; that they were prepared expressly as the heralds of his advent, and to summon all nations to unite with them in the expectation of this Saviour.

The meeting with such a people surprises me, and on account of the many wonderful and singular events connected with them, they seem to me worthy of the greatest attention.

They are a nation of brethren; and whilst other nations are found of an infinite number of families, this people, though so extraordinarily populous, are all descended from one man; and being thus one flesh, and members one of another, they compose a mighty power, concentrated in one single family. This is an instance without parallel.

This is the most ancient people, within the memory of man; a circumstance which makes them worthy of peculiar regard, and especially with reference to our present inquiry: *for if God did in all previous time, communicate with man, then it is to this, the most ancient people, that we must come to ascertain the tradition.*

This people is not only considerable for its antiquity, but for its duration, which has ever continued from its origin till now; for whilst the nations of Greece, of Italy, of Lacedemon, Athens or Rome, and others that have arisen much later, have long since passed away; this nation still subsists, and notwithstanding the efforts of many mighty kings, who, according to historic testimony, have tried a hundred times to destroy them; an event, also, which is easy to suppose would have occurred in the natural course of events in so many years; yet they have been always preserved; and their history, extending from the primitive times to the present, involves the period of all other histories within its own.

The law by which this people is governed, is at the same time the most ancient, the most perfect, and the only one which has been recognised without interruption in a state. Philo, the Jew, shews this in several places; and so does Josephus against Appion, where he observes that it is so ancient, that even the term of *law* was not known by the most ancient nations, till more than 1000 years afterwards; so that Homer, who speaks of so many nations, never uses it. And it is easy to form an idea of its perfection, by simply reading it; where we see that it had provided for all things with so much wisdom, equity and prudence, that the most ancient Greek and Roman legislators, having received a measure of its light, have borrowed from it their chief and best institutions. This appears from the twelve tables, and from the other proofs adduced by Josephus.

This law is also, at the same time, the most severe and rigorous of all; enjoining on this people, under pain of death, a thousand peculiar and painful observances, as the means of keeping them in their duty. So that it is very wonderful, that this law should have been preserved for so many ages, amidst a people so rebellious and impatient of the yoke; whilst all other nations have repeatedly changed their laws, though much more easy of observance.

2. This people also must be admired for their sincerity. They keep with affection and fidelity, the book in which Moses declares, that they have ever been ungrateful to their God, and that he knows they will be still more so, after his death; but that he calls heaven and earth to witness against them, that he had given them an ample warning: that at length God, becoming angry with them, would scatter them among all the nations of the earth; and that as they had angered him in worshipping those as Gods who were no Gods, he would anger them in calling a people who were not his people. Yet this book, which so copiously dishonours them, they preserve at the expence of their life. This is a sincerity which has no parallel in the world, and has not its radical principle in mere human nature.

Then, finally, I find no reason to doubt the truth of the book, which contains all these things; for there is a great difference between a book which an individual writes and introduces among a people, and a book which actually forms that people.

There can be no doubt that this book is as old as the nation. It is a book written by cotemporary authors. All history that is not cotemporary, is questionable, as the books of the Sybil, of Trismegistus, and many others that have obtained credit with the world, and in the course of time, have been proved to be false. But this is not the case with cotemporary historians.

3. How different this from other books! I do not wonder that the Greeks have their Iliad, or the Egyptians and Chinese their histories. We have only to observe how this occurs. These fabulous historians are not cotemporary with the matters which they record. Homer writ

a romance, which he sends forth as such; for scarcely any one doubts that Troy and Agamemnon no more existed, than the golden apple. His object was not to write a history, but a book of amusement. It was the only book of his day. The beauty of the composition preserved it. Every one learned it and spoke of it. It must be known. Every one knew it by heart. Then four hundred years afterwards, the witnesses of things have ceased to exist. No one knew by his own knowledge whether it was truth or fable. All they knew was, that they learned it from their ancestors. It may pass then for truth.

CHAPTER XII.

THE JEWS.

THE creation and the deluge having taken place, and God not purposing again to destroy or to create the world, nor again to vouchsafe such extraordinary evidences of himself, began to establish a people on the earth, formed expressly to continue till the coming of that people whom Messiah should form to himself by his Spirit.

2. God, willing to make it evident that he could form a people possessed of a sanctity invisible to the world, and filled with eternal glory, has exhibited a pattern in temporal things, of what he purposed to do in spiritual blessings; that men might learn from his excellent doings in the things which are seen, his ability to do his will in the things which are not seen.

With this view, in the person of Noah, he saved his people from the deluge; he caused them to be born of

Abraham; he redeemed them from their enemies, and gave them rest.

The purpose of God was not to save a people from the flood, and to cause them to spring from Abraham, merely that he might plant them in a fruitful land; but that as nature is in a measure symbolical of grace, these visible wonders might indicate the unseen wonders which he purposed to perform.

3. Another reason of his choosing the Jewish people is, that as he purposed to deprive his own people of carnal and perishable possessions, he would shew by this series of miracles, that their poverty was at least not imputable to his impotence.

This people had cherished these earthly conceits, that God loved their father Abraham personally, and all who descended from him: that on this account, he had multiplied their nation, and distinguished them from all others, and forbidden their intermingling with them; and that therefore he led them out of Egypt with such mighty signs; that he fed them with manna in the wilderness; that he brought them into a happy and fruitful land; that he gave them kings, and a beautiful temple for the sacrifice of victims, and for their purification by the shedding of blood; and that he purposed ultimately to send them a Messiah, to make them masters of the whole world.

The Jews being accustomed to great and splendid miracles, and having considered the events at the Red Sea, and in the land of Canaan, but as a sample of the great things to be done by Messiah, expected from him the accomplishment of wonders far more brilliant, and compared with which, the miracles of Moses should be but as a spark.

THE JEWS.

When the Jewish nation had grown old in these low and sensual views, Jesus Christ came at the time predicted, but not with the state which they had anticipated; and, consequently, they did not think that it could be he. After his death, St. Paul came to teach men that all the events of the Jewish history were figurative; that the kingdom of God was not carnal, but spiritual; that the enemies of men were not the Babylonians, but their own passions; that God delighteth not in temples made with hands, but in a pure and penitent heart; that the circumcision of the body was unavailing, but that he required the circumcision of the heart.

4. God, not willing to discover these things to a people unworthy of them, but willing, nevertheless, to announce them that they might be believed, did clearly predict the time of their fulfilment, and did sometimes even clearly express the truths themselves; but ordinarily he did so in figures, that those who preferred the things which prefigured, might rest in them; whilst they who really loved the things prefigured, might discover them. And hence it followed, that at the coming of Messiah, the people was divided. The spiritually-minded Jew received him; the carnal Jews rejected him; and have been ordained to remain, to this day, as his witnesses.

5. The carnal Jews understood not either the dignity or the degradation of Messiah, as predicted by their prophets. They knew him not in his greatness; as when it is said of him, that Messiah, the son of David, shall be David's Lord; that he was before Abraham, and had seen Abraham. They did not believe him to be so great, as to have been from everlasting. Neither did they know him

in his humiliation and death. "Messiah," they said, "abideth ever; and this man says that he must die." They did not believe him to be either mortal or eternal. They expected nothing beyond an earthly carnal greatness.

They so loved the material figure, and so exclusively devoted themselves to it, that they knew not the reality, even when it came both at the time and in the manner foretold.

6. Sceptical men try to find their excuse in the unbelief of the Jews. "If the truth was so clear," it is said, "why did they not believe?" But their rejection of Christ is one of the foundations of our confidence. We had been much less inclined to believe, if they had all received him. We should thus have had a much ampler pretext for incredulity and distrust. It is a wonderful confirmation of the truth, to see the Jews ardently attached to the things predicted, yet bitterly hostile to their fulfilment; and to see that this very aversion was itself foretold.

7. To establish the Messiah's claim to confidence, it required that there should be prophecies going before him, and that these should be in the hands of men altogether unsuspected, and of diligence, fidelity and zeal extraordinary in their degree, and known to all men.

To attain this object, God chose this sensual nation, to whose care he committed the prophecies which foretold the Messiah as a deliverer, and a dispenser of those earthly blessings which this people loved. They felt, therefore, an extraordinary regard for their prophets, and exhibited to the whole world those books in which

iah was foretold; assuring all nations that he would
, and that he would come in the mode predicted in
books, which they laid open to the inspection of the
l. But being themselves deceived by the mean and
ninious advent of Messiah, they became his greatest
ies. So that we have the people which would be,
1 mankind, the least suspected of favouring the
stian scheme, directly aiding it; and by their zeal
ie law and the prophets, preserving with incorrupti-
rupulosity, the record of their own condemnation,
he evidences of our religion.

Those who rejected and crucified Jesus Christ, as an
ce to them, are they who possess the books that bear
ess of him, and that testify that he would be rejected
offence to them. Thus by their rejection of him,
marked him as Messiah; and he has received testi-
' both from the righteous Jew who believed, and
the unrighteous who rejected him: both those facts
; foretold in their scriptures.
r the same reason, the prophecies have a hidden
—a spiritual meaning, to which the people were ad-
', concealed under the carnal meaning which they
. Had the spiritual meaning been evident, they had
he capacity to love it: and as they would not have ap-
d it, they would have had little zeal for the preserva-
f their scriptures and their ceremonies. And even if
had loved these spiritual promises, and had preserved
uncorrupted to the days of Messiah, their witness,
e witness of friends, would have wanted its present
rtance. On this account, it seems good that the
ual sense was concealed. But on the other hand, if
ense had been so hidden, as not to be seen at all, it

E

could not have served as a testimony to the Messiah. What, then, has God done? In the majority of passages, the spiritual was veiled under the temporal sense, whilst in a few, it was clearly discovered. Moreover, the time and the state of the world, at the period of fulfilment, were so clearly foretold, that the sun itself is not more evident. The spiritual meaning also is in some places so plainly developed, that not to discover it, there needed absolutely such a blindness, as the flesh brings upon the spirit that is entirely enslaved by it.

This then is the way which God has taken. This spiritual meaning is in most places concealed; and in some, though rarely, it is disclosed. But then this is done in such a way, that the passages where the meaning is concealed, are equivocal, and equally admit both senses; whilst the places where the spiritual import is displayed are unequivocal, and will only bear the spiritual interpretation. So that this method could not properly lead to error, and that none but a people as carnal as they, could have misunderstood it.

For when good things are promised in abundance, what forbad them to understand the true riches, except that cupidity which at once eagerly restricted the sense to earthly blessings? But they who had no treasure but in God, referred them exclusively to God. For there are two principles which divide the human will, covetousness and charity. It is not that covetousness cannot co-exist with faith, or charity with earthly possessions: but covetousness makes its use of God, and enjoys the world; whilst charity uses the world, but finds its joy in God.

It is the ultimate end which we have in view, that gives names to things. Whatever prevents our obtaining this end, is called an enemy. Thus creatures, though in themselves good, are the enemies of the just, when they withdraw them from God; and God is accounted the enemy of those whose passions he counteracts.

Hence the word *enemy* in the Scripture, varies in its application with the end sought; the righteous understand by it their own passions, and carnal men, the Babylonians; so that these terms were only obscure to the wicked. And this Isaiah means when he says, *Seal the law among my disciples*. And when he prophesies that Christ should be *a stone of stumbling, and a rock of offence, but blessed are they who shall not be offended in him*. Hosea says the same thing very plainly: *Who is wise, and he shall understand these things; prudent, and he shall know them. For the ways of the Lord are right, and the just shall walk in them; but transgressors shall fall therein*.

And yet this Testament which is so composed, that in enlightening some, it blinds others, did stamp the truth upon those whom it blinded, so plainly that others might read it. For the visible external blessings which they received from God, were so great and God-like, as to render it abundantly evident, that he could give them invisible blessings, and a Messiah, according to his word.

9. The time of Christ's first advent was accurately foretold; the time of the second is not: because the first was to be private, but the second was to be splendid, and so evident that even his enemies should acknowledge him. But since it became him to come in obscurity, and to be revealed only to those who sincerely searched the Scriptures, God had so ordered things, that all contributed to make him known. The Jews bore witness to him, by receiving him, for they were the depository of the prophecies; and they confirmed the truth by rejecting him, for *by this they* fulfilled the prophecies.

10. The Jews had in their favour, both miracles and prophecies which they saw fulfilled; the doctrine also of their law required them to worship and to serve but one God. Their religion had been of perpetual duration. Thus it had every mark of being the true religion; and so it was. But we must distinguish between the doctrine of the Jews, and the doctrine of the Jewish law; for the doctrine actually held by the Jews, was not true; though associated with miracles, prophecies, and the perpetuity of their system; because it wanted the fourth essential characteristic—the exclusive love and service of God.

The Jewish religion, then, must be differently estimated, according as it appears in the traditions of their saints, and the traditions of the people. Its moral rule and its promised happiness, as stated in the traditions of the people, are quite ridiculous; but in the authentic traditions of their holy men, they are admirable. The basis of their religion is excellent. It is the most ancient, and the most authentic book in the world; and whilst Mahomet, to preserve his Scriptures from ruin, has forbidden them to be read; Moses, to establish his, ordered every one to read them.

11. The Jewish religion is altogether divine in its authority, its continuance, its perpetuity, in its morals, its practice, its doctrine, and its effects. It was framed as a type of the reality of the Messiah; and the truth of the Messiah was recognised by the religion of the Jews, which prefigured him. Among the Jews, the truth dwelt only typically. In heaven it exists unveiled. In the church, it is veiled, but made known by its symbolising with the figure. The type was framed according to the pattern of the truth, and the truth was disclosed by the type.

THE JEWS.

12. He who should estimate the Jewish religion by externals, would be in error. It may be seen in the Holy Scriptures; and in the traditions of their prophets, who have amply shewn that they did not understand the law literally. Thus, our religion, seen in the gospels, the epistles, and in its traditions, is divine; but it is sadly distorted among the many who misuse it.

13. The Jews were divided into two classes. The dispositions of the one were only heathen; those of the other Christian.

Messiah, according to the carnal Jews, should have been a great temporal prince. According to the carnal Christians, he is come to release us from the obligation to love God, and to give us Sacraments effective without our concurrence. The one is not the Jewish religion; the other is not the Christian.

True Jews and true Christians have equally recognised a Messiah, who inspires them with the love of God, and causes them by that love to overcome their enemies.

14. The veil that is upon the Scripture to the Jews, is there also to the false and faithless Christian, and to all who do not abhor themselves. But how well disposed are we to understand the record, and to know Jesus Christ, when we do cordially hate ourselves!

15. The carnal Jews occupy a middle place between Christians and heathens. The heathens know not God, and love this world only. The Jews know the true God, yet love this world only. Christians know the true God, and love not the world. The Jew and the heathen love the same object. The Jew and the Christian know the same God.

16. Evidently the Jews are a people formed expressly to be witnesses to the Messiah. They possess the Scriptures, and love them, but do not comprehend them. And all this has been expressly foretold; for it is written, that the oracles of God are committed to them, but as a book that is sealed.

Whilst the prophets were continued for the preservation of the law, the people neglected it. But when the line of prophets failed, the zeal of the people arose in their stead. This is a wonderful providence.

17. When the creation of the world began to be a remote event, God raised up a cotemporary historian, and commissioned a whole nation to preserve his work; that this history might be the most authentic in the world; and that all men might learn a fact so necessary to be known, and which could be known in no other way.

18. Moses evidently was a man of talent. If then he had purposed to deceive, he would have adopted a course not likely to lead to detection. He has done just the reverse; for if he had put forth falsehoods, there was not a Jew that would not have discovered the imposture.

Why, for example, has he described the lives of the first men so long, and their generations so few? He might have veiled his fraud in a multitude of generations, but he could not in so few. It is not the number of years, but the frequent succession of generations, which gives obscurity to history.

Truth suffers no change, but by a change of men. And yet Moses places two events as memorable as possible—the creation and the flood—so near, that owing to the *paucity* of generations, they were almost tangible things.

So that at the period when he wrote, the memory of these events must have been quite recent in the minds of all the Jews.

Shem, who had seen Lamech, who had seen Adam, lived at the least to see Abraham; and Abraham saw Jacob, who lived to see those who saw Moses. Then the deluge and the creation are facts. This is conclusive to those who comprehend the nature of such testimony.

The length of the patriarchal life, instead of operating to the loss of historic facts, served to preserve them. For the reason why we are not well versed in the history of our ancestors, is commonly that we have seldom lived with them; or that they died before we reached maturity. But when men lived so long, children lived a long while with their parents, and necessarily conversed much with them. Now, of what could they speak, but of the history of their ancestors? For this was all the history that they had to tell: and as to sciences, they had none, nor any of those arts which occupy so large a portion of human intercourse. We see also, that in those days, men took especial care to preserve their genealogies.

19. The more I examine the Jews, the more of truth I find in their case, and the more plainly I discover this Scriptural mark, that they are without prophets, and without a king; and, that as our enemies, they are the best witnesses to the truth of those prophecies, in which both their continuance and their blindness is foretold. I see in their judicial expulsion, that this religion is divine in its authority, in its continuance, in its perpetuity, in its morals, in its practice, in its effects. And hence I stretch forth my hands to my deliverer, who, having been predicted for 4000 years, came at last to suffer and to die

for me, at the time, and under all the circumstances that have been predicted; and, by his grace, I now wait for death in peace, hoping to be eternally with him. And I ever live rejoicing, either in the blessings which he is pleased to bestow, or in the sorrows which he sends for my profit, and which I learn from his own example to endure.

By that fact, I refute all other religions. By that, I give an answer to all objections. It is just that a pure and holy God should not reveal himself, but to those whose hearts have been purified.

I find it satisfactory to my mind, that ever since the memory of man, here is a people that has subsisted longer than any other people; that this people has constantly announced to man that they are in a state of universal corruption, but that a deliverer will come; and it is not one man that has said this, but an infinite number: a whole people prophecying through a period of 4000 years.

CHAPTER XII.

OF FIGURES.

SOME figures are clear and demonstrative; others are less simple and natural, and tell only upon those who have been previously persuaded by other means. These last resemble the prophetic figures borrowed by some men from the Apocalypse, and explained according to their own views. But between them and the true, there is this difference, they have no figures that are unquestionably established, by which to support their interpretation. It is very unjust, therefore, to pretend that theirs are as well sustained as ours, when they have no figures of established interpretation to refer to as we have. The two cases are not parallel. Men should not parallelize and confound two things, because in one respect they appear similar, seeing that in another, they are so different.

2. One of the main reasons why the prophets have veiled the spiritual blessings, which they promised, under the type of temporal blessings, is that they had to deal with a carnal people, and to commit to their care a spiritual deposit.

Jesus Christ was typically represented by Joseph, the beloved of his father, sent by his father to seek for his brethren; innocent, yet sold by his brethren, for twenty pieces of silver; and, by that means, constituted their Lord, their Saviour; the Saviour of strangers; the Saviour of the world; which he could not have been, but for the purpose to destroy him, and the sale, and the abandonment, of which his brethren were guilty.

Joseph was innocent, and imprisoned with two criminals. Jesus was crucified between two robbers. Joseph foretold to men, in the same cirstumstances, the saving of the one, and the death of the other. Jesus saved one, and left the other to his fate, though both were guilty of the same crime. Joseph, however, could only foretel. Jesus fulfilled also. Joseph also requested him who was to be saved, to remember him when he was come to prosperity; and he whom Jesus Christ saved, prayed that he would remember him when he came to his kingdom.

3. Grace is the type of glory. It is not itself the ultimate end. Grace was typified by the law, and is itself

typical of glory; but so as to be, at the same time, a means of obtaining that glory.

4. The synagogue is not altogether destroyed, because it was a type of the church; but because it was only a type, it has fallen into bondage. The type was continued till the reality came, that the church might be always visible, either in the shadow or the substance.

5. To prove, at once, the authority of both Testaments, we need only inquire, if the prophecies of the one, are accomplished in the other.

To examine the prophecies, we should understand them; for, if they have but one meaning, then certainly the Messiah is not come; but if they have a double sense, then as certainly he is come in Jesus Christ.

The question then is, Have they a twofold meaning? Are they types, or literal realities? that is, are we to inquire for something more than at first appears, or must we, invariably, rest satisfied with the literal sense which they directly suggest?

If the law and the sacrifices were the ultimate reality, they must be pleasing to God; they could not displease him. If they are typical, they must both please and displease him.* Now, throughout the Scripture, they appear to do both. Then they can only be typical.

6. To discern clearly that the Old Testament is figurative, and that by temporal blessings, the prophets mean something further, we need only notice, *First*, That it

---

* That is according to the circumstances of different cases.

OF FIGURES.

would be beneath the Deity, to call men only to the enjoyment of temporal happiness. *Secondly,* That the language of the prophets most distinctly expresses the promise of temporal good, whilst they, at the same time declare, that their discourses are really obscure; that the ostensible meaning is not the real one, and that it would not be understood till the latter days. (Jeremiah xxiii. 20.) Then evidently they speak of other sacrifices, and another Redeemer.

Besides, their discourses are contradictory and suicidal, if by the words *law* and *sacrifice*, they understood only the law and sacrifices of Moses. There would be a manifest and gross contradiction in their writings, and sometimes even in the same chapter; whence, it follows, that they must mean something else.

7. It is said that the law shall be changed; that the sacrifice shall be changed; that they shall be without a king, without a prince, without a sacrifice; that a new covenant shall be established; that there shall be a new law; that the precepts which they had received were not good; that their sacrifices were an abomination; that God had not required them.

On the other hand, it is said, that the law shall endure for ever; that this covenant is an everlasting covenant; that the sacrifice shall be perpetual; that the sceptre should never leave them, seeing that it could not depart till the arrival of the Everlasting King. Do these passages prove the then present system to be the substance? No! Do they prove it to be figurative? No! They only shew that it is either a substance, or a figure; but as the former passages conclude against the reality, they shew that the law is a figure.

All these passages, taken together, cannot be predicated of the substance; all may be affirmed of the shadow. Then they do not relate to the substance, but to the shadow.

8. To ascertain whether the law and its sacrifices be the substance, or a figure, we should examine if the views and thoughts of the prophets terminated in these things, so that they contemplated only this original covenant; or whether they did not look for something beyond, of which these were a pictural representation; for in a portrait we see the thing presented typically. With this view, we have only to examine what they say.

When they speak of the covenant as everlasting, do they mean to speak of that covenant, of which they affirm, that it shall be changed? and so of the sacrifices, &c.

9. The prophets say distinctly, that Israel shall always be loved of God, and that the law shall be eternal. They say also, that their meaning in this is not comprehended, and that it is, in fact, hidden.

A cypher, for secret correspondence, has frequently two meanings. If, then, we intercept an important letter, in which we find a plain meaning, and in which it is said, at the same time, that the sense is hidden, and obscured, and that it is so veiled purposely, that seeing we might not see, and perceiving, we might not understand; what would we think, but that it was written in a cypher of two fold signification, and much more so, if we found in the literal sense some manifest contradictions? How thankful should we be then to those who would give us the key to the cypher, and teach us to discern the hidden meaning, especially when the principles on which they proceed are quite natural, and approved principles! Jesus Christ and his apostles have done precisely this. They have broken the seal: they have rent the veil: they have disclosed the meaning: they have taught us that man's enemies are his passions; that the Redeemer was a spiritual Redeemer; that he would have two advents—the one, in humiliation to abase the proud, the other, in glory to elevate the humble; that Jesus Christ was both God and man.

10. Jesus Christ taught men, that they were lovers of themselves; that they were enslaved, blinded, sick, miserable, and sinful; that they needed him to deliver, enlighten, sanctify, and heal them; and, that to obtain this, they must deny themselves, and take up the cross, and follow him through suffering and death.

The letter killeth: the sense lies hidden in the cypher. A suffering Saviour; a God in humiliation; the circumcision of the heart; a true fast; a true sacrifice; a true temple; two laws; a twofold table of the law; two temples; two captivities;—there is the key to the cypher, which Jesus Christ has given to us.

Christ has at length taught us, that these things were but figures, and has explained the true freedom, the true Israelite, the true circumcision, the true bread from heaven, &c.

11. Each one finds in these promises, that which lies nearest to his heart, spiritual or temporal blessings, God or the creature; but with this difference, they who desire the creature, find it promised, but with many apparent contradictions—with the prohibition to love it, and with the command to love and worship God only; whilst they who seek God in the promises, find him without any contradiction, and with the command to love him exclusively.

110   OF FIGURES.

12. The origin of the contrarieties in Scripture, is found in a Deity humbled to the death of the cross; a Messiah, by means of death, triumphant over death; two natures in Jesus Christ; two advents; and two states of the nature of man.

As we cannot ascertain a man's character, but by reconciling its contrarieties, and as it is not sufficient to infer from a train of congruous qualities, without taking the opposite qualities into the account, so to determine the meaning of an author, we must shew the harmony of the apparently contradictory passages.

So that to understand the Scripture, there must be a sense in which the seemingly contradictory passages agree. It is not enough to find a sense which is borne out by many analogous passages; we must find one which reconciles those that seem to differ. Every author has a meaning with which all his seemingly incongruous passages harmonize, or he has no meaning at all. We cannot say that the Scriptures or the prophets have no meaning. They had too much good sense for that. Then we must look out for a meaning, which reconciles all their incongruities.

Now the Jewish interpretation is not that true meaning; but, in Jesus Christ, all the apparent contradictions completely harmonize.

The Jews would not know how to reconcile the termination of the kingdom and principality predicted by Hosea, with the prophecy of Jacob.

If we take the law, the sacrifices, and the kingdom for the ultimate reality, it were impossible to reconcile all the assertions of the same author, the same book, or the same chapter. This sufficiently indicates the meaning of the writer.

13. It was not allowed to sacrifice out of Jerusalem, which was the place that the Lord had chosen, nor even to eat the tenths elsewhere.

Hosea predicted that they should be without a king, without a prince, without a sacrifice, and without a teraphim. This is now accomplished, for they cannot legally sacrifice out of Jerusalem.

14. When the word of God, which is necessarily true, is false literally, it is true spiritually. *Sit thou on my right hand.* Literally this is false; it is spiritually true. The passage speaks of God after the manner of men, and means no more than that God has the same intention, as men have when they cause another to sit at their right hand. It indicates the purpose of God, not the mode of fulfilling it.

So when it is said, God has received the odour of your incense, and will recompense you with a good and fruitful land; it is only affirmed, that the same intention, which a man has, who, pleased with your incense, promises a fruitful land, God will have for you, because you have had the same intention with respect to him, that a man has to him to whom he gives perfume.

15. The end of the commandment is charity. Whatever in it appears to fall short of this end is figurative; for since there is but one end, all that does not bear upon it in express terms, must do so figuratively.

God diversifies the mode of inculcating this one precept, to satisfy that weakness in us, which seeks variety, by giving a variety which leads us ever towards the one thing needful. For one thing only is necessary, and we love variety; God has met both difficulties, by giving a variety which leads to that one thing needful.

16. The Rabbins only regard as figurative, the breasts of the spouse, and such things as do not literally express the sole object of temporal good which they have in view.

17. There are men who see plainly that the only enemy of man is his concupiscence, which leads him away from God; and that the only good is not a fertile land, but God. As for those who believe that man's supreme joy is in the flesh, and his bane in that which robs him of sensual delight, let them take their fill and die; but for those who seek God with all their heart, who have no sorrow but absence from him, and no desire but to enjoy him, no enemies but those who hinder their approach to him, and who mourn, that by such enemies, they are surrounded and oppressed; let them be comforted. For them there is a deliverer; for them there is a God. A Messiah has been promised to deliver man from his enemies. A Messiah is come, but it is to deliver him from his iniquities.

18. When David foretels that the Messiah shall deliver his people from their enemies, a carnal mind might understand him to mean the Egyptians; and in that case, I could not shew that the prophecy was accomplished. But it is very possible also, to understand that he meant our iniquities. For in truth, the Egyptians are not men's real enemies, but their iniquities are. The term *enemy* then is equivocal.

But if, in common with Isaiah and others, he says also, that Messiah shall deliver his people from their *iniquities*, then the ambiguity is removed, and the equivocal sense of the word " enemy," is reduced to the simple sense of iniquities. If he had really meant sins, he might properly convey the idea by the term *enemies;* but if *enemies* were his simple meaning, iniquities would not express it.

Now, Moses, David, and Isaiah, all use the same terms. Who then is prepared to say that they have not the same meaning, and that the meaning of David, who, beyond a doubt, intends iniquities, when he speaks of enemies, is not the same with that of Moses, when he speaks of enemies?

Daniel in chapter ix. prays for the deliverance of his people from the bondage of their enemies; but he evidently meant their sins: and in proof of this, we find it said, that Gabriel came to assure him, that his prayer was heard, and that but seventy weeks were determined to finish the transgression, and to make an end of *sins;*— and that then the Redeemer—the Holy of Holies, should bring in an everlasting righteousness—a righteousness, not merely legal, but eternal.

When once this mystery of a twofold meaning is disclosed to us, it is impossible not to perceive it. Read the Old Testament with this notion, and see if the sacrifices were the true sacrifice; if descent from Abraham was the true cause of the love of God; if the land of promise were the true place of rest: certainly not. Then they were types. Look then in the same way at all the ordained ceremonies, and all the commandments which speak not directly of love; you will find them all typical.

CHAPTER XIV.

JESUS CHRIST.

THE infinite distance between body and mind, figuratively represents the infinitely more infinite distance between mere intellect, and pure love; for that love is supernatural.

The pomp of external shew has no attraction to men engaged deeply in intellectual research. The greatness of intellectual men is imperceptible to the rich, to kings and conquerors who are but carnally great. The grandeur of that wisdom, which comes from God, is invisible both to merely sensual, and merely intellectual men. Here then are three different orders of distinction.

Great minds have their peculiar empire, their renown, their dignity, their conquests. They need not the sensual splendours of this world, between which, and the things that they seek, there is little similarity. It is the mind, and not the eye which appreciates their excellence; but then this satisfies them.

The saints also have their empire, their renown, their greatness, and their victories, and need not either sensual or intellectual splendour, to make them great. Such things are not of their order, and neither increase or diminish the greatness which they seek. God and his angels discern them, whilst, to the bodily eye, or the philosophic mind, they are alike invisible; but to them, God is every thing.

Archimedes is venerated independently of the distinction of his birth. He won no battles; but he has given

ronderful inventions to the world. How great,
istrious, is he to the scientific mind!
i Christ, without wealth, without the adventitious
ness of scientific discovery, comes in his order—
holiness. He publishes no inventions, he wears
rn; but he was humble, patient, holy in the sight
l, terrible to wicked spirits, and free from sin.
what mighty splendour, and with what prodigious
icence has he come forth before the eyes of the
-the optics of true wisdom.

ough Archimedes was of princely birth, it would
:en idle to have brought this forward in his book of
:ry.

id been useless also for our Lord Jesus Christ to
n earth as a monarch, in order to add dignity to
gn of holiness.* But how becoming is the peculiar
of his own order.

folly indeed to be offended at the low condition of
Christ, as if that meanness were of the same order
he glory that he came to manifest. Contemplate
:andeur in his life, in his passion, in his obscurity,
death, in the choice of his disciples, in their for-
him, in his unseen resurrection, and all the other
istances of his case; you will find him so truly
that there is little cause to complain of meanness.
no existence.

there are men who can only admire the distinc-
if external pomp, to the exclusion of all mental ex-
:e. And there are others who reverence only in-

---

t is, holiness exhibited alone and independent of all adventitious dis-

tellectual greatness: as if in the true wisdom there were not a far loftier worth.

All organized bodies, the heavens, the earth, the stars, taken together, are not equal in value to the meanest mind; for mind knows these things; it knows itself: but matter knows nothing. And all bodies, and all minds united, are not worth one emotion of love. It is of an order of excellence infinitely higher.

We cannot elicit from universal matter a single thought. It is impossible. Thought is of a higher order of creation. Again, all bodies, and all spirits combined, could not give birth to a single emotion of real love. This also is impossible. Love is of another and still higher order of being. It is supernatural.

2. Jesus Christ lived in such obscurity, (we use the word in the worldly sense) that historians who record none but important events, scarcely discerned him.

3. What man ever had more renown than Jesus Christ? The whole Jewish people foretold his coming. The Gentiles when he came adored him. Both Jews and Gentiles look to him as their centre. And yet what man ever enjoyed so little of such a fame. Out of thirty-three years, he passed thirty unseen; and the remaining three, he was accounted an impostor. The priests and rulers of his nation rejected him. His friends and relations despised him: and at length, betrayed by one of his disciples, denied by another, and abandoned by all, he died an ignominious death.

In how much then, of this splendour, did he participate? No man was ever so illustrious; no man was ever so degraded: but all this lustre was for our sakes, that we might know him; none for his own.

4. Jesus Christ speaks of the most sublime subjects with such simplicity, that he seems not to have thought on them; and yet with such accuracy, that what he thought is distinctly brought out. This union of artlessness with perspicuity, is perfectly beautiful.

Who taught the evangelists the qualities of a truly heroic mind, that they should paint it to such perfection in Jesus Christ? Why have they told of his weakness during his agony? Could they not describe a resolute death? Undoubtedly. St Luke himself paints St Stephen's death with more of fortitude than that of Christ. They have shewn him to be capable of fear, before the hour of death was come; but afterwards perfectly calm. When they tell of his being in affliction, that sorrow proceeded from himself; but when *men* afflicted him, he was unmoved.

The church has at times had to prove to those who denied it, that Jesus Christ was man, as well as that he was God; and appearances were as much against the one truth as against the other.

Jesus Christ is a God to whom we can approach without pride; and before whom we abase ourselves without despair.

5. The conversion of the heathen was reserved for the grace of the Messiah. Either the Jews did not try it, or they were unsuccessful. All that Solomon and the prophets said on this subject, was vain. Their wise men, also, as Plato and Socrates, could not lead them to worship the one true God.

The gospel speaks only of the virginity of Mary, up to the period of the Saviour's birth. Every thing has reference to Jesus Christ.

118   JESUS CHRIST.

The two Testaments contemplate Jesus Christ; one as its expectation; the other as its exemplar: as their centre.

The prophets predict, but were not predicted. saints were predicted, but do not predict. Jesus Cl predicts, and is predicted.

Jesus Christ for all men; Moses for one people.

The Jews are blessed in Abraham; *I will bless them bless thee.* Gen. xii. 3. But all nations are blessed in seed. Gen. xviii. 18. He is *a light to lighten the Gen* Luke ii. 32.

He has not done so to any nation, (Psalm cxlvii. said David, when speaking of the law. But in speal of Jesus Christ, we may say, He hath done so to all tions.

Jesus Christ is an universal blessing. The church mits her sacramental services to the apparently faith Christ gave himself a ransom for all.

Let us then open our arms to our Redeemer, who, l ing been promised for 4000 years, is come at length suffer and to die for us, at the period, and under all circumstances predicted. And while, through his gr we await a peaceful death, in the hope of being unite him for ever, let us receive with joy either the prosp ties which it pleases him to give, or the trials that sends for our profit, and which, from his own examp we learn to endure.

CHAPTER XV.

PROPHETICAL PROOFS OF JESUS CHRIST.

THE most powerful evidence in favour of Jesus Christ, is the prophecies; and to them also God appears to have had the most special regard; for the occurrence of those events which fulfil them, is a miracle which has subsisted from the beginning of the church to the end. God raised up a succession of prophets, during a period of 1600 years, and during four subsequent centuries, he scattered these prophecies, with the Jews who possessed them, throughout all parts of the world. Such, then, was the preparation for the birth of Christ; for as his gospel was to be believed by all the world, it required not only that there should be prophecies to render it credible, but that these prophecies should be diffused throughout the world, in order that all the world might believe.

If one individual only had written a volume of predictions respecting Jesus Christ, and the time and manner of his coming, and then Jesus Christ had come, in accordance to these predictions, the proof would be infinitely powerful. But we have more than this. In this case there is a series of men for 4000 years, who constantly and without discrepancy foretel successively the same advent. He is announced by a whole people, who subsist for 4000 years, to yield a successive cumulative testimony to their certain expectation of his coming; and from which neither threat nor persecution could turn them. This is much ampler proof.

2. The appointed period was predicted by the **state of the Jews, by the state of the heathen, by the state of the temple, and by the precise number of years.**

The prophets having given several signs which should happen at the coming of Messiah, it follows that all these signs should occur at the same time; and hence it followed, that the fourth monarchy should be come, at the expiration of the seventy weeks of Daniel; that the sceptre should then depart from Judah; and that then Messiah should come. At that very crisis, Jesus Christ came, and declared himself the Messiah.

It is predicted, that during the fourth monarchy, before the destruction of the second temple, before the dominion of the Jews had ceased, and in the seventieth week of Daniel, the heathen should be instructed and led to the knowledge of that God, whom the Jews worshipped, and that they who loved him, should be delivered from their enemies, and filled with his love and his fear.

And it did happen, that during the fourth monarchy, and before the destruction of the second temple, multitudes of the heathen worshipped God, and lived a heavenly life; women devoted to God their virginity, and their whole life; men renounced a life of pleasure; and that which Plato could not accomplish with a few chosen and well disciplined individuals, was now effected by a secret influence, operating through a few words, on hundreds of thousands of illiterate men.

And what is all this? It is that which has been foretold long before. *I will pour out my Spirit upon all flesh.* All men were lying in wretchedness and unbelief. Now the whole earth kindles into love. Princes laid aside *their* splendour: the wealthy parted with their abundance:

girls submitted to martyrdom: children forsook their homes to live in the deserts. Whence is this energy? It is that Messiah is come. This is the effect and the proof of his arrival.

For 2000 years the God of the Jews was unknown to the countless multitudes of the heathen; but, at the time predicted, the heathen rushed in crowds to worship this only God. The temples are thrown down; and kings themselves bend before the cross. Whence comes this? The Spirit of God has been poured out upon the earth.

It was foretold that Messiah should come to establish a new covenant, which should cause them to forget their departure from Egypt. Jer. xxiii. 7. That he should write his law, not on an exterior tablet, but on their hearts, Isaiah li. 7.; and put his fear, which, till then, had been only superficial, in their hearts also. Jer. xxxi. 33. That the Jews should reject Christ, and that they should be rejected of God, because the chosen vine brought forth wild grapes only. Isaiah v. That the chosen people should be faithless, ungrateful, and incredulous,—*an unbelieving and gainsaying people.* Isaiah lxv. 2. That God should smite them with blindness, and that they should stumble like blind men at noon-day. Deut. xxviii. That the church should be small at its commencement, and increase gradually. Ezek. xlvii.

It was foretold that then idolatry should be overthrown; that Messiah should overturn all the idols, and bring men to the worship of the true God. Ezek. xxx. 13.

That the temples and the images should be caused to cease, and in every place a pure offering should be offered, and not the blood of beasts. Mal. i. 11.

That he should teach men the perfect way. Isa. ii. 3. Micah iv. 2. That he should be the king, both of Jews and Gentiles. Psalm ii. 6—8. Psalm lxxi. And never has there come either before Jesus Christ, or since, any man who has taught any thing like this.

And at length, after so many individuals have predicted this advent, Jesus Christ appeared and said, I am he, and the time is fulfilled. He came to teach men that they had no enemies but themselves; that their sinful inclinations separate them from God; that he came to deliver them, to give them grace, and to gather all men into one holy church; to unite in this church both Jews and Gentiles; and to destroy the idols of the one, and the superstitions of the other.

"What the prophets have foretold, my apostles," said he, "will shortly accomplish. The Jews shall be rejected; Jerusalem will soon be destroyed; the Gentiles shall come to the knowledge of God; and when you shall have slain the heir of the vineyard, my apostles shall turn from you to them."

Afterwards we find the apostles saying to the Jews: a curse is coming upon you; and to the Gentiles, you shall know the Lord.

To this dispensation all men were adverse, owing to the natural antipathy of their sinfulness. This king of both Jews and Gentiles, was oppressed by both, who conspired to kill him. All that was mighty in the world, the learned, the wise, the powerful, all confederated against this nascent religion. Some wrote, some censured, and others shed blood. But notwithstanding all opposition, in a short time, we see Jesus Christ reigning over both,—destroying the Jewish worship in Jerusalem, which was its centre and erecting there his first church; and destroying the worship of idols, at Rome, where idolatry centred, and establishing in it his principal church.

The apostles and the primitive Christians, a simple and powerless people, resisted all the powers of the earth; overcame monarchs, philosophers, and sages, and destroyed an established idolatry. And all this was wrought by the alone energy of that word which had foretold it.

The Jews, by slaying Christ, that they might not acknowledge him as Messiah, have completed the proof of his Messiahship. Their perseverance in denying him, makes them irrefragable witnesses in his behalf. And both by their killing him, and persisting to reject him, they have fulfilled the prophecy.

Who does not recognize Jesus Christ in a great variety of particulars predicted of the Messiah? For it is said,

That he should have a forerunner. Mal. iii. 1. That he should be born as an infant. Isaiah ix. 6. That he should be born in Bethlehem. Micah v. 2. That he should spring from the family of Judah and of David: that he should appear chiefly in Jerusalem. Mal. iii. 1. Hag. ii. 10. That he should hide these things from the wise and prudent, and reveal them to the poor and to babes. That he should open the eyes of the blind, should heal the sick, Isaiah xxxv. and lead those who languished in darkness, into light. Isaiah xlii. 8, 9.

That he should teach a perfect way, and be the instructor of the Gentiles. Isaiah lv. 4.

That he should be the victim offered for the sins of the world. Isaiah liii.

That he should be the precious foundation stone. Isaiah xxviii. 26.

That he should be a stone of stumbling, and a rock of offence, Isaiah viii. 14.

That the inhabitants of Jerusalem shall fall on it. Isaiah viii. 15.

That the builders shall reject this stone, and that God shall make it the head stone of the corner. Psalm cxviii. 22. And that this stone should become a great mountain, and fill the earth. Dan. ii. 35.

That he should be rejected, Psalm cxviii. 22.; disowned, Isaiah liii. 2.; betrayed, Psalm xl. 9.; sold, Zach. xi. 12.; stricken, Isaiah l. 6.; mocked and afflicted in many different ways, Psalm lxix. That they should give him gall to drink, Psalm lxix. 21.; that they should pierce his hands and his feet, Psalm xxii. 16.; that they should spit upon him, Isaiah l. 6.; and kill him, Dan. ix.; and cast lots for his vesture, Psalm xxii. 18. That he should rise again the third day, Psalm xvi. Hosea vi. 2. That he should ascend to heaven, Psalm xlvii. 5.—lxviii. 18.; and sit down at the right hand of God, Psalm cx. 1. That the kings of the earth should take counsel against him, Psalm ii. That sitting at the right hand of God, he should make his foes his footstool. Psalm cx. 1. That all kings shall fall down before him—all nations shall worship him. Psalm lxxii. That the Jews should subsist perpetually as a people. Jer. xxxi. 36. That they should wander about, Amos ix. 9.; without a prince, without a sacrifice, without an altar, Hosea iii. 4.; and without prophets, Psalm lxxiv. 9.; looking for redemption, but looking in vain, Isaiah lix. 9. Jer. viii. 15.

3. The Messiah was to form to himself a numerous people, elect and holy; to lead them, to nourish them, to bring them into a place of rest and holiness; to make them holy to the Lord, to make them the temple of God; to reconcile them to God; to save them from the wrath of God; to rescue them from the slavery of sin, which evidently reigns over men; to give a law to them, and

to write it in their hearts; to offer himself to God for them; to sacrifice himself for them; to be both the spotless victim, and the offering priest; he was to offer himself, both his body and his blood to God. Jesus Christ has done all this.

It was foretold that a deliverer should come, who should bruise the serpent's head, who should deliver his people from all their iniquities, Psalm cxxx. 8.; that he should establish a new covenant, which should be everlasting; and a new priesthood after the order of Melchisedec, to abide for ever; that the Messiah should be glorious, powerful, and mighty, and yet so abject, as to be disowned; that he should not be esteemed for what he really was; that he should be rejected, that he should be slain; that his people who denied him, should be his people no longer; that the idolatrous Gentiles should believe, and fly to him for refuge; that he should abandon Zion, to reign in the centre of idolatry; that the Jewish nation, notwithstanding, should still subsist; and that this person so predicted, should spring out of Judah, at the time when the kingdom ceased.

4. Now consider, that from the beginning of the world, the expectation, or the actual worship of Messiah, has continued without interval; that he was promised to the first man, immediately after his fall; that other men appeared subsequently, who declared that God had revealed to them also, that a Redeemer should be born, who would save his people; that Abraham then came, who affirmed the fact of a revelation made to him, that the Redeemer should descend from him, by a son of his, who was yet unborn; that Jacob said, that out of his twelve sons, Judah should be the direct ancestor of the Messiah; that

Moses and the prophets, at length pointed out the time and manner of his coming; that they declared the then present law, to be only a provisional appointment till the coming of Messiah; that, till then only it should endure, but that the other should last for ever; but so that either the old law, or that of Messiah, of which the first was a typical pledge, should be ever on the earth; that such has been the fact; and that at length Jesus Christ did come, in circumstances entirely conformed to all these minute predictions. Surely this is wonderful!

But it will be said, If all this was so clearly foretold to the Jews, why did they not believe, or why are they not utterly destroyed for having resisted so clear a testimony? I answer, that both these facts are in the prediction; both, that they would not believe this ample testimony, and that they should not be exterminated. And nothing could more effectually subserve the glory of Messiah; for it was not sufficient to have the testimony of prophecy on his behalf; but those prophecies must be preserved in circumstances actually free from the slightest taint of suspicion.

5. The prophetic writings have, blended with the predictions concerning Messiah, some others that were local and peculiar, in order that the prophecies, concerning Messiah, might not be without some other evidence; and that the local predictions might have their use in the system.

We have no king but Cæsar, said the Jews. Then Jesus was the Messiah. For their avowed king was an alien, and they recognized no other.

A doubt hangs on the beginning of the seventy weeks of Daniel, on account of the wording of the prophecy itself; and also on the termination of that period, on

OF JESUS CHRIST. 127

to the differences among chronologists. But the utmost limits of the difference is not more than 200 years.

The prophecies which tell of Messiah's poverty, describe him also as lord of all nations.

The prophecies which announce the time of his advent, only speak of him as the king of the Gentiles, and as a sufferer; not as a judge coming in the clouds of heaven; and those which describe him as judging the nations on the throne of his glory, say nothing of the precise period of his coming.

When they speak of Messiah's advent in glory, it is evidently his coming to judge the world, not to redeem it. Isaiah lxvi. 15, 16.

CHAPTER XVI.

OTHER PROOFS OF JESUS CHRIST.

IF we do not give credit to the apostles, we must hold either that they are deceived or deceivers. But either alternative has its difficulties. In the first case, it is scarcely possible to be cheated into a belief, that a dead man had risen again; and in the other, the supposition that they were themselves impostors, is very absurd. Let us follow out the case. Let us suppose these twelve men assembling after the death of Christ, and conspiring together to maintain that he had risen from the dead. We know, that by this doctrine, they attacked all the powers of this world. The heart of man also is strangely disposed to levity and to change, and easily influenced by promises and gifts. Now, if in these circumstances of risk, but one of them had been shaken by those allurements, or what is more likely, by imprisonment, torture, or the pain of death, they were all lost.

While Jesus Christ was with them, he could sustain them; but afterwards, if he did not appear to them, who did encourage them to action?

2. The style of the gospel is admirable in many respects; and, amongst others, that there is not a single invective indulged by the historians against Judas or Pilate, or any of the enemies or murderers of Jesus Christ.

Had this delicacy on the part of the evangelical historians been only assumed, together with all the other features of their amiable character; and had they only assumed it, that it might be observed,—then, even though they had not dared in some way or other to point the attention to it themselves, they could not have failed to procure some friend to notice it to their advantage. But as they were quite unaffected and disinterested, they never provided any one to make such a comment. In fact, I know not that the remark was ever made till now; and this is a strong proof of the simplicity of their conduct.

3. Jesus Christ wrought miracles; so did his apostles. So also did the primitive saints; because, as the prophecies were not fulfilled, and were in fact only fulfilling in them, there was as yet no testimony to the truth but miracles. It was foretold that Messiah should convert the nations. How could this prophecy be fulfilled, but by the conversion of nations; and how were the first nations to be *converted* to Messiah, not seeing this conclusive result of *the* prophetic testimony in support of his mission? Th

his death and resurrection, then, and even till some nations had been converted, the whole evidence was not complete; and hence miracles were necessary during the whole of that time. Now, however, they are no longer needed. Prophecy fulfilled is a standing miracle.

4. The state of the Jews strikingly proves the truth of our religion. It is wonderful to see this people, subsisting for so many centuries, and to see them always wretched: it being essential to the evidence in support of Jesus Christ, that they should subsist as witnesses to him; and that they should be miserable, because they slew him. And though their misery presses against their existence, they exist still, in spite of their misery.

But were they not almost in the same state at the time of the captivity? No. The continuance of the sceptre was not interrupted by the captivity in Babylon; because their return was promised and predicted. When Nebuchadnezzar led them captive, lest it should be supposed that the sceptre had departed from Judah, it was previously declared to them, that they should be there for a short time only, and that they should be re-established. They had still the consolation of their prophets, and their kings were not taken away. But the second destruction of their polity, is without any promise of restoration, without prophets, without kings, without comfort, and without hope; for the sceptre is removed for ever.

That was scarcely a captivity which was alleviated by the promise of deliverance in seventy years; but now they are captive without hope.

God had promised them, that even though he scattered them to the ends of the earth, yet if they were faithful to his law, he would bring them back again. They are faithful to the law, and yet remain in oppression. It follows, then, that Messiah must be come, and that the law which contained these promises, has been superseded by the establishment of a new law.

5. Had the Jews been all converted to the faith of Christ, we should have had none but suspected witnesses, and had they been extirpated, we should have had no witnesses at all.

The Jews rejected Christ, yet not all of them. Those who were holy, received him; those who were carnal did not: and so far is this from militating against his glory, that it gives to it the finishing touch. The reason of their rejection, and the only one which is found in their writings, in the Talmud, and in the Rabbins, is that Jesus Christ did not subdue the nations by force of arms. "Jesus Christ," they say, "has been slain; he has fallen; he has not subdued the heathen by his might; he has not given us their spoils; he has given no wealth." Is that all they can say? It is for this that I love him. A Messiah such as they describe, I have no wish for.

6. How delightful it is to see with the eye of faith, Darius, Cyrus, Alexander, the Romans, Pompey, and Herod, labouring unwittingly for the glory of the Gospel.

7. The Mohammedan religion has for its foundation the Koran and Mohammed. But has this man, who was said to be the last prophet expected in the world, been at all the subject of prediction? And what mark has he to accredit him, more than any other man who chooses to set up for a prophet? What miracles does he himself affirm that he performed? What mystery has he taught

even by his own account? What morality did he teach, and what blessedness did he promise?

Mohammed is unsupported by any authority. His reasons then had need to be powerful indeed, since they rest solely on their own strength.

8. If two men utter things which appear of a common place and popular kind, but the discourse of one has a twofold sense understood by his disciples, whilst the discourses of the other have but one meaning; then any one, not in the secret, hearing the two persons saying similar things, would judge in a similar way of both. But if, in conclusion, the one utters heavenly things, whilst the other still brings forward only common-place, and mean notions, and even fooleries, he would then conceive that the one spoke with a mystic meaning, and the other did not; the one having sufficiently proved himself to be incapable of absurdity, but capable of having a mystic sense; the other, that he can be absurd, but not a setter forth of mysteries.

9. It is not by the obscurities in the writings of Mohammed, and which they may pretend have a mystic sense, that I would wish him to be judged, but by his plain statements, as his account of paradise, and such like. Even in these things he is ridiculous. Now, it is not so with the Holy Scriptures. They also have their obscurities; but then there are many clear and lucid statements, and many prophecies in direct terms which have been accomplished. The cases then are not parallel. We must not put on an equal footing, books which only resemble each other in the existence of obscurities, and not in those brilliancies, which substantiate their own di-

vine origin, and justly claim a due reverence also for the obscurities, by which they are accompanied.

The Koran itself, says that Matthew was a good man. Then Mohammed was a false prophet, either in calling good men wicked, or in rejecting as untrue, what they affirm of Jesus Christ.

10. Any man may do what Mohammed did; for he wrought no miracles, he fulfilled no previous prophecy. No man can do what Jesus Christ did.

Mohammed established his system by killing others; Jesus Christ by exposing his disciples to death; Mohammed by forbidding to read; Jesus by enjoining it. In fact, so opposite were their plans, that, if according to human calculation, Mohammed took the way to succeed, Jesus Christ certainly took the way of failure. And instead of arguing, that because Mohammed succeeded, therefore Jesus Christ might; it follows rather, that since Mohammed succeeded, Christianity must have failed, if it had not been supported by an energy purely Divine.

CHAPTER XVII.

THE PURPOSE OF GOD TO CONCEAL HIMSELF FROM SOME, AND TO REVEAL HIMSELF TO OTHERS.

IT was the purpose of God to redeem mankind, and to extend salvation to those who will seek it. But men render themselves so unworthy of it, that he is equitable in refusing to some, because of the hardness of their hearts, that which he bestows on others, by a mercy to which they have no claim. Had he chosen to overpower

DIVINE SOVEREIGNTY. 133

the obstinacy of the most hardened, he could have done so, by revealing himself to them so distinctly, that they could no longer doubt the truth of his existence. And he will so appear at the last day, with such an awful storm, and such a destruction of the frame of nature, that the most blind must see him.

He did not, however, choose thus to appear at the advent of grace; because, as so many men rendered themselves unworthy of his clemency, he determined that they should remain strangers to the blessing which they did not desire. It would not then have been just to appear in a mode manifestly divine, and such as absolutely to convince all men; nor would it have been just on the other hand, to come in a mode so hidden, that he could not have been recognized by those who sought him in sincerity. It was his will to make himself perfectly cognizable to all such; and hence, willing to be revealed to those who seek him with their whole heart, and hidden from those who, as cordially fly from him, he has so regulated the means of knowing him, as to give indications of himself, which are plain to those who seek him, and shrouded to those who seek him not.*

2. There is light enough for those whose main wish is to see; and darkness enough to confound those of an opposite disposition.

There is brightness enough to enlighten the elect, and sufficient obscurity to keep them humble.

There is mystery enough to blind the reprobate; but light enough to condemn them, and to make them inexcusable.

---

* The pillar of cloud and of fire, is a beautiful illustration of this idea.

If this world subsisted only to teach men the existence of God, his divinity would have shined forth in every part of it with resistless splendour. But since the world only exists by Jesus Christ, and for him, and to teach men their fall and their redemption, the whole abounds with proofs of these two truths. The appearance of things indicates neither the total abandonment, nor the plenary presence of the Divinity, but the presence of a God that hideth himself. Every thing wears this character.

If God had never appeared at all, such a total concealment might have been ambiguous, and might have been referred equally to the non-existence of Deity, as to the unworthiness of men to know him. But his occasional manifestations remove the ambiguity. If he has appeared once, then he *is* always. And we are shut up to the conclusion, that there is a God, and that men are unworthy of his manifested presence.

3. The purpose of God was more to rectify the will, than the understanding of man. Now, an unclouded brightness would have satisfied the understanding, and left the will unreformed. Had there been no obscurity, man would not have been sensible of his corruption. Had there been no light, man would have despaired of a remedy. It is then not only equitable, but profitable for us, that God should be partly hidden, and partly revealed; since it is equally dangerous for man to know God, without the consciousness of his misery; or to know his misery, without knowing his God.

4. All things around man teach him his real state; if he should read them rightly. For it is not true either that God is wholly revealed, or wholly hidden. But h

these assertions are true together, that he hides himself from those who tempt him, and that he discovers himself to those who seek him. Because men are, at the same time, unworthy of God, and yet capable of receiving him; unworthy in consequence of their corruption; capable by their original nature.

5. Every thing on earth proclaims the misery of man, or the mercy of God; the powerlessness of man without God, or his might when God is with him.

The whole universe teaches man, either that he is corrupt, or that he is redeemed. All things teach him his greatness or his misery. In the heathen he sees the withdrawment of God; in the Jews, his presence and protection.

6. All things work together for good to the elect; even the obscurities of Scripture; for they reverence them on account of those portions which are manifestly Divine. All things are evil to the reprobate, even the plainest truths of Scripture, because they blaspheme them on account of those obscurities, which they cannot comprehend.

7. If Jesus Christ had only come to sanctify and save, the whole of Scripture, and all other things, would have tended to that object, and it would have been easy indeed to convince the infidel. But since, as Isaiah says, chap. viii. 14. he became both as *a sanctuary* (for salvation) and *a rock of offence*, we cannot expect to overcome the obstinacy of infidelity. But this does not militate against us, since we ourselves affirm, that God's dealings with us were not meant to carry conviction to those stubborn, self-satisfied spirits, who do not sincerely seek for truth.

Jesus is come, *that those who see not, may see; and that those who see, may become blind.* He came to heal the diseased, and to let *the whole* perish: to *call sinners to repentance* and justification, and to leave *the righteous, those* who think themselves righteous, in their sins: *to fill the hungry with good things, and to send the rich empty away.*

What say the prophets of Jesus Christ? That he should be manifestly God? No. But that he is the true God veiled; that he shall be unrecognised; that men shall not think that this is he; that he shall be *a stone of stumbling,* on which *many shall fall.*

It is that Messiah might be known by the good, and unknown by the wicked, that he is foretold as he is. If the mode of his coming had been fully unfolded, there would have been no obscurity even to the wicked. If the period had been foretold obscurely, there would have been darkness on the minds of the good, for their moral state would not convey to them the idea of Hebrew notation; for instance, that a ס should signify 600 years. The time therefore was foretold plainly—the mode mystically.

Thus, the wicked erroneously supposing, that the blessings promised were temporal, were misled, although the time was so distinctly foretold; while the righteous avoided the error, because the comprehension of such blessings is with the heart, which always calls that good, that it really loves; but the knowledge of the time was not a matter for the comprehension of the heart. And thus the clear pointing out of the time, together with an obscure description of the blessing, could only mislead the wicked.

8. Why was it necessary with respect to Messiah, that it should be stated of him, that in him the sceptre was to

remain perpetually in Judah; and yet, that at his coming, the sceptre should be taken from Judah?

As a provision, *That seeing, they might not see; and that hearing, they might not understand,* nothing could be more effectual.

Instead of lamenting that God is hidden, we should thank him that he has been so far revealed; we should thank him that he has not revealed himself to the prudent and the proud of this world, who were unworthy to know a holy God.

9. The genealogy of Jesus Christ in the Old Testament, is blended with so many others apparently useless, as to be scarcely discernible. If Moses had only registered the ancestry of Jesus Christ, the fact would have been too plainly exhibited. But even to an accurate observer, it may be distinctly traced through Thamar, Ruth, Bathsheba, &c.

Even the apparently weak points in the chain of evidence, have their peculiar force to a well constituted mind. Witness the two genealogies by Matthew and Luke, which prove that there has not been collusion.

10. Let them not reproach us any longer, with the want of clearness in our evidence. We own the fact as part of our system. But let them recognize the truth of our religion, even in its obscurities, in the little light that we have; and in the indifference respecting the discovery of it, which is so generally manifested.

Had there been but one religion, God would have been too manifest. The case were the same, if *our* religion only had its martyrs.

Jesus Christ so far left the wicked to their wilful blindness, in that he did not say he was not of Nazareth, nor that he was not the son of Joseph.

As Jesus Christ dwelt unrecognized among men, so the truth dwells undistinguished among the crowd of vulgar opinions.

If the mercy of God is so great, that it makes us wise unto salvation, even while he hideth himself, what illumination may we not expect when he is fully revealed!

We can know nothing of the work of God, if we do not admit as a first principle, that he blinds some, while he enlightens others.

CHAPTER XVIII.

THAT THE RELIGION OF REAL CHRISTIANS, AND REAL JEWS, IS ONE AND THE SAME.

THE Jewish religion *seemed* to consist essentially in descent from Abraham, in circumcision, in sacrifices, and ceremonies, in the ark, and the temple at Jerusalem, and in the law, and the covenant of Moses.

I affirm that it did not consist in all, or any of these things, but simply in the love of God; and that God disallowed all the rest.

That God did not choose the people who sprung from Abraham according to the flesh.

That the Jews were to be punished by the Almighty, as strangers would be, if they offended. *If thou forget the Lord thy God, and walk after other gods, and serve them, and worship them; I testify against you this day, that ye shall surely perish; as the nations which the Lord destroyeth before your face, so shall ye perish.*

That strangers would be accepted, even as the Jews, if they loved God.

That the true Jews ascribed their safety to God, and not to Abraham. *Doubtless thou art our father, though Abraham be ignorant of us, and Israel acknowledge us not: thou, O Lord, art our Father, our Redeemer.* Isa. lxiii. 16.

Moses also had said, *God accepteth not persons, nor taketh rewards.*

I affirm that the Jewish religion enjoins also the circumcision of the heart. *Circumcise, therefore, the foreskin of your heart, and be no more stiff-necked. For the Lord your God is God of gods, and Lord of lords, a great God, a mighty, a terrible, &c.* Deut. x. 16, 17.

That God promised to do this for them at some future day. *And the Lord thy God will circumcise thy heart, and the heart of thy seed, to love the Lord thy God with all thy heart.* Deut xxx. 6.

That the uncircumcised in heart shall be judged and punished. *God will punish them which are circumcised with the uncircumcised; for all these nations are uncircumcised, and all the house of Israel are uncircumcised in heart.*

2. I affirm that circumcision was a sign, instituted to distinguish the Jewish people from all other nations. And therefore it was that, while they wandered in the wilderness, they were not circumcised, because they could then not intermingle with strangers; and that since the coming of Jesus Christ, it is no longer necessary.

The love of God is every where enjoined. *I call heaven and earth to record this day against you, that I have set before you life and death, blessing and cursing; therefore choose life, that both thou and thy seed may live; that thou mayest love the Lord thy God, and that thou mayest obey his voice,* and that thou mayest cleave unto him; for he is thy life. Deut. xxx. 19, 20.

It is said also, that the Jews, from the want of this love, shall be rejected for their crimes, and the Gentiles chosen in their stead. *I will hide my face from them, for they are a very froward nation, and unbelieving. They have moved me to jealousy with that which is not God,—and I will move them to jealousy with those which are not a people. I will provoke them to anger with a foolish nation.* Deut. xxxii. 20, 21.

That temporal blessings are fallacious, but that the true good is to be united to God. That their feasts were displeasing to God. That the sacrifices of the Jews displeased God; and not only those of the wicked Jews, but that he had no pleasure in the sacrifices of the righteous, for, in Psalm 50th, previously to his special address to the wicked, beginning, *But to the wicked God saith, &c.* verse 16th, it is stated that God will not accept the sacrifices of beasts, nor their blood. 1 Sam. xv. 22.

That the offerings of the Gentiles shall be accepted of God. Mal. i. 11. And that the offerings of the Jews were not acceptable to him. Jer. vi. 20.

That God would make a new covenant by Messiah, and that the old one should be abolished, Jer. xxxi. 31.

That the former things shall be forgotten. Isa. xliii. 18.

That the ark shall be no more remembered. Jer. iii. 16.

That the temple shall be rejected. Jer. vii. 12—14.

That the sacrifices should be done away, and a purer sacrifice established. Mal. i. 10, 11.

That the order of the Aaronic priesthood should be rejected, and that of Melchisedec introduced by the Messiah, and that this should be an everlasting priesthood.

That Jerusalem shall be rejected. Isaiah v. That a new name shall be given. That it shall be a better and an eternal name. Isaiah lvi. 5.

That the Jews shall continue without prophet, priest, king, prince, sacrifice or altar; and that they should subsist, notwithstanding, as a distinct people.

CHAPTER XIX.

WE CANNOT KNOW GOD SAVINGLY, BUT BY JESUS CHRIST.

IT is usual for the greater part of those who try to convince the ungodly of the being of a God, to begin with the works of nature; and they seldom succeed. Not that I question the substantiality of that class of proofs, for they are consecrated by the Scripture; and they consist with sound reason: but frequently they are not well adapted to the disposition of mind, of those to whom they are so applied.

For it should be observed, that this line of argument is not applied to those who have a living faith in the heart, and who see clearly that every thing which exists is the work of the God whom they adore. To such, all nature speaks for its author. To them the heavens declare the glory of God. But for those in whom this light is extinct, and in whom we wish it to revive; those men who are without faith and charity, and who find nothing but clouds and darkness throughout nature; for such it seems scarcely the right way to reclaim them, that we should ply them on a subject so great and important, with proofs drawn from the course of the moon and the planets, or with any of those common-place arguments, against which they have invariably revolted. The hardness of their hearts has rendered them deaf to this voice of nature, ringing constantly upon their ear; and experience proves, that far from carrying them by these means, nothing is more likely to disgust them, and to destroy the hope of their discovering the truth, than professing to convince them simply by such reasonings, and telling them that they will find truth altogether unveiled.

Certainly this is not the way in which the Scriptures speak of God, which are far better prepared to speak of him than we are. They tell us, we allow, that the beauty of creation declares its author; but, they do not say, that it does so to the whole world. On the contrary, they affirm, that the creature does not make God known by its own light, but by that light which God, at the same time, pours into the minds of those whom he thus instructs. *That which may be known of God, is manifest in them; for God hath shewed it to them.* Rom. i. 19. The Scripture teaches us in general, that *God is a God that hideth himself;* and, that since the corruption of human nature, he has left men in a state of blindness, from which they cannot escape, but through Jesus Christ, without whom, all communion with God is impracticable. *No man knoweth the Father, but the Son, and he to whomsoever the Son will reveal him.* Matt. ii. 27.

The Scripture teaches the same truth also, where, in so many different passages, it affirms, that they who seek God shall find him. But we do not speak thus of a clear and self-evident light. It needs no *seeking*. It compels observation by its own brilliancy.

2. Metaphysical arguments, in proof of Deity, are so

remote from the common habits of reasoning, and so intricate and involved, that they produce little impression; and even though they may influence a few, it is only at the time when they are actually considering the demonstration, and an hour afterward, they fear they have deceived themselves. *Quod curiositate cognoverant superbia amiserunt.*

Besides, this sort of proof can only lead to a speculative knowledge of God; and to know him only in this way, is not to know him at all.

The God whom Christians worship, is not merely the divine author of geometric truths, and of the order of the elements. This is the belief of the heathen. He is not merely a God who watches providentially over the lives and fortunes of men, to bestow a succession of happy years on his worshippers. This is the belief of the Jew. But the God of Abraham and of Jacob, the God of the Christian, is a God of love and of consolation. He is a God who fills the soul and the heart which he possesses. He is a God who makes them feel within, their own misery; whose infinite grace unites itself with their inmost soul; fills it with humility, and joy, and confidence, and love; and makes it impossible for them to seek any other end than himself.

The God of the Christians is a God who causes the soul to feel that he is its only good, that he is its only rest; and that it can have no joy but in his love; and who teaches it, at the same time, to abhor every obstacle to the full ardour of that affection. That self-love and sensual affections which impede it, are insufferable to it. God discloses to the soul this abyss of selfishness, and that he himself is the only remedy.

That is to know God as a Christian. But to know

God thus, a man must know also his misery and unworthiness, and the need he has of a mediator, by whom he may draw near to God, and be again united to him. These two branches of knowledge must not be separated, for when separate, they are not only useless, but injurious. The knowledge of our ruin, without the knowledge of Jesus Christ, is despair. But the knowledge of Christ delivers us both from pride and despair, because in him we discern, at once, our God, our own guilt, and the only way of recovery.

We may know God without knowing our wretchedness, or our wretchedness without knowing God; or both without knowing the way of deliverance from those miseries by which we are overwhelmed. But we cannot know Jesus Christ, without knowing, at once, our God, our ruin, and our remedy, because Jesus Christ is not a mere God; but God our Saviour from misery.

Hence, therefore, they who seek God without a Saviour, will discover no satisfactory or truly beneficial light. For either they never discover that there is a God; or, if they do, it is to little purpose; because they devise to themselves some mode of approaching without mediation, that God, whom, without the aid of a mediator, they have discovered: and thus they fall either into Atheism or Deism, two evils equally abhorrent to the Christian system.

We should aim then, exclusively, to know Jesus Christ, since, by him only, we can expect ever to obtain a beneficial knowledge of God.

He is the true God of mankind; that is, of miserable sinners. He is the centre of all, and to him every thing points: and he who knows him not, knows nothing of the economy of this world, or of himself. For not only we not know God, but by Jesus Christ, but we cannot know ourselves except by him.

Without Jesus Christ, man must remain in sin and misery. In Jesus Christ, man is delivered from sin and misery. In him is treasured up all our happiness, our virtue, our very life, and light, and hope; and out of him there is nothing for us but sin, misery, darkness, and despair; without him, we see nothing but obscurity and confusion in the nature of both God and man.

CHAPTER XX.

THOUGHTS ON MIRACLES.

WE must judge of doctrine by miracles, and of miracles by doctrine. The doctrine attests the miracles, and the miracles attest the doctrine. Both sides of the assertion are true, and yet there is no discrepancy between them.

2. There are miracles which are indubitable evidences of truth, and there are some which are not. We should have a mark to distinguish those which are, or they would be useless. But they are not useless; they are of the nature of a foundation. The test then which is given to us, should be such as not to destroy that proof which true miracles give to the truth, and which is the chief end of miracles.

If no miracles had ever been adduced in support of falsehood, they would have been a certain criterion. If there were no rule for discrimination, miracles would have been useless; there would have been no just ground to credit them.

Moses has given us one test, which is, when the miracle

G

leads to idolatry. *If there arise among you a prophet, or a dreamer of dreams, and giveth thee a sign or a wonder, and the sign or the wonder come to pass, whereof he spake to thee, saying, Let us go after other gods, which thou hast not known, and let us serve them; thou shalt not hearken unto the words of that prophet, or that dreamer of dreams: for the Lord your God proveth you.* Deut. xiii. 1, 2, 3. Jesus Christ also has given us one in Mark ix. 39. *There is no man who shall do a miracle in my name, that can lightly speak evil of me.* Whence it follows, that whoever declares himself openly against Jesus Christ, cannot do a miracle in his name. So that, if he works miracles, it is not in the name of Jesus Christ, and he should not be listened to. We see then the limits marked out to our faith in miracles, to which we must add no others. In the Old Testament, when they turn away from God. In the New, when they turn men from Jesus Christ.

So that if we see a miracle, we must at once receive it, or discover some plain reason to the contrary. We must examine if he who does it, denies God or Jesus Christ.

3. Every religion is false, which does not in its belief worship one God as the author of all things; and in its morals, love one God as the end of all things. Every religion now which does not recognize Jesus Christ is notoriously false, and miracles can avail it nothing.

The Jews had a doctrine from God, as we have from Jesus Christ, and confirmed similarly by miracles. They were forbidden to believe in any worker of miracles, who should teach a contrary doctrine; and, moreover, they were required to have recourse to their priests, and to adhere to them strictly. So that, apparently, all the reasons which we have for rejecting workers of miracles, they had with respect to Jesus Christ and his apostles.

Yet, it is certain, that they were very highly blamable for refusing to believe them on the testimony of their miracles; for Jesus Christ said, That they would not have been blamable if they had not seen his miracles. John xv. 22—24.

It follows, then, that he regarded his miracles as an infallible proof of his doctrine, and that the Jews were bound by them to believe him. And, in fact, it was these miracles especially which made their unbelief criminal. For the proofs that they might have adduced from Scripture, *during the life of Christ*, were not alone conclusive. They might see there that Moses had said, Another prophet should come; but that would not have proved Jesus Christ to be that prophet, which was the whole matter in question. Such passages of Scripture, however, would have shewn them that Jesus Christ might be that prophet; and this, taken together with his miracles, should have determined their belief that he really was so.

4. Prophecy alone was not a sufficient testimony to Jesus Christ, during his life; and hence the Jews would not have been criminal in not believing him before his death, if his miracles had not decided the point. Miracles, then, are sufficient when we detect no contrariety in doctrine, and they should be received.

Jesus Christ had proved himself to be the Messiah, by confirming his doctrine more by his own miracles, than by an appeal to the Scriptures and the prophets.

It was by his miracles that Nicodemus knew his doctrine to be from God. *We know that thou art a teacher come from God; for no man can do the things that thou doest, except God be with him.* John iii. 2. He did not judge of the miracles by the doctrine, but of the doctrine by the miracles.

148 THOUGHTS ON MIRACLES.

So that even though the doctrine was suspected, as that of Jesus Christ might be by Nicodemus, because it seemed to threaten with destruction the traditions of the Pharisees, yet if there were clear and evident miracles on its side, the evidence for the miracle ought to carry it against any apparent difficulty in respect to the doctrine. This rule has its foundation in the indubitable principle, that God cannot lead into error.

There is something reciprocally due between God and man. God says in Isaiah i. 18. *Come now and let us reason together.* And in another place, *What could I have done more to my vineyard, that I have not done in it?* v. 4.

Men owe it to God, to receive the religion which he sends; God owes it to men not to lead them into error. Now, they would be led into error, if any workers of miracles set forth a false doctrine, which did not manifestly appear false to the apprehensions of common sense, and if a greater worker of miracles had not already enjoined upon them not to believe it. So that, if the church were divided, and the Arians, for instance, who affirm that they are founded upon the Scripture, equally with the orthodox, had wrought miracles, and the orthodox had not, men would have been led into error. For, as a man who professes to make known the secret things of God, is not worthy of credit on his own private authority, so a man, who, in proof of the communication that he has from God, raises the dead, predicts future events, removes mountains, and heals diseases, is worthy of credit; and we are impious to refuse it, so long as he is not contradicted by some other teacher who works still greater wonders.

But is not God said to prove us? And may he not *prove us by miracles which seem to uphold error?*

THOUGHTS ON MIRACLES. 149

There is a great difference between proving us, and leading us into error. God proves us; but he never leads into error. To prove, is to present the occasion which does not impose a necessity to act. To lead into error, is to place man under the necessity of assuming and approving a falsehood. This God cannot do; and yet he would do this, if in an obscure question, he permitted miracles to be wrought on the side of falsehood.

We are warranted then to conclude, that it is impossible for a man who conceals his false doctrine, with a view to make it appear like truth, and who affirms himself to be conformed to the will of God and the rule of his church, to work miracles, in order gradually and insensibly to insinuate a false and subtle error. This cannot be; still less can it be, that God who knoweth the heart, should work miracles in favour of such a deceiver.

5. There is a great difference between not being for Jesus Christ, and avowing the infidelity; and not being for Jesus Christ, but pretending to be so. In the first case, perhaps, miracles might be permitted, but not in the other; for it is quite clear of the one class, that they are opposed to the truth, but it is not so of the other; and thus, such miracles may be rightly estimated.

Miracles, then, have been the test in doubtful points, between the Jew and the heathen, the Jew and the Christian.

We have seen this in all the combats of truth against error. In those of Abel against Cain; of Moses against the magicians of Egypt; of Elijah against the prophets of Baal; of Jesus Christ against the Pharisees; of St Paul against Elymas; of the Apostles against the Exorcists; and the primitive Christians against infidels. The truth always surpassed in a contest of miracles; and never in a contest for the true God, and for the truth of religion, has a miracle been wrought in support of error, but a greater miracle has been wrought in support of truth.

By this rule it is clear, that the Jews were under obligation to believe in Christ. He was suspected by them, but his miracles were infinitely more strong than the suspicions against him. They ought therefore to have believed him.

In the days of Jesus Christ, some believed in him, but others would not, because the prophecies said, that Messiah should be born in Bethlehem; instead of which, they conceived that Jesus Christ was born in Nazareth. But they should have examined more narrowly, whether he might not yet have been born in Bethlehem; for his miracles being such, as to carry conviction, the alleged contradictions of his doctrine to Scripture, and this obscurity, did not operate to excuse, but merely to blind them.

Jesus Christ healed him that was born blind, and did many other miracles on the Sabbath-day, by means of which, the Pharisees were blinded, who affirmed that it was right to try the miracles by the doctrine.

The same rule which renders imperative the belief in Christ, equally forbids the belief of antichrist.

Jesus Christ did not speak either against God, or against Moses. The antichrist and the false prophets foretold in the Old and New Testaments, will speak openly against God, and against Jesus Christ. But to a concealed enemy, God will not give the power of openly working miracles.

Moses foretold Jesus Christ, and commanded to follow him. Jesus Christ foretold the antichrist, and forebad to follow him.

The miracles of Jesus Christ were not predicted by antichrist, but the miracles of antichrist were predicted by Jesus Christ. And thus, if Jesus Christ were not the Messiah, he would have led into error; but we could not be reasonably led into error by the miracles of antichrist. Therefore the miracles of antichrist, do not affect the miracles of Jesus Christ. In fact, when Jesus Christ predicted the miracles of antichrist, did he think to injure the faith of his own?

There is no reason to believe in antichrist, that there is not for believing in Christ; but there are reasons for believing in Christ, which there are not for believing in antichrist.

6. Miracles assisted in the foundation, and will assist in the preservation of the church to the days of antichrist, and even to the end.

Wherefore, God, to preserve this testimony in his church, has either confounded all false miracles, or foretold them in his word; and, in both ways, has elevated his cause, and us who believe in it, above those false wonders which appear to us supernatural.

It will be the same in future time. Either God will not permit, or he will confound false miracles, or he will work greater; for miracles have such weight, that however evident the truth of God may be, yet it is necessary that he should warn us against them, when they are wrought against him; without this, they might disturb us.

And thus, however much the passage in the 15th of Deuteronomy, which forbids to believe, and to hear those who work miracles, and who thereby seduce from the service of God; and that in St Mark xiii. 22. which says, *There shall rise up false Christs and false prophets, who shall do many signs and wonders, and seduce, if it were possible, the very elect,* and some similar ones, may appear to make against the authority of miracles; nothing more directly proves their force.

The true reason why real miracles are not believed, is the want of love to God. *Ye believe not,* said Christ, *because ye are not of my sheep.* The same reason holds, why men believe false miracles. *Because they received not the love of the truth that they might be saved, God shall send them strong delusion, that they shall believe a lie.* 2 Thes. ii. 10.

When I have considered how it is that men repose such faith in impostors, who profess to have certain remedies for disease, as to put their lives in their hands, it has appeared to me, that the true reason is, that there are some *real* remedies; for it could not be, that there should be so many fallacious ones, and that they should obtain so much credit, if there were none that were true. Had there never been a real remedy, and all our diseases had been incurable, it is impossible that any men could have supposed themselves able to cure; or that so many others should have reposed confidence in their boasted powers. As, for instance, if any man professed to be able to prevent us from ever dying, no one would believe this, because there is not a single instance of success. But since many effectual remedies have been attested by the wisest of men, the disposition to believe has been thus created; because, as the fact cannot generally be denied, that there are successful cures which are undoubted, the people who are unable to discriminate between the false and the true, believe all. In the same way, the belief of so many imaginary influences of the moon, originates in the fact, that some do exist, as the flux and reflux of the waters of the ocean.

In the same way, it appears to me that there could

have been so many false miracles, false revelations predictions, if there had not been some that were ; nor so many false religions, if there had not been ue one. For had there been nothing of the kind, it most impossible that men could have invented these gs, and still more so, that others should have believed n. But since there have been some very remarkable gs which were true, and that they have been believed he greatest among men, such an effect has been pro- d, that almost all the world has acquired a tendency elieve those that are untrue. And thus, instead of luding that because there are many false miracles, e are none true, we must, on the contrary conclude, there are some true miracles, because there are so y false; and that there are false ones, only from this e, that there are some true; and that, in the same , there are false religions, only because one religion rue. The real cause of this is, that the human mind, g prejudiced towards that side of the que e things that are true, acquires a predisposition ive even what is counterfeit.

CHAPTER XXI.

MISCELLANEOUS THOUGHTS ON RELIGION.

RRHONISM has been useful to religion, for after men, before the coming of Christ, did not know where were, nor whether they were great or insignificant. l those who affirmed the one or the other, knew nothing ly, and conjectured without reason, and at a venture. l whichever they denied, they were still compelled to *ut the principle of faith.*

2. Who would blame Christians for their inability to give a reason for their belief, when they profess to hold a religion, that they cannot altogether explain. On the contrary, they declare when they propose it to the Gentiles, that it is foolishness; and should you then complain that they do not go into the proof of it? If they prove it, they contradict their own words. It is in the failure of proof, that they maintain their consistency. Yes, but while that excuses those who present the Christian religion as such, and cancels the blame of producing it without a full and rational explanation; it does not excuse those, who, upon the offer of it made to them, refuse to believe.

3. Do you conceive it impossible that God is infinite, and without parts? Yes. I will shew you then a thing which is infinite and indivisible. It is a point moving every where with infinite velocity. Let this effect of nature, which at first, seemed impossible to you, teach you that there may be others which you do not know. Do not infer from these your days of apprenticeship, the conclusion that there is nothing more to be known, but rather that there is infinitely more.

4. The way of God, who does all things well, is to plant religion in the understanding by reasoning, and in the heart by his grace. But to seek to introduce it, either to the head or the heart by violence, and by threatening, is not to infuse religion, but terror. Begin by pitying the incredulous. They are sufficiently unfortunate. We should not rail at them, but when it may profit them; but it injures them.

The whole of our faith is to be found in Jesus Christ and Adam. The whole of morals, in the ideas of corruption and grace.

5. The heart has its reasonings, which reason does not apprehend. We feel this in a thousand instances. It loves universal being naturally, and self naturally, just as it takes a fancy; and it hardens itself against either as it will. You have chosen one, and renounced the other. Was this a matter of reason with you?

6. The world exists for the exercise of mercy and judgment upon men; not as beings now issuing pure from the hands of God, but as the enemies of God, to whom he gives, as a matter of grace, sufficient light for their return, if they will seek and follow it: but sufficient to warrant their punishment if they refuse.

7. After all, it must be acknowledged, that the Christian religion has something very wonderful in it. It is, says one, because you were born to it. Far from it. I resist it for that very reason; lest I should be biassed by a prepossession. But though I were born to it, I believe that I should have felt the same.

8. There are two ways of inculcating the truths of our religion, one by the force of reason, the other by the authority of Him who declares them. Men do not use the latter, but the former. They do not say, We must believe this, for the Scriptures which teach it are Divine; but we must believe for this and the other reason, our own weak arguments; for reason itself is easily perverted.

Those who appear most hostile to the glory of religion, are not altogether useless to others. We would conclude, in the first place, that there is something supernatural in their hostility, for a blindness so great is not natural. But if their own folly makes them such enemies to their own welfare, it may serve as a warning to others, by the dread of an example so melancholy, and a folly so much to be pitied.

9. Without Jesus Christ, the world could not continue to exist. It must either be destroyed, or become a hell.

Does he who knows human nature, know it only to be miserable? And will he only who knows it, be the only miserable?

It was not necessary that man should see nothing at all. It was not necessary that he should see sufficient to believe that he had hold of truth; but it was necessary that he should see sufficient to know that he has lost it. To ascertain what he has lost, he must both see and not see; and this is precisely the state of human nature.

It was necessary that the true religion should teach us both our greatness and our misery, and lead us both to the esteem and contempt, the love and the hatred, of self.

10. Religion is a matter of such importance, that it is quite just, that they who will not be at the pains to seek it, if it is obscure, should not discover it. What can they complain of, if it is such, that it may be found for seeking?

Pride counterbalances and cancels all our miseries. How monstrous this is, and how manifestly man is astray! He is fallen from his high estate, and he seeks it again restlessly.

After we had become corrupt, it was right that we who are in that state should know it; both those who delight in it, and those who do not. But it is not necessary that all should see the way of redemption.

When you say that Christ did not die for all, you give

occasion to a vice of the human heart, which constantly applies to itself the exception. Thus you give rise to despair, instead of cherishing hope.

11. The wicked who abandon themselves, blindly to their lusts, without the knowledge of God, and without troubling themselves to seek him, verify in themselves this fundamental principle of the faith which they oppose, that human nature is corrupt. And the Jews who oppose so stubbornly the Christian religion, confirm also this other fundamental truth of the religion which they oppose,—that Jesus Christ is the true Messiah, and that he is come to redeem men, and to deliver them from corruption and misery,—as much by their state at the present day, which is found predicted in their prophetic writings, as by those same prophecies which they hold, and which they scrupulously preserve, as containing the marks by which they are to recognize Messiah. And thus, the proofs of human corruption, and of the redemption of Jesus Christ, which are the two leading truths of the system, are drawn from the profane who boast their utter indifference to this religion, and from the Jews, who are its avowed and irreconcileable enemies.

12. The dignity of man in his state of innocence, consisted in the dominion of the creatures, and in using them; but now, it consists in avoiding and subduing them.

13. Many persons go so much the more dangerously astray, because they assume a truth as the foundation of their error. Their fault is not the following a falsehood; but the following of one truth, to the exclusion of another.

158 MISCELLANEOUS THOUGHTS

There are many truths, both in faith and morals, which seem repugnant and contrary to each other, and which are yet linked together in a most beautiful order.

The source of all heresies, is the exclusion of some one or other of these truths; and the source of all the objections, which heretics bring forward, is the ignorance of some of these truths. And it usually happens, that being unable to conceive the relation between two apparently opposing truths, and believing that the adoption of one, involves the rejection of the other; they do actually embrace the one, and renounce the other.

The Nestorians maintained, that there were two persons in Jesus Christ, because there were two natures; and the Eutychians, on the contrary, that there was but one nature, because there was but one person. The orthodox unite the two truths, of two natures, and one person.

The shortest way to prevent heresy, is to teach the whole truth; and the surest way of refuting heresy, is to meet it by an unreserved declaration of truth.

Grace will be ever in the world, and nature also. There will always be Pelagians, and always men of the Catholic faith; because our first birth makes the one, and the second birth the other.

It will be one of the severest pangs of the damned, to find that they are condemned, even by their own reason, by which they pretended to condemn the Christian religion.

14. It is a common feature of the lives of ordinary men, and of saints, that they are all seeking happiness; they differ only in respect to the point where they place it. Each counts him an enemy, who prevents his attaining the desired object.

We should determine what is good or evil by the will of God, who can neither be unjust or blind, and not by our own will, which is always full of wickedness and error.

15. Jesus Christ has given in the gospel, this criterion of those who have faith, that they speak a new language; and, in fact, the renewing of the thoughts and wishes, alters the conversation also. For these new things, which cannot be displeasing to God, in the same way as the old man could not please him, differ widely from earthly novelties. The things of the world, however novel, soon grow old in the using; while this new spiritual nature becomes newer and fresher as it goes forward. *Our outward man perishes,* says St Paul, *but the inner man is renewed day by day.* And it will never be completely renewed, but in eternity, where they sing without ceasing, the new song of which David speaks in his Psalms; (Psalm xxxiii. 3.) the song which flows spontaneously from the pure spirit of love.

16. When St Peter and the apostles (Acts xv.) deliberated on the abolishing of circumcision, where the point in question involved an apparent contradiction of the law of God; they did not consult the prophets, but held by the simple fact of the gift of the Holy Ghost, to those who were uncircumcised. They judged it a more certain way of settling the question, that God approved those whom he had filled with his Spirit, than that it did not become them to observe the law. They knew that the end of the law was but the gift of the Spirit; and that since they had received it without circumcision, the ceremony was not essentially necessary.

17. Two laws are better fitted to govern the whole Christian republic, than all political codes whatever. These are, The love of God, and the love of our neighbour.

Our religion is adapted to minds of every order. The multitude looks only at its present state and establishment; and our religion is such, that its establishment is a sufficient evidence of its truth. Others trace it up to the apostles. The best informed follow it up to the creation of the world. The angels see better and farther still; they trace it up to God himself.

Those to whom God has given religion as the feeling of the heart, are happy indeed, and thoroughly satisfied of its truth. But for those who have not this experience, we can only reason with them, and wait till God himself shall stamp this impression on the heart, without which, faith cannot be saving.

God, to reserve to himself the sole right of teaching us, and to render this difficult problem of our being, more completely incomprehensible to us, has concealed the clue to it, so high, or rather so low, that we cannot reach it; so that it is not by the energies of reason, but by the simple submission of reason, that we shall at length really know ourselves.

18. The wicked, who profess to follow the dictates of reason, had need be wonderfully strong in their reasoning. What do they say then? Do we not see, say they, that brutes live and die like men, and Turks like Christians. Have not the Turks their ceremonies, prophets, doctors, saints, and religionists as we have? Well, and is this contrary to Scripture? Do not the Scriptures affirm all this? If you have little care to know the truth,

you know enough now to allow you still to slumber. But you wish with all your heart to know the truth, it is not enough. You must examine minutely. This might be enough for some mere question of a vain philosophy. But here, where every thing is at stake, it is not. And yet, many a man, after a flimsy reflection like this, returns to trifles.

It is dreadful to feel every thing we possess, and every thing we learn to value, gliding continually away, without a serious wish, on our parts, to inquire, if there is nothing else that is permanent.

A different mode of life in this world, should surely follow these different suppositions, either that we may abide here for ever, or that it being sure that we cannot be here long, it is doubtful whether we shall be here another hour. This last supposition is our actual case.

19. You are bound by your circumstances to make your best exertions for the discovery of the truth. For if you die without the worship of Him, who is the true principle of all things, you are lost. But, you say, if he had wished me to worship him, he would have given me some indications of his will. And so he has; but you neglect them. The least you can do, is to seek them; and it will well repay you.

The Atheists ought to be able to say their things with absolute certainty. Now, it seems to me, that a man must be insane, who could affirm it as absolutely certain, that the human soul is mortal. I can quite understand a man's not seeing it necessary to fathom the Copernican system; but the knowledge, whether the soul be mortal or immortal, is essential to every step in life.

20. Prophecies, miracles, and all the other proofs of our religion, are not of that sort, that we can say they are geometrically convincing. But, at present, it is sufficient if you grant me, that it is not contrary to sound reason to believe them. They have their brightness and their obscurity, calculated to illuminate some, and to darken others. But the brightness is such, that it outshines, or, at the least, equals the clearest presumption to the contrary; so much so, that sound reason never can determine not to accept the evidence, and probably it is only the corruption and depravity of the heart that do. There is in the evidence, also, sufficient plainness to condemn those who refuse to believe, though not enough to compel belief; and hence it is evident, that in those who follow the light, it is grace, and not reason, which causes them to pursue; and in those who turn away, it is their corruption, and not their reason, that makes them fly from it.

Who can hesitate to admire a religion, which is evidently so thoroughly informed on matters, the truth of which we recognize increasingly, in proportion to the increase of our light.

A man who discovers proofs of the Christian religion, is like a heritor finding the titles to his property. Will he say that they are invalid, or neglect to examine them?

21. Two sorts of persons know God; those whose hearts are humbled, and who, whatever be the measure of their intellect, whether common or elevated, love reproach and self-abasement; and those who have sufficient determination to seek out, and maintain the truth, whatever opposition they meet with.

Those wise men among the heathen, who affirmed th

unity of God, were persecuted; the Jews were hated; and Christians even more so.

22. The resurrection of the dead, and the conception by the Virgin Mary, appear to me to present no greater obstacle to belief, than the creation of the world. Is it more difficult to reproduce a man, than to create man at first? And if we had not become familiar with the notion of natural generation, would it have been more strange to us, that a child should spring from a woman only, than from a man and a woman?

23. There is a vast difference between peace and assurance of conscience. Nothing short of a sincere search after truth, should give peace; but nothing short of an actual possession of truth itself can give assurance.

There are two articles of faith, equally unquestionable; the one, that man in his primitive state, or in a state of grace, is elevated above all the natural world, is assimilated to God, and made a partaker of the divine nature; the other, that in this state of corruption and of sin, he is fallen from that elevation, and become like the brute creation. These two propositions are equally true. The Scripture affirms both of these unequivocally. In Prov. viii. 31. *My delight is with the sons of men.* In Joel ii. 28. *I will pour out my Spirit upon all flesh.* In Psalm lxxxii. 6. *I have said, ye are gods; and all of you are children of the Most High.* Then again, it is said, in Isaiah xl. 6. *All flesh is grass, &c.* In Psalm xlix. 12. *Man is like unto the beasts that perish.* And in Eccles. iii. 18, 19. *I said in my heart concerning the estate of the sons of men, that God might manifest them, and that they might see that they themselves are beasts. For that which befalleth the sons of men befalleth beasts, even one thing befalleth them: as the one dieth, so dieth the other, yea, they have all one breath, so that a man hath no pre-eminence above a beast: for all is vanity.*

24. The instances of the heroic death of the Spartans and others, affect us very little; for in what way do they bear upon our case? But the death of the martyrs comes home to our bosoms, for they are our very members; we have one common interest with them; their resolution may go to form our own. There is nothing of this in the instances of heathen heroism; we have no point of union with them. In the same way as I am not made wealthy by the enriching of a stranger, but I am by the wealth of a parent or a husband.

25. We can never break off an attachment without pain. As St Augustin says, A man does not feel the chain, when he voluntarily follows him who leads him by it; but when he begins to resist, and to go the other way, then he suffers—the chain tightens, and suffers violence. Such a chain is our body, which breaks only by death. Our Lord has said, from the coming of John the Baptist, (i. e.[*] from his entrance into the heart of each believer,) *The kingdom of heaven suffereth violence, and the violent take it by force.* Before the heart is touched, we have only the dead weight of our corruption, dragging us down to the earth. But when God draws us from above, there arises between these opposing influences, that fearful struggle in which God alone can overcome. But, as St Leon says, We can do every thing through him, without

---

[*] This is an accommodation of the text, but it is ingenious.

whom we can do nothing. We must resolve, then, to sustain this warfare all our life long, for here there cannot be peace. Jesus Christ is *not come to bring peace on earth, but a sword.* But yet we must admit, that as the wisdom of men is foolishness with God, so even this warfare which seems so trying to men, is actually peace with God; it is the very experience of that peace, which Jesus Christ has accomplished. It cannot, however, be perfected in us, till the body is dissolved. And this it is which gives rise to the wish for death, even while we cheerfully endure a lengthened life for the love of him, who underwent both life and death for us; *and who,* as St Paul says, *is able to do for us far more abundantly than we can ask or think.*

26. We should try never to be afflicted at any thing, but to consider every event as happening for the best. I believe this to be a duty, and that we sin in not performing it. For, in fact, the reason why sin is sin, is merely its contrariety to the will of God; and thus, the essence of sin consisting in opposition to that which we know to be the will of God, it appears to me evident, that when He discovers to us his will by the events of his Providence, it is a sin not to approve it.

27. When truth is abandoned and persecuted, then is the time apparently, when our services in its defence are most pleasing in the sight of God. We may judge of grace by the analogies of nature; and hence, we are allowed to conclude, that as an expatriated prince feels a peculiarly kind esteem for the few of his subjects who continue faithful amidst a general revolt; so will God regard, with a peculiar favour, those who defend the purity

of religion in a day of rebuke and blasphemy. But there is this difference between the kings of the earth, and the King of kings, that princes do not make their subjects faithful, they find them so; whilst God finds all men faithless, who are without his grace, and makes them faithful when they are so. So that, whilst on the one hand, kings must confess their obligation to those who remain dutiful and obedient; on the other, those who remain steadfast in the service of God, owe it as a matter of infinite obligation to him only.

28. Neither the discipline of the body, nor the distresses of the mind, are really meritorious. It is only the gracious emotions of the heart, that sustain the body and the mind in suffering, and attach a value to such sorrows. For, in fact, these two things, pains and pleasures, are needful for sanctification. St Paul has said, that we must, through much tribulation, enter the kingdom of God. This should comfort those who experience trial, because having learned that the way to the heaven which they seek, is full of trouble, it should rejoice them to recognize such proofs that they are in the right road. But those very pains are not without their pleasures, and the overcoming of them is always accompanied with pleasure. For, as those who forsake God, to return to the world, do so only because they find more delight in the pleasures of earth, than in those which flow from union with God, and that such charms carry them triumphantly away, and causing them to repent their former choice, make them, at last, as Tertullian says, the devil's penitents; so no one ever quits the pleasures of the world, to embrace the cross of Christ, if he has not found more de-*light* in reproach, and poverty, and destitution, and the

sborn of men, than in all the pleasures of sin. And thus, as Tertullian says, we must not suppose the Christian's life to be a life of sorrow. He abandons not the pleasures of earth, but for others far more noble. St Paul says, *Pray without ceasing ; in every thing give thanks ; rejoice ever more.* It is the joy of having found God, which is the real principle of our regret at having offended him, and of our whole change of life. He who has found the *treasure hid in a field, has,* according to Jesus Christ, *such joy thereof, that he sells all that he hath to buy it.* Matth. xiii. 44. The men of the world have their sorrow; but they have not that joy, which, as Jesus Christ says, *the world can neither give, nor take away.* The blessed in heaven have this joy, without any alloy of grief. Christians here have this joy, mingled with regret, at having sought after questionable pleasures, and with the fear of losing it, through the influence of those indulgences, which still minister unceasing temptation. We should endeavour then continually to cherish this fear, which husbands and regulates our joy ; and according as we find ourselves leaning too much to the one, we should incline towards the other, that we may be kept from falling.

Remember your blessings in the day of your sorrow, and in the day of prosperity remember your afflictions, till that day, when the promise of Jesus, that our joy in him shall be full, is accomplished. Let us not give way to melancholy. Let us not conceive that piety consists in unmitigated bitterness of soul. True piety, which is only perfected in heaven, is so full of consolations, that they are showered on its beginning, its progress, and its crown. It is a light so brilliant, that it reflects illumination on all which belongs to it. If some sorrow mingles with it, especially at the commencement, this originates in us, not in the way that we take. It is not the result of piety newly infused into us, but of the impiety which yet remains. Take away sin, and unmingled joy is left. If we mourn then, let us not lay the blame upon our religion, but upon ourselves; and let us seek only in our own amendment for relief.

29. The past should present to us no difficulties, since we have but one duty towards it—regret for our errors; the future should still less trouble us; because it is not in the least degree, under our controul, and we may never reach it. The present is the only moment which is really ours, and we ought to occupy it for God. To this our thoughts should chiefly be directed. Yet man, in general, is so restless, that he scarcely ever thinks of the life present and the actual instant of his existence now, but only of that in which he will live hereafter. His propensity is always to live prospectively, but never to live now. Yet our Lord did not wish our forethought to go beyond the day in which we now live. These are the limits which he requires us to keep, both for our future safety, and our present peace.

30. We sometimes learn more from the sight of evil than from an example of good; and it is well to accustom ourselves to profit by the evil which is so common, while that which is good is so rare.

31. In the 13th chapter of Mark, Jesus Christ speaks largely to his apostles of his second coming; and as the experience of the church in general, is the experience of every Christian in particular, it is certain that this chapter predicts, not only the entire destruction of the world, so

make way for a new heavens and a new earth, but also the state of each individual, in whom, at his conversion, the old man is destroyed. The prediction which it contains of the ruin of the reprobated temple, which represents the ruin of the old and reprobate man in each of us; and of which it is said, that not one stone shall be left upon another, indicates that not one affection of the old man shall be suffered to remain; and those fearful, civil, and domestic wars which are there foretold, are a too accurate picture of the inward conflict that they feel who give themselves up to God.

33. The elect are unconscious of their virtues; the reprobate of their crimes. Both will say at the last day, *Lord, when saw we thee an hungred.* Matth. xxv.

Jesus Christ did not desire the testimony of devils, nor of those who were not called; but of God, and of John the Baptist.

34. The faults of Montaigne are very great. He abounds with improper and impure expressions. His thoughts on wilful murder, and on death, are dreadful. He inspires an indifference about salvation, without fear or repentance. As his book was not written to inculcate religion, he need not have pressed it; but a man is bound not to write against it. Whatever may be said to excuse the licence of his opinions on many subjects, it is impossible in any way to palliate his heathen notions about death. For a man must have utterly renounced all religion, who does not, at all events, wish to die like a Christian: now throughout his whole book, he thinks only of dying basely and contemptibly.

36. With those who have an aversion to religion, we should begin by shewing them, that it is not contrary to reason; then that it is venerable and worthy of their respect; next, we should put it before them in an amiable light, and lead them to wish that it were true; and lastly, shew them by positive proof that it is true; point out its antiquity and purity, its dignity and elevation; and finally, its loveliness, as promising to us the true good.

One word from David or from Moses, such as, *God will circumcise your hearts*, serves to determine men's views. Let all the rest of a man's discourse be doubtful, and let it be uncertain whether he is a Philosopher or a Christian; one sentence like this gives a colour to all the rest. Up to that point there may be doubt; but not afterwards.

Though we should be in error in believing the Christian religion true, we should lose but little by it. But how sad to have been in error, in believing it false.

37. Those circumstances in life, which, according to the world, are the easiest to live in, are the most difficult according to the will of God. On the contrary, nothing is so difficult in the estimation of the world as the religious life; whilst, according to God's rule, there is nothing more easy. Nothing is easier than to perform important duties, and manage great wealth, according to the morality of the world. Nothing is more difficult than to live to God in such a situation, without acquiring an interest, and a conformity of taste for such pursuits.

38. The Old Testament contained a typical presentation of future happiness, and the New Testament the way to obtain it. The typical scene was full but the way to the reality is penitence. And yet

then, the Pascal Lamb was eaten with bitter herbs; a perpetual lesson, that bitterness and sorrow are the road to joy.

39. The apparently casual utterance of the word Galilee by the Jewish crowd, when they accused Jesus before Pilate, gave occasion to Pilate to send him to Herod, by which event, the mystery was fulfilled, that he should be judged both by the Jews and the Gentiles. A mere accident, as far as we see, led to the fulfilment of the predetermined mystery.

41. It is pleasant to be in a vessel beaten by the storm, when we have the assurance of safety. This is precisely the character of the persecutions of the church.

The history of the church, should be called a history of truth.

42. The two great sources of our sins are pride and indolence; and God has been pleased to make known, in himself, two corresponding means of cure, his mercy and his justice. The proper effect of his justice is to abase our pride; and that of his mercy, is to overcome our indolence, by stimulating us to good works according to that text, Romans ii. 4. *The goodness of God leadeth thee to repentance;* and that of the Ninevites, Jonah iii. 9. *Who can tell if God will return and repent, and turn away from his fierce anger, that we perish not.* And thus, so far is the mercy of God from encouraging licentiousness, that, on the contrary, nothing is so directly opposed to it. And instead of saying, " If there had not been mercy in God, we must have made a more strenuous effort to obey

his laws;" we ought, on the contrary, to say, "Because He is a God of mercy, we must do our utmost to obey him."

43. All that is in the world is the *lust of the flesh, the lust of the eyes, and the pride of life*. Woe for that land of curse, along which these three streams pour forth their waves of kindling flame. Happy they, who, though they lie upon the bosom of these streams, are neither engulphed nor hurried down by them, but remain immoveably secure; not however standing boldly erect, but occupying a safe, though humble seat, from which they rise not till the light shall dawn; but who, resting there in peace, spread forth their hands to Him who can, and will deliver them, and plant their feet firmly within the gates of the holy city, where they need fear the assaults of human pride no more;—and who yet weep, not to see the perishing goods of this world rolling down that fearful tide, but at the remembrance of that land, a better land, the heavenly Jerusalem, for which they sigh incessantly, through the period of a lengthened exile.

44. A miracle, they say, would determine our belief. Men speak thus, while they see no further. But those reasons, which, when seen at a distance, seem to limit our range, do not limit us when we have attained to them. We begin a fresh prospect from that very point. Nothing bounds the rapid march of mind. There is scarcely, it is said, a rule without an exception; nor a truth so general, but that there are some cases in which its application is questionable. It is sufficient that it is *not* absolutely universal, to give us a pretext for assuming that the case in point is the exception, and to say,

"That is not always true; then there are cases when it is not true:" then it only remains to shew, that this is one of such cases, and it were inexpert indeed not to manage that some way.

45. Charity is not a metaphorical precept. To say that Jesus Christ, who came to supersede types, by realities, is only come to teach a metaphorical charity, and to annul the real virtue which existed before, is abominable.

46. How many stars have our glasses discovered, which were formerly invisible to our philosophers! They boldly attacked the Scripture, because they found it frequently speaking of the great number of the stars. They said, "There are but one thousand and twenty-two in all; we have counted them."

47. Man is so constituted, that by merely telling him he is a fool, he will, at length, believe it; and, if he tells himself so, he will make himself believe it. For man holds an inward communication with himself, which ought to be well regulated, since even here, *Evil communications corrupt good manners.* We ought to keep silence as much as possible, and commune with ourselves of God, and thus we shall soon convince ourselves of what we really are.

49. Our own will, even in the possession of all that it can desire, would not be satisfied. But the instant we renounce it, we are content. With it, we cannot but be dissatisfied; without it, we cannot but be happy.

The true and only virtue, consists in self-abhorrence; because corruption has made us hateful; and in seeking a being truly worthy of love, that we may love him. But as we cannot love that which is beyond us, we must love a being who is within us, but not identified with us. Now, none but the Omnipresent Being can be such. *The kingdom of God is within us.* The universal Good dwells in us, yet is He distinct from us.

It is unwise in any one to become fondly attached to us, though it be, on their part, a matter of voluntary choice and of delight. We cannot but deceive those in whom we have created such an affection—for we cannot be to any one their ultimate object, or give them plenary enjoyment. Are we not ourselves ready to perish? And so the object of their regard must die. As we should be criminal in making any one believe a falsehood, though we persuaded him to it kindly, and he believed it with pleasure, and gave us pleasure by believing; so are we guilty, if we make others love us, and try to allure their affections to ourselves. Whatever advantage might accrue to us by a falsehood, we ought to inform those who are about to believe it, that it is not true. And so also should we warn our fellows against an attachment to ourselves, when their whole life should be spent in seeking after God, or in studying to please him.

50. It is superstition to repose our confidence in forms and ceremonies; but not to submit to them is pride.

51. All other sects and religions have had natural reason for their guide. Christians only have been compelled to look beyond themselves for a rule of guidance, and to study that which Jesus Christ delivered to the primitive saints, for transmission to his people. There are some who fret under this control. They wish, like other people,

to follow their own inclinations. It is vain for us to say to them, *Stand ye in the way, and ask for the old paths, where is the good way, and walk therein.* They answer like the Jews, *We will not walk therein; but we will certainly do according to the thoughts of our own heart, like the nations round about us.*

52. There are three means of faith, reasoning, custom, and inspiration. The Christian religion, which alone has reason to support it, admits not as its true converts, those who believe without inspiration. Not that it excludes the influences of reasoning and custom: on the contrary, it is right that the mind be open to rational proof, and acquire strength of faith by habit. Still our religion requires, that we humble ourselves to ask those spiritual influences which alone can produce a true and saving faith. As St. Paul says, *Not with wisdom of words, lest the cross of Christ be of none effect.*

53. We never do evil so thoroughly and cordially, as when we are led to it by a false principle of conscience.

54. The Jews who were called to subdue nations and their kings, have been the slaves of sin; and Christians whose calling was to serve, and be subject, are " the children that are free."

55. Is it courage in a dying man, to go in his weakness, and in his agony, and face the Omnipotent and eternal God?

56. I readily believe that history, the witnesses of which have died a violent death in its support.

57. A proper fear of God originates in faith; a wrong fear, in doubt;—a right fear tends towards hope, because it springs from faith, and we do hope in the God whom we really believe;—an improper fear leads to despair, because we dread him in whom we have not faith. This fears to lose God, and that to find him.

58. Solomon and Job knew best, and exhibited most accurately the misery of man; the one being the happiest, the other the most wretched of men: the one knowing experimentally the vanity of this world's pleasure; the other, the reality of its afflictions.

59. The heathen spoke ill of Israel; and so also did the prophet,—and so far from the Israelites having a right to say, "You speak as the heathen," it appears that one of his strongest arguments was drawn from the fact, that the heathen spake like him.

60. God does not propose that we should submit to believe him contrary to our reason, or that he should make us the subjects of a mere tyrannical authority. At the same time, he does not profess to give us reasons for every thing he does. And to reconcile these contrarieties, he is pleased to exhibit to us clear and convincing proofs of what he is, and to establish his authority with us, by miracles and proofs which we cannot honestly reject; so that subsequently, we may believe without hesitation, the mysteries which he teaches, when we perceive that we have no other ground for rejecting them, but that we are not able of ourselves to ascertain whether they are so they appear or not.

61. Mankind is divided into three classes of persons; those who have found out God, and are serving him; those who are occupied in seeking after God, and have not yet found him; and those who have not only not found God, but are not seeking him. The first are wise and happy; the last are foolish and unhappy; the middle class are wise, and yet unhappy.

62. Men frequently mistake their imagination for their heart, and believe that they are converted as soon as they begin to think of turning to God.

Reason acts so tardily, and on the ground of so many different views and principles, which she requires to have always before her, that she is continually becoming drowsy and inert, or going actively astray for want of seeing the whole case at once. It is just the reverse with feeling; it acts at once, and is ever ready for action. It were well then, after our reason has ascertained what is truth, to endeavour to feel it, and to associate our faith with the affections of the heart; for without this it will ever be wavering and uncertain.

The heart has its reasons, of which reason knows nothing. We find this in a thousand instances. It is the heart which feels God, and not the reasoning powers. And this is faith made perfect :—God realized by feeling in the heart.

63. It is an essential feature of the character of God, that his justice is infinite, as well as his mercy. Yet certainly his justice and severity towards the impenitent, is less surprising than his mercy towards the elect.

64. Man is evidently made for thinking. Thought is

all his dignity, and all his worth. To think rightly, is the whole of his duty; and the true order of thought, is to begin with himself, with his author, and his end. Yet on what do men in general think? Never on these things; but how to obtain pleasure, wealth, or fame; how to become kings, without considering what it is to be a king, or even to be a man.

Human thought is in its nature wonderful. To make it contemptible, it must have some strange defects; and yet it has such, that nothing appears more ridiculous. How exalted in its nature? How degraded in its misuse.

65. If there is a God, we ought to love him—not his creatures. The reasonings of the wicked in the Book of Wisdom, are founded on their persuasion, that there is no God. They say, Grant this, and our delight shall be in the creature. But, had they known that there is a God, they would have drawn a different conclusion; and that is the conclusion of the wise. "There is a God; seek not for happiness in creatures." Then every thing which allures us towards the love of the creature, is evil, because it so far hinders us from serving God if we know him; or from seeking him if we do not. Now, we are full of concupiscence. Then we are full of evil. We must learn, then, to abhor ourselves, and all that would attach us to any other than God only.

66. When we would think of God, how many things we find which turn us away from him, and tempt us to think otherwise. All this is evil; yet it is innate.

67. That we are worthy of the love of others, is false. To wish for their love, is unjust. Had we been born in

a right state of mind, and with a due knowledge of ourselves and others, we should not have felt this wish. Yet we are born with it. We are then born unjust. Each one regards himself. That is contrary to all order. Each should regard the general good. This selfish bias is the source of all error, in war, in government, and in economy, &c.

If the members of each national and civil community should seek the good of the whole body, these communities themselves should seek the good of that whole body of which they are members.

He who does not hate in himself that self-love, and that propensity which leads him to exalt himself above all others, must be blind indeed; for nothing is more directly contrary to truth and justice. For it is false that we deserve this exaltation; and to attain it, is both unjust and impossible; for every one seeks it. This disposition with which we are born, is manifestly unjust—an evil from which we cannot, but from which we ought, to free ourselves.

Yet, no other religion but the Christian has condemned this as a sin, or shewn that we are born with it; and that we ought to resist it, or suggested a means of cure.

68. There is in man, an internal war between his reason and his passions. He might have enjoyed some little repose, had he been gifted with reason, without the passions, or with passions independently of reason. But, possessed as he is of both, he cannot but be in a state of conflict, for he cannot make peace with the one, without being at war with the other.

If it is an unnatural blindness to live without inquiry as to what we really are; it is surely a far more fearful state, to live in sin, while we acknowledge God. The greater part of men are the subjects of one or other of these states of blindness.

69. It is certain that the soul is either mortal or immortal. The decision of this question must make a total difference in the principles of morals. Yet philosophers have arranged their moral system entirely independent of this. What an extraordinary blindness!

However bright they make the comedy of life appear before, the last act is always stained with blood. The earth is laid upon our head, and there it lies for ever.

70. When God had created the heavens and the earth, which could feel no happiness in their own existence, it pleased him to create also a race of beings who should feel this, and who should constitute a compound body of thinking members. All men are members of this body; and in order to their happiness, it was requisite that their individual and private will be conformed to the general will by which the whole body is regulated. Yet it often happens, that one man thinks himself an independent whole; and that, losing sight of the body with which he is associated, he believes that he depends only on himself, and wishes to be his own centre, and his own circumference. But he finds himself in this state, like a member amputated from the body, and that having in himself no principle of life, he only wanders and becomes more confused in the uncertainty of his own existence. But when, at length, a man begins rightly to know himself, he is, as it were, returned to his senses; then he feels that he is not the body; he understands then that he is only a member of the universal body, and that to be a member, is to have no life, being, or motion, but by the spirit of the

body, and for the body,—that a member separated from the body to which he belongs, has only a remnant and expiring existence; and that he ought not to love himself, but for the sake of the body, or rather that he should love only the whole body, because in loving that, he loves himself, seeing that in it, for it, and by it, only has he any existence whatever.

For the regulation of that love which we should feel towards ourselves, we should imagine ourselves a body composed of thinking members, for we are members one of another; and thus, consider how far each member should love itself.

The body loves the hand, and if the hand had a will of its own, it should love itself precisely in that degree, that the body loves it. Any measure of love that exceeds this, is unjust.

If the feet and the hands had a separate will, they would never be in their place, but in submitting it to the will of the whole body; to do otherwise, is insubordination and error. But in seeking exclusively the good of the whole body, they cannot but consult their individual interest.

The members of our body are not aware of the advantage of their union, of their admirable sympathy, and of the care that nature takes to infuse into them vitality, and make them grow and endure. If they could know this, and availed themselves of their knowledge, to retain in themselves the nourishment which they received, without distributing it to the other members, they would not only be unjust, but actually miserable—they would be hating, and not loving themselves: their happiness, as well as their duty, consisting in submission to the guidance of that all pervading soul, which loves them better than they can love themselves.

He who is joined to the Lord is one spirit. I love myself, because I am a member of Jesus Christ. I love Jesus Christ, because he is the head of the body of which I am the member. All are in one; each one is in the other.

Concupiscence and compulsion are the sources of all our actions, purely human. Concupiscence gives rise to voluntary, and compulsion to involuntary actions.

71. The Platonists, and even Epictetus and his followers maintained, that God only was worthy of love and admiration; yet they sought for themselves the love and admiration of men. They had no idea of their own corruption. If they feel themselves naturally led to love and adore him, and to seek in them their chief joy, they are welcome to account themselves good. But if they feel a natural aversion to this, if they have no manifest bias, but to wish to establish themselves in the good opinion of men; and that all their perfection comes to this, to lead men, without compulsion, to find happiness in loving them; then I say, that such perfection is horrible. What, have they known God, and have not desired exclusively that his creatures should love him? Have they wished that the affections of men should stop at themselves? Have they wished to be to men, the object of their deliberate preference for happiness?

72. It is true, that there is difficulty in the practice of piety. But this difficulty does not arise from the piety that is now begun within us, but from the impiety that yet remains. If our sensuality were not opposed to penitence, and our corruption to the divine purity, there would be nothing painful in it. We only suffer just in propor-

tion as the evil which is natural to us, resists the supernatural agency of grace. We feel our heart rending under these opposing influences. But it were sadly unjust to attribute this violence to God, who draws us to himself, rather than to the world, which holds us back. Our case is like that of an infant, whom its mother drags from the arms of robbers; and who, even in the agony of laceration, must love the fond and legitimate violence of her who struggles for its liberty, and can only detest the fierce and tyrannical might of those who detain it so unjustly. The most cruel war that God can wage against men in this life is, to leave them without that war which he has himself proclaimed. *I am come*, said Christ, *to bring war;* and to provide for this war, he says, *I am come to bring fire and sword.* Matth. x. 34. Luke xii. 49. Before this, the world lived in a false and delusive peace.

73. God looks at the interior. The church judges only by the exterior. God absolves us as soon as he sees penitence in the heart. The church only when she sees it in our works. God makes a church, which is pure within, and which confounds, by its internal and spiritual sanctity, the impious superficial pretences of the self-sufficient and the Pharisee. And the church forms a company of men, whose outward manners are so pure, as to condemn the habits of the heathen. If there are within her border, hypocrites so well concealed, that she detects not their malignity, she permits their continuance, for though they are not received by God, whom they cannot deceive, they are received by men, whom they can. In such cases, however, the church is not outwardly dishonoured, for their conduct has the semblance of holiness.

74. The law has not destroyed natural principle; it in-

structs nature. Grace has not abrogated the law; it enables us to fulfil it.

We make an idol even of truth itself; for truth, apart from charity, is not God. It is but his image, an idol that we ought neither to love nor worship; still less should we love and adore its contrary, which is falsehood.

75. All public amusements are full of danger to the Christian life; but amongst all those which the world has invented, none is more to be feared than sentimental comedy. It is a representation of the passions so natural and delicate, that it awakens them, and gives them fresh spring in the heart,—especially the passion of love, and still more so, when it is exhibited as eminently chaste and virtuous. For the more innocent it is made to appear to innocent minds, the more are they laid open to its influence. The violence of it gratifies our self-love, which speedily desires to give rise to the same effects, which we have seen represented. In the mean while, also, conscience justifies itself by the honourable nature of those feelings which have been pourtrayed, so far as to calm the fears of a pure mind, and to suggest the idea that it can surely be no violation of purity to love with an affection so apparently rational. And thus, we leave the theatre with a heart teeming with the delights and the tendernesses of love; and with the understanding so persuaded of its innocence, that we are fully prepared to receive its first impressions, or rather to seek the opportunity of giving birth to them in the heart of another, that we may receive the same pleasures, and the same adulation which we saw so well depicted on the stage.

76. Licentious opinions are so far naturally p

ON RELIGION. 185

...en, that it is strange that any should be displeased
...them. But this is only when they have exceeded all
...lerate bounds. Besides, there are many people who
...ceive the truth, though they cannot act up to it.
...there are few who do not know that the purity of
...ion is opposed to such lax opinions, and that it is
... to affirm, that an eternal reward awaits a life of
...

... I feared that I might have written erroneously,
... I saw myself condemned; but the example of so
... persons ... has made me think differently. It is
... write truth.
... tirely corrupt or ignorant. It is
... in vain. I fear nothing. I hope
... Royal feared. It was bad policy
... when they feared the least, they
... most.
... persecution. But the saints
... It is true that their should
... are not to learn this from the
... from the necessity of speaking.
... at Rome, that which I
... in heaven.
... points of doubts, are the two

... accused of having written
... to-
...
... the au-
... passages.

which I have cited? I answered, If I were in a town where there were a dozen fountains, and I knew for certain that one of them was poisoned, I should be under obligation to tell the world not to draw from that fountain; and, as it might be supposed, that this was a mere fancy on my part, I should be obliged to name him who had poisoned it, rather than expose a whole city to the risk of death.

I was asked, *thirdly*, why I adopted an agreeable, jocose, and entertaining style? I answered, If I had written dogmatically, none but the learned would have read my book; and they had no need of it, knowing how the matter stood, at least as well as I did. I conceived it therefore my duty to write, so that my letters might be read by women, and people in general, that they might know the danger of all those maxims and propositions which were then spread abroad, and admitted with so little hesitation.

Finally, I was asked If I had myself read all the books which I quoted? I answered, No. To do this, I had need have passed the greater part of my life in reading very bad books. But I have twice read Escobar throughout; and for the others, I got several of my friends to read them; but I have never used a single passage without having read it myself in the book quoted, without having examined the case in which it is brought forward, and without having read the preceding and subsequent context, that I might not run the risk of citing that as an answer, which was, in fact, an objection, which would have been very unjust and blameable.

79. The Arithmetical machine produces results which come nearer to thought, than any thing that brutes can

do; but it does nothing that would, in the least, lead one to suppose that it has a will like them.

80. Some authors, speaking of their works, say, " My book, my commentary, my history." They betray their own vulgarity, who have just got a house over their heads, and have always, " My house," at their tongue's end. It were better to say, " Our book, our history, our commentary, &c. for generally there is more in it belonging to others than to themselves.

81. Christian piety annihilates the egotism of the heart; worldly politeness veils and represses it.

82. If my heart were as poor as my understanding, I should be happy, for I am thoroughly persuaded, that such poverty is a great means of salvation.

83. One thing I have observed, that let a man be ever so poor, he has always something to leave on his deathbed.

84. I love poverty, because Jesus Christ loved it. I love wealth, because it gives the means of assisting the wretched. I wish to deal faithfully with all men. I render no evil to those who have done evil to me; but I wish them a condition similar to my own, in which they would not receive from the greater portion of men either good or evil. I aim to be always true, and just, and open towards all men. I have much tenderness of heart towards those whom God has more strictly united to me. Whether I am in secret, or in the sight of men, I have set before me in all my actions, the God who will judge them, and to whom I have consecrated them. These are

my feelings; and I bless my Redeemer every day of m[y]
life, who has planted them in me; and who, from a ma[n]
full of weakness, misery, lust, pride, and ambition, ha[s]
formed one victorious over these evils by the power o[f]
that grace, to which I owe every thing, seeing that i[n]
myself there is nothing but misery and horror.

85. Disease is the natural state of Christians; for b[y]
its influence, we become what we should be at all time[s]
we endure evil; we are deprived of all our goods, and [of]
all the pleasures of sense; we are freed from the excit[e]
ment of those passions which annoy us all through life
we live without ambition and without avarice, in the con[
stant expectation of death. And is it not thus, th[at]
Christians should spend their days? And is it not re[al]
happiness to find ourselves placed by necessity in th[e]
state in which we ought to be, and that we have nothin[g]
to do, but humbly and peaceably submit to our lot. Wit[h]
this view, I ask for nothing else but to pray God th[at]
he would bestow this grace upon me.

86. It is strange that men have wished to dive into t[he]
principles of things, and to attain to universal know[
ledge; for surely it were impossible to cherish such [a]
purpose, without a capacity, or the presumption of a c[a]
pacity, as boundless as nature itself.

87. Nature has many perfections to shew that it is [the]
image of the Deity. It has defects, to shew that it is b[ut]
an image.

88. Men are so completely fools by necessity, that [he]
is but a fool in a higher strain of folly, who does not c[on]
fess his foolishness.

89. Do away the doctrine of probability, and you please the world no longer. Give them the doctrine of probability, and you cannot but please them.

90. If that which is contingent were made certain, the zeal of the saints, for the practice of good works, would be useless.

91. It must be grace indeed that makes a man a saint. And who, even in his most doubtful mood, does not know what constitutes a saint, and what a natural man?

96. The smallest motion is of importance in nature. The whole substance of the sea moves when we throw in a pebble. So in the life of grace, the most trifling action has a bearing in its consequences upon the whole. Every thing then is important.

97. Naturally men hate each other. Much use has been made of human corruption, to make it subserve the public good. But then, all this is but deception; a false semblance of charity; really it is only hatred after all. This vile resource of human nature, this *figmentum malum* is only covered. It is not removed.

98. They, who say that man is too insignificant to be admitted to communion with God, had need be more than ordinarily great to know it assuredly.

99. It is unworthy of God to join himself to man in his miserable degradation; but it is not so to bring him forth from that misery.

100. Who ever heard such absurdities? sinners puri-

fied without penitence; just men made perfect without the grace of Christ; God without a controlling power over the human will; predestination without mystery; and a Redeemer without the certainty of salvation.

103. That Christianity is not the only religion, is no real objection to its being true. On the contrary, this is one of the means of proof that it is true.

104. In a state established as a republic, like Venice, it were a great sin to try to force a king upon them, and to rob the people of that liberty which God had given them. But in a state where monarchical power has been admitted, we cannot violate the respect due to the king, without a degree of sacrilege; for as the power that God has conferred on him, is not only a representation, but a participation of the power of God, we may not oppose it without resisting manifestly the ordinance of God. Moreover, as civil war, which is the consequence of such resistance, is one of the greatest evils that we can commit in violation of the love of our neighbour, we can never sufficiently magnify the greatness of the crime. The primitive Christians did not teach us revolt, but patience, when kings trampled upon their rights.

I am as far removed from the probability of this sin, as from assassination and robbery on the highway. There is nothing more contrary to my natural disposition, and to which I am less tempted.

105. Eloquence is the art of saying things in such a manner, that in the *first* place, those to whom we speak, may hear them without pain, and with pleasure; and, in the *second*, that they may feel interested in them, and be led by their own self-love, to a more willing reflection

on them. It consists in the endeavour to establish a correspondence between the understanding and heart of those to whom we speak, on the one hand, and the thoughts and expressions of which, we make use on the other; an idea which supposes, at the outset, that we have well studied the human heart, to know all its recesses, and rightly to arrange the proportions of a discourse, calculated to meet it. We ought to put ourselves in the place of those to whom we speak, and try upon our own heart, the turn of thought which we give to a discourse, and thus ascertain if the one is adapted to the other, and if we can in this way acquire the conviction, that the hearer will be compelled to surrender to it. Our strength should be, in being simple and natural, neither inflating that which is little, nor lowering that which is really grand. It is not enough that the statement be beautiful. It should suit the subject, having nothing exuberant, nothing defective.

Eloquence is a pictural representation of thought; and hence, those who, after having painted it, make additions to it, give us a fancy picture, but not a portrait.

106. The Holy Scripture is not a science of the understanding, but of the heart. It is intelligible only to those who have an honest and good heart. The veil that is upon the Scriptures, in the case of the Jews, is there also in the case of Christians. Charity is not only the end of the Holy Scriptures, but the entrance to them.

107. If we are to do nothing, but where we have the advantage of certainty, then we should do nothing in religion; for religion is not a matter of certainty. But how many things we do uncertainly, as sea-voyages,

battles, &c. I say then, that we should do nothing at all, for nothing is certain. There is more of certainty in religion, than in the hope that we shall see the morrow; for it is not certain that we shall see the morrow. But it is certainly possible, that we may not see to-morrow.* And this cannot be affirmed of religion. It is not certain that religion is; but who will dare to say, that it is certainly possible that it is not. Now when we labour for to-morrow, and upon an uncertainty, reason justifies us.

108. The inventions of men progressively improve from age to age. The goodness and the wickedness of men in general remain the same.

109. A man must acquire a habit of more philosophic speculation and thought on what he sees, and form his judgment of things by that, while he speaks generally to others in more popular language.

111.† Casual circumstances give rise to thoughts, and take them away again; there is no art of creating or preserving them.

112. You think that the church should not judge of the inward man, because this belongs only to God; nor of the outward man, because God judges of the heart; and thus, destroying all power of discriminating human character, you retain within the church the most dissolute of men, and men who so manifestly disgrace it, that even the synagogues of the Jews, and the sects of philosophers

---

* That is, we know of possible events by which this might be the case.
† The thought 110, is not found in the MSS. but only in the edition of Condorcet, an authority certainly not to be followed.

would have ejected them as worthless, and consigned them to abhorrence.

113. Whoever will, may now be made a priest, as in the days of Jeroboam.

114. The multitude which is not brought to act as unity, is confusion. That unity which has not its origin in the multitude, is tyranny.

115. Men consult only the ear, for want of the heart.

116. We should be able to say in every dialogue or discourse, to those who are offended at it, " Of what can you complain ?"

117. Children are alarmed at the face which they have themselves disguised ; but how is it, that he who is so weak, as an infant, is so bold in maturer years ? Alas, his weakness has only changed its subject !

118. It is alike incomprehensible that God is, and that he is not; that the soul is in the body, and that we have no soul; that the world is, or is not created ; that there is, or is not such a thing as original sin.

119. The statements of Atheists ought to be perfectly clear of doubt. Now it is not perfectly clear, that the soul is material.

120. Unbelievers the most credulous ! They believe the miracles of Vespasian, that they may not believe the miracles of Moses.

On the Philosophy of Descartes.

We may say generally, the world is made by figure and motion, for that is true; but to say what figure and motion, and to specify the composition of the machine, is perfectly ridiculous; for it is useless, questionable, and laborious. But, if it be all true, the whole of the philosophy is not worth an hour's thought.

CHAPTER XXII.

THOUGHTS ON DEATH, EXTRACTED FROM A LETTER OF M. PASCAL, ON THE OCCASION OF THE DEATH OF HIS FATHER.

WHEN we are in affliction, owing to the death of some friend whom we loved, or some other misfortune that has happened to us, we ought not to seek for consolation in ourselves, nor in our fellow-creatures, nor in any created thing; we should seek it in God only. And the reason is, that creatures are not the primary cause of those occurrences which we call evils. But that the providence of God being the true and sole cause of them, the arbiter and the sovereign, we ought, undoubtedly, to have recourse directly to their source, and ascend even to their origin, to obtain satisfactory alleviation. For, if we follow this precept, and consider this afflicting bereavement, not as the result of chance, nor as a fatal necessity of our nature, not as the sport of those elements and atoms of which man is formed (for God has not abandoned his elect to the risk of caprice or chance) but as the indispensible, inevitable, just, and holy result of a decree of the providence of God, to be executed in the fulness of time;

and, in fact, that all which happens has been eternally present and pre-ordained in God; if, I say, by the teachings of grace we consider this casualty, not in itself, and independently of God, but viewed independently of self, and as in the will of God, and in the justice of his decree, and the order of his Providence; which is, in fact, the true cause, without which it could not have happened, by which alone it has happened, and happened in the precise manner in which it has; we should adore in humble silence the inaccessible elevation of His secrecy; we should venerate the holiness of His decrees; we should bless the course of His providence; and, uniting our will to the very will of God, we should desire with Him, in Him, and for Him, those very things which He has wished in us, and for us, from all eternity.

2. There is no consolation but in truth. Unquestionably there is nothing in Socrates or Seneca which can soothe or comfort us on these occasions. They were under the error, which, in blinding the first man, blinded all the rest. They have all conceived death to be natural to man; and all the discourses that they have founded upon this false principle, are so vain and so wanting in solidity, that they have only served to shew, by their utter uselessness, how very feeble man is, since the loftiest productions of the greatest minds are so mean and puerile.

It is not so with Jesus Christ; it is not so with the canonical Scriptures. The truth is set forth there: and consolation is associated with it, as infallibly as that truth itself is infallibly separated from error. Let us regard death then, by the light of that truth which the Holy Spirit teaches. We have there a most advantageous means of knowing that really and truly death is the penalty of sin, appointed to man as the desert of crime, and necessary to man for his escape from corruption: that it is the only means of delivering the soul from the motions of sin in the members, from which the saints are never entirely free, while they live in this world. We know that life, and the life of Christians especially, is a continued sacrifice, which can only be terminated by death. We know that Jesus Christ, when he came into this world, considered himself, and offered himself to God as a sacrifice, and as a real victim; that his birth, his life, his death, resurrection and ascension, and his sitting at the right hand of the Father, are but one and the same sacrifice. We know that what took place in Jesus Christ, must occur also in all his members.

Let us consider life then as a sacrifice, and that the accidents of life make no impression on the Christian mind, but as they interrupt or carry on this sacrifice. Let us call nothing evil but that which constitutes the victim due to God a victim offered to the devil; but let us call that really good, which renders the victim due in Adam to the devil, a victim sacrificed to God; and by this rule, let us examine death.

For this purpose we must have recourse to the person of Jesus Christ: for as God regards men only in the person of the mediator, Jesus Christ, men also should only regard either others, or themselves, mediately through him.

If we do not avail ourselves of this mediation, we shall find in ourselves nothing but real miseries or abominable evils: but if we learn to look at every thing thr[ough] Jesus Christ, we shall always obtain comfort, satisfact[ion] and instruction.

Let us look at death then through Christ, and not without him. Without Christ it is horrible, detestable; it is the abhorrence of human nature. In Jesus Christ it is very different; it is lovely, holy, and the joy of the faithful. All trial is sweet in Jesus Christ, even death. He suffered and died to sanctify death and suffering; and as God and man, he has been all that is great and noble, and all that is abject, in order to consecrate in himself all things, except sin, and to be the model of all conditions of life.

In order to know what death is, and what it is in Jesus Christ, we should ascertain what place it holds in his one eternal sacrifice; and with a view to this, observe, that the principal part of a sacrifice is the death of the victim. The offering and the consecration which precede it, are preliminary steps, but the actual sacrifice is death, in which the creature, by the surrender of its life, renders to God all the homage of which it is capable, making itself nothing before the eyes of His majesty, and adoring that Sovereign Being which exists essentially and alone. It is true that there is yet another step after the death of the victim, which is God's acceptance of the sacrifice, and which is referred to in the Scripture, as Gen. viii. 21. *And God smelled a sweet savour.* This certainly crowns the offering; but then this is more an act of God towards the creature, than of the creature to God; and does not therefore alter the fact that the last act of the creature is his death.

All this has been accomplished in Jesus Christ. When he came into the world he offered himself. So Heb. ix. 14. *Through the eternal Spirit, he offered himself to God. When he cometh into the world, he saith, Sacrifice and offering thou wouldst not, but a body thou hast prepared me.* Then, said

I, Lo I come, in the volume of the book it is written of me, to do thy will, O God; yea, thy law is within my heart. Heb. x. 5. Psalm xl. 7, 8. Here is his oblation; his sanctification followed immediately upon his oblation. This sacrifice continued through his whole life, and was completed by his death. So Luke xxiv. 26. *Ought not Christ to have suffered these things, and entered into his glory.* And again, Heb. v. *In the days of his flesh, when he had offered up prayers and supplications, with strong crying and tears unto him that was able to save him from death, he was heard in that he feared;* and *though he were a son, yet learned he obedience by the things which he suffered.* And God raised him from the dead, and caused his glory to rest upon him, (an event formerly prefigured by the fire from heaven which fell upon the victims to burn and consume the body,) to quicken him to the life of glory. This is what Jesus Christ has obtained, and which was accomplished at his resurrection.

This sacrifice, therefore, having been perfected by the death of Jesus Christ, and consummated even in his body by the resurrection, in which the likeness of sinful flesh has been swallowed up in glory, Jesus Christ had done all on his part; it remained only that the sacrifice be accepted of God; and that, as the smoke arose and carried the odour to the throne of God, so Jesus Christ should be in this state of complete immolation, offered, carried up, and received at the throne of God itself; and this was accomplished in his ascension, in which, by his own strength, and by the strength of the Holy Spirit, supplied to him continually, he ascended up on high. He was borne up as the smoke of those victims who were typical of Jesus Christ, was carried up buoyant on the air, which is a type of the Holy Spirit. And the Acts of the Apostles state expressly, that he was received into heaven, to assure us that this holy sacrifice, offered on the earth, was accepted and received into the bosom of God.

Such is the fact with regard to our Almighty Lord. Now, let us look at ourselves. When we enter into the church, which is the company of all faithful people, or to speak more particularly, of God's elect, into which Jesus Christ, by a privilege peculiar to the only Son of God, entered at the moment of his incarnation, we are offered and sanctified. This sacrifice continues through life, and is perfected in death, in which the soul, quitting entirely the vices and the corrupt affections of earth, whose contagion still, throughout life, ministered some infection, perfects her own immolation, and is received into the bosom of God.

Let us not then sorrow for the death of the faithful, as the heathen who have no hope. We have not lost them at their death. We lost them, so to speak, from that moment when they were really given to God. From that time they were the Lord's. Their life was devoted to him; their actions to mankind regarded only the glory of God. Then in their death they have become entirely separated from sin, and in that moment they have been received of God, and their sacrifice received its completion and its crown.

They have performed their vows; they have done the work which God gave them to do; they have accomplished the work for which alone they were created. The will of God has been done in them, and their will has been absorbed in the will of God. That then which God has joined together, let not our will put asunder: let us destroy or subdue, by a right comprehension of the truth, that sentiment of our corrupted and fallen nature which presents to us only false impressions, and which disturbs by its delusions, the holy feelings that evangelical truth inspires.

Let us not then regard death as heathens, but as Christians, with hope, as St Paul ordains; for this is the special privilege of believers. Think not of a corpse as a putrid carcase, as lying nature represents it to us; but count it, according to the apprehensions of faith, as the sacred and eternal temple of the Spirit of God.

For we know that the bodies of the saints are preserved by the Holy Spirit unto the resurrection, which will be accomplished by that Spirit dwelling in them for that purpose. It was on this account that some reverenced relics of the dead; and for this same reason, formerly, the eucharist was placed in the mouth of the dead. But the church has given up this custom, because the eucharist being the bread of life, and of the living, ought not to be administered to the dead.

Do not consider the faithful, who have died in the grace of God, as having ceased to live, though nature suggests this; but as now beginning to live, for so the truth assures us. Do not regard their souls as perished and annihilated, but as quickened and united to the sovereign source of life. And in this way, correct by the belief of these truths, those erroneous opinions which are so impressed upon our minds, and those feelings of dread which are so natural to us.

3. God created man with two principles of love; the love of God, and the love of self; but governed by this law, that the love of God should be infinite, having only the infinite God for its end; the love of self finite and subordinate to God.

Man, in that state, not only loved himself without sinning; but not to have loved himself, would have been criminal.

But since sin entered into the world, man has lost the former principle of love; and this love of self, having dwelt alone in this noble mind, made originally capable of an infinite love, has spread forth inordinately in the void which the love of God left desolate; and hence man now loves himself, and all other things for his own sake, i. e. in an infinite degree.

There is the origin of self-love. It was natural to Adam; and in his state of innocence it was quite justifiable; but in consequence of sin, it has become criminal and unbounded. We see then both the source of this love, and the cause of its enormity and guilt. It is the same with the desire of dominion, with inactivity, and all other vices; and this idea may be easily transferred to the dread which we have of death. This dread was natural and proper in Adam, when innocent; because as his life was approved of God, it ought to be so by man; and death would have been dreadful, as terminating a life conformed to the will of God. But since man has sinned, his life has become corrupt, his body and soul mutually hostile to each other, and both hostile to God.

But while this change has poisoned a life once so holy, the love of life has yet remained; and that dread of death, which has remained the same also, and which was justifiable in Adam, is not justifiable in us.

We see, then, the origin of the dread of death, and the cause of its guilt. Let the illumination of faith correct the error of nature.

The dread of death is natural to man; but it was in his state of innocence, because death could not enter paradise, without finishing a life perfectly pure. It was right, then, to hate it, when it went to separate a holy soul from a holy body: but then it is right to love it, when it separates a holy soul from an impure body. It was right to shrink from it when it would have broken up the peace between the soul and the body; but not when it terminates an otherwise irreconcileable dissension. In fact, when it would have afflicted an innocent body; when it would have deprived the body of the power of knowing God; when it would have separated from the soul a body submissive to its will, and co-operating with it; when it would have terminated all the blessings of which man knew himself capable, then it was right to abhor it. But, when it terminates an impure life; when it takes away from the body the liberty of sinning; when it rescues the soul from the might of a rebel, who counteracts all his efforts for salvation, it is very improper to retain towards it the same opinions.

We must not then give up this love of life which was given us by nature; for we have received it from God. But then, let it be a love for that same life which God gave, and not for a life directly contrary to it. And whilst we approve the love which Adam felt to the life of innocence, and which Jesus Christ also had for his life, let it be one business to hate a life, the reverse of that which Jesus Christ loved, and to attain to that death which Jesus Christ experienced, and which happens to a body approved of God; but let us not dread a death, which, as it operates to punish a guilty body, and to cleanse a vitiated body, ought to inspire in us very different feelings, if we have but the principles, in however small a degree, of faith, hope, and charity.

It is one of the great principles of Christianity, that

all which happened to Jesus Christ, should take place in the soul and body of each Christian: that as Jesus Christ has suffered during his mortal life, has died to this mortal life, has risen to a new life, has ascended to heaven, where he has sat down at the right hand of the Father; so ought both the body and soul to suffer, die, rise again, and ascend to heaven.

All these things are accomplished during this life in the soul, but not in the body. The soul suffers and dies to sin; the soul is raised to a new life; and then, at last, the soul quits the earth, and ascends to heaven in the holy paths of a heavenly life; as St Paul says, *Our conversation is in heaven.*

But none of these things take place in the body during this present life; they will occur hereafter. For, in death, the body dies to its mortal life: at the judgment, it shall rise to new life; and after the judgment, it shall ascend to heaven, and dwell there for ever. So that the same train of events happens to the body as to the soul, only at different times: and these changes in the body do not take place till those of the soul are complete—that is, after death. So that death is the coronation of the beatification of the soul, and the dawn of blessedness to the body also.

These are the wonderful ways of Divine wisdom respecting the salvation of souls! And St Augustin teaches us here, that God has adopted this arrangement to prevent a serious evil; for if the period of the act of the spiritual regeneration of the soul had been made the period of the death and resurrection of the body also, men would only have submitted to the obedience of the gospel from the love of life; but by the present arrangement, the power of faith is much more manifested, whilst the way to immortality is traced through the shades of death.

4. It were not right that we should not feel and mourn over the afflictions and misfortunes of life, like angels who have not the passions of our nature. It were not right either that we should sorrow without consolation like the heathens, who know not the hope of grace. But it is right that we should be afflicted and comforted as Christians, and that the consolations of grace should rise superior to the feelings of nature; so that grace should not only be in us, but victorious in us; so that, in hallowing our heavenly Father's name, his will should become ours; so that his grace should reign over our imperfect nature, and that our afflictions should be, as it were, the matter of a sacrifice which grace completes, and consumes to the glory of God: and that these individual sacrifices should honour and anticipate that universal sacrifice, in which our whole nature shall be perfected by the power of Jesus Christ.

And hence we derive benefit from our imperfections, since they serve as matter for such sacrifices.[a] For it is the object of true Christians to profit by their own imperfections, in as much as *all things work together for good to the elect.*

And if we are careful, we shall find great profit and edification in considering this matter as it is in truth. For since it is true, that the death of the body is only the image of the death of the soul, and that we build on this principle, that we have good ground to hope for the salvation of those whose death we mourn; then it is certain, that if we cannot check the tide of our grief and distress, we may at least derive from it this benefit, that if the death of the body is so dreadful, as to give rise to

---

[a] 1 Corinthians xii. 9, 10.

such emotions, that of the soul would have caused us agonies far less consolable. God has sent the former to those for whom we weep; but we hope that the latter he has averted. See then in the magnitude of our woes, the greatness of our blessings; and let the excess of our grief, be the measure of our joy.

5. Man is evidently too weak to judge accurately of the train of future events. Let our hope, then, be in God; and do not let us weary ourselves by rash and unjustifiable anticipations. Let us commit ourselves to God for the guidance of our way in this life, and let not discontent have dominion over us.

Saint Augustin teaches us that there is in each man, a Serpent, an Eve, and an Adam. Our senses and natural propensities are the Serpent; the excitable desire is the Eve; and reason is the Adam. Our nature tempts us perpetually; criminal desire is often excited; but sin is not completed till reason consents.

Leave then this Serpent and this Eve to distress us if they will; but let us pray to God so to strengthen our Adam by his grace, that he may abide victorious,—that Jesus Christ may be his conqueror, and may dwell in us for ever.

CHAPTER XXIII.

PRAYER, FOR THE SANCTIFIED USE OF AFFLICTION BY DISEASE.

O LORD, whose Spirit is in all things so good and gracious, and who art so merciful, that not only the prosperities, but even the humiliations of thy elect are the results of thy mercy: graciously enable me to act in the state to which thy righteous hand has reduced me, not as a heathen, but as a true Christian; that I may recognize thee as my Father and my God, in whatever state I am; since the change in my condition, makes no change in thine; since thou art always the same, though I am ever variable; and that thou art no less God, when thou ministerest affliction or punishment, than in the gifts of consolation and peace.

2. Thou hast given me health to serve thee, and I have profanely misused it. Thou hast now sent disease to correct me. Suffer me not so to receive it as to anger thee by my impatience. I have abused my health, and thou hast rightly punished me: let me not abuse thy correction also. And since the corruption of my nature is such, that it renders thy favours hurtful to me, let thy Almighty grace, O God, make these thy chastenings profitable. If in the vigour of health, my heart was filled with the love of this world, destroy that vigour for my safety's sake, and unfit me for the enjoyment of this world, either by weakness of body, or by overcoming love, that I may rejoice in thee only.

3. O God, to whom at the end of my life, and at the end of this world, I must give an account of all that I have done; O God, who permittest this world to exist, only for the trial of thine elect, and the punishment of the wicked; O God, who leavest hardened sinners to the luxurious, but criminal enjoyments of this world; O God, who causest this body to die, and at the hour of death separatest our souls from all that in this world I loved; O God, who at the last moment of my li

cut me off from all those things to which I am attached, and on which my heart has been fixed; O God, who wilt consume, at the last day, the heavens and the earth, and all the creatures that are therein, to shew to all the world that nothing subsists but thyself, and that nothing but thyself is worthy of love, because thou only dost endure; O God, who wilt destroy all these vain idols, and all these fatal objects of our affections; I praise thee, and I will bless thee, O my God, all the days of my life, that it hath pleased thee to anticipate in my favour, the event of that awful day, by destroying already, as it respects me, all these things, through the weakness to which thou hast reduced me. I praise thee, O my God, and I will bless thee all the days of my life, that it hath pleased thee to reduce me to a state of inability to enjoy the sweets of health, and the pleasures of the world; and that thou hast in a manner destroyed for my profit, those deceitful idols which thou wilt hereafter effectually destroy, to the confusion of the wicked in the day of thine anger. Grant, Lord, that I may henceforth judge myself according to this destruction, which thou hast wrought in my behalf; that thou mayest not judge me after that entire destruction which thou wilt make of my natural life, and of the whole world. For seeing, O Lord, that at the instant of my death, I shall find myself separated from this world, stripped of all things, and alone in thy presence, to answer to thy justice for all the thoughts of my heart; grant that I may consider myself in this disease, as in a kind of death, separated from the world, stripped of all the objects of my affection, and alone in thy presence, to implore from thy compassion the conversion of my heart; and that hence I may have great comfort from the thought, that thou visitest me now with a species of death, as the result of thy mercy, before thou appointest me really and finally to death as the result of thy justice. Grant then, O my God, that since thou hast anticipated my death, I may anticipate the rigour of thy sentence; and that I may examine myself before thy judgment, to find mercy in thy presence.

4. Grant, O my God, that I may adore in silence, the order of thy providence, in the guidance of my life; that thy rod may comfort me; and that, if I have lived in the bitterness of my own sins during my prosperity, I may now taste the heavenly sweetness of thy grace, during the salutary evils with which thou hast chastened me. But I confess, O my God, that my heart is so hardened, and so full of the thoughts, and cares, and anxieties, and attachments of the world, that neither sickness, nor health, neither sermons, nor books, nor thy holy Scriptures, nor thy gospel, nor its holiest mysteries, nor alms, nor fastings, nor mortifications, nor the sacraments, nor thy death, nor all my efforts, nor those of the whole world put together, can effect any thing whatever, even to begin my conversion, if thou dost not accompany all these things by the extraordinary assistance of thy grace. For this, O my God, I address myself to thee, the Almighty, to ask from thee a gift, that all thy creatures together could not bestow. I should not have the daring to direct my cry to thee, if any other being could answer it. But, O my God, since the conversion of my heart, for which I now entreat, is a work which surpasses all the efforts of nature; I can apply to none but to the Author and Almighty master of nature, and of my heart. To whom should I cry, Lord, to whom should I have recourse, but to thee? Nothing short of God can fulfil my

desire. It is God himself that I need, and that I seek; and to thee only, O my God, do I address myself, that I may obtain thee. Open my heart, Lord. Enter this rebel place, where sin has reigned. Sin holds it in subjection. Enter as into the house of a strong man; but first bind the strong and mighty enemy who ruled it, and then take possession of the treasures which are there. O Lord, regain those affections which the world has stolen. Seize this treasure thyself, or rather resume it; for it belongs to thee as a tribute that I owe thee, as stamped by thine own image. Thou hast imprinted it at the moment of my baptism, which was my second birth; but it is all effaced. The image of the world is graven there so deeply, that thine is scarcely cognizable. Thou only couldst create my soul; thou only canst create it anew. Thou only couldst impress there thine image; thou only canst reform it, and refresh the lineaments of thy obliterated likeness; that is, Jesus Christ my Saviour, who is thine image, and the very character of thy subsistence.

5. O my God, how happy is a heart that can love so lovely an object, with an honourable and a beneficial love! I feel that I cannot love the world without displeasing thee, without injuring and dishonouring myself; and yet the world is still the object of my delight. O my God, how happy is the soul who finds his delight in thee, since he may abandon himself to thy love, not only without scruple, but with commendation. How firm and lasting is his happiness, since his hope cannot be disappointed, because thou wilt never be destroyed, and neither life nor death shall separate him from the object of his desires; and that the same moment which overwhelms the wicked and their idols in one common ruin, shall unite

the just with thee in one common glory; and that as the one shall perish with the perishable objects to which they were attached; the others, shall subsist eternally in the eternal and self-existent object to which they were so strictly united. Blessed are they, who, with perfect freedom, and an invincible bias of their will, love perfectly and freely, that which they are incessantly constrained to love.

6. Perfect, O my God, the holy emotions that thou hast given me. Be their end, as thou art their beginning. Crown thine own gifts; for thine I admit them to be. Yes, O my God, far from assuming that my prayers have any merit, which could constrain thee to answer them, I most humbly confess, that having given to the creature that heart, which thou didst form for thyself only, and not for the world, nor for myself, I could look for no blessing but to thy mercy; since I have nothing in me which could deserve it; and that all the natural emotions of my heart, inclining towards the creatures or myself, can only anger thee. I thank thee, then, O my God, for the holy emotions that thou hast given me, and even for that disposition which thou hast also given me to feel thankful.

7. Touch my heart with repentance for its faults; for without this inward grief, the outward evils with which thou hast smitten my body, will be but a new occasion of sin. Make me to know that the diseases of my body are only the chastening, and the emblem of the diseases of my soul. But grant, Lord, also, that they may be the r⸻ by making me consider, amidst these pains that I ⸳ the evil which I did not previously perceive in

though totally diseased and covered with *putrifying sores*. For, O Lord, the greatest of its evils is that insensibility, and that extreme weakness which has deprived it of all consciousness of its own miseries. Make me then to feel them deeply; and let the remainder of my life be a continued penitence, to bewail the sins which I have committed.

8. O Lord, though my life past has been exempt from gross crimes, from the temptations to which thou hast preserved me; it has been very hateful in thy sight, from my continual negligence, my misuse of thy holy sacraments, my contempt of thy word, and of thy holy influence, by the listlessness and uselessness of my actions and thoughts, by the total loss of that time which thou hast given me for thy worship, to seek, in all my ways, the means of pleasing thee, and to repent of the sins which I daily commit; sins from which, even the most righteous are not exempt; so that even their life had need be a continual penitence, or they run the risk of falling from their stedfastness. In this way, O my God, I have ever been rebellious against thee.

9. Yes, Lord, up to this hour I have been ever deaf to thy inspirations; I have despised thy oracles; I have judged contrary to what thou judgest; I have contradicted those holy precepts which thou didst bring into the world, from the bosom of thy eternal Father, and by which thou wilt judge the world. Thou sayest, *Blessed are they that mourn, and woe to them that are comforted;* and I have said, Wretched are those that mourn, and blessed are those who are comforted. I have said, Happy are they who enjoy a fortunate lot, a splendid reputation,

and robust health. And why have I thought them happy, except that all these advantages furnished them an ample facility for enjoying the creature, that is, for offending thee. Yes, Lord, I confess that I have esteemed health a blessing, not because it was a ready means of serving thee usefully, by devoting more care and watchfulness to thy service, and by the ready assistance of my neighbour; but that, by its aid, I could abandon myself, with less restraint, to the abounding delights of life, and taste more freely its deadly pleasures. Graciously, O Lord, reform my corrupted reason, and conform my principles to thine. Grant that I may count myself happy in affliction, and that in this inability for external action, my thoughts may be so purified, as no longer to be repugnant to thine; and that in this way, I may find thee within me, when from my weakness I cannot go forth to seek thee. For, Lord, thy kingdom is within thy believing people; and I shall find it within myself, if I discover there thy Spirit and thy precepts.

10. But, Lord, what shall I do to constrain thee to pour forth thy Spirit upon this wretched earth? All that I am is hateful in thy sight; and I find nothing in me which can please thee. I see nothing there, Lord, except my griefs which bear some faint resemblance to thine. Consider then the ills that I suffer, and those which threaten me. Look with an eye of pity on the wounds which thy hand hath made. O my Saviour, who didst love thy sufferings even in death; O my God, who didst become man, only to suffer more than any man, for man's salvation; O God, who didst become incarnate after the sin of men, and who didst take a body only to suffer in it all that our sins deserved; O God, who lovest so much

the suffering bodies of men, that thou didst choose for thyself the most afflicted body that ever was in the world; graciously accept my body, not for its own sake, nor for any thing in it,—for all deserves thine indignation,—but for the miseries which it endures, which only can be worthy of thy love. Kindly regard my sufferings, O Lord, and let my distresses invite thee to visit me. But to complete the sanctification of thy dwelling, grant, O my Saviour, that if my body is admitted to the common privilege with thine, that it suffers for my offences, my soul also may have this in common with thy soul, that it may be in bitterness for them also; and that thus, I may suffer with thee, and like thee, both in my body and my soul, for the sins which I have committed.

11. Graciously, O Lord, impart thy consolations during my sufferings, that I may suffer as a Christian. I ask not exemption from distress; for this is the reward of the saints: but I pray not to be given up to the agonies of suffering nature, without the consolations of thy Spirit; for this is the curse of Jews and heathens. I ask not a fulness of consolation, without any suffering; for that is the life of glory. I ask not a full cup of sorrow, without alleviation, for that is the present state of Judaism. But I ask, Lord, to feel, at the same time, both the pangs of nature for my sins, and the consolations of thy Spirit through grace; for this is true Christianity. Let me not experience pain, without consolation; but let me feel pains and consolations at the same time, so that ultimately I may experience consolation only, free from all suffering. For formerly, Lord, before the advent of thy Son, thou didst leave the world to languish without comfort under natural sufferings: now thou dost console and

temper the sufferings of thy saints, by the grace of thine only Son; and hereafter, thou wilt crown thy saints with a beatitude, perfectly pure, in thy Son's eternal glory. These are the marvellous degrees through which thou dost carry thy works. Thou hast withdrawn me from the first; cause me to pass through the second; that I may reach the third. This, Lord, is the mercy that I ask.

12. Suffer me not to be so far alienated from thee, as to be able to contemplate thy soul, sorrowful even unto death, and thy body laid low by death for my sins, without rejoicing to suffer also both in my body and my mind. For there is nothing more disgraceful, and yet nothing more usual among Christians, than that while thou didst sweat blood for the expiation of our offences, we should be living luxuriously at ease; and that Christians, who make a profession of being devoted to thee; that those who, in their baptism, have renounced the world to follow thee; that those who have vowed solemnly, before the church, to live and die for thee; that those who profess to believe that the world persecuted and crucified thee; that those who believe that thou didst give thyself up to the wrath of God, and to the cruelty of men, to redeem them from all iniquity; that those, I say, who believe all these truths, who consider thy body as the sacrifice offered for their salvation; who consider the indulgences, and the sins of this world, as the only cause of thy sufferings, and the world itself as thy executioner; that they should seek to indulge their own bodies with these same delights, and in this same world; and that they who could not, without horror, see a man caress and cherish the murderer of his own father, who had surrendered

himself to secure his life, should live as I have done; should live joyously amidst that world, which I know unquestionably to have been the murderer of him whom I recognize as my Father and my God, who gave himself up for my salvation, and who has borne in his own body the punishment of my transgressions. It is right, O Lord, that thou hast interrupted a joyousness so criminal as that in which I have indulged amidst the shadows of death.

13. Take from me then, O Lord, the grief that selflove may feel on account of my own sufferings, and on account of those human events which do not fall out precisely according to the wishes of my heart, and which do not make for thy glory. But awaken within me a sorrow assimilated to thine own. Let my sufferings mollify thine anger. Make them the means of my safety and my conversion. Let me wish no more for health and life, but to employ and expend them for thee, with thee, and in thee. I do not ask of thee health or sickness, life or death; but merely that thou wouldst dispose of my health or sickness, of my life or death, for thy glory, for my salvation, and for the benefit of thy church, and of thy saints, among whom I would hope, by thy grace, to be found. Thou only knowest what is needful for me: thou art the sovereign Lord; do with me what thou wilt. Give or take; only conform my will to thine; and grant, that in humble and entire submission, I may accept the ordinances of thy eternal providence, and that I may regard with equal reverence, whatever comes from thee.

14. Grant, O my God, that in uniform equanimity of mind, I may receive whatever happens; since we know

not what we should ask, and since I cannot wish for one thing more than another without presumption, and without setting up myself as a judge, and making myself responsible for those consequences which thy wisdom has determined properly to conceal from me. O Lord, I know that I know but one thing; and that is, that it is good to follow thee, and evil to offend thee. After that, I know not what is better or worse in any thing. I know not which is more profitable for me, sickness or health, wealth or poverty, nor any other of the things of this world. This were a discovery beyond the power of men or angels, and which is veiled in the secrets of thy providence which I adore, and which I do not desire to fathom.

15. Grant then, O Lord, that such as I am, I may be conformed to thy will; and that, diseased as I am, I may glorify thee in my sufferings. Without these, I cannot reach thy glory; and even thou, my Saviour, wouldst not attain to glory but by this means. It was by the scars of thy sufferings that thy disciples knew thee; and it is by their sufferings that thou wilt recognize those who are thy disciples. Recognize me, O Lord, amidst the evils that I suffer, both in body and mind, for the sins that I have committed; and because nothing is acceptable to God, that is not offered by thee, unite my will to thine, and my agonies to those which thou hast endured. Let mine become thine. Unite me to thyself; and fill me with thyself, and with thy Holy Spirit. Dwell in my heart and soul, to endure within me my sufferings, and to continue to endure in me, all that remains yet unsuffered of thy passion, which thou completest in all thy members, even to the entire perfection of thy mystical body; that being

thus at length full of thee, it may be no more I that live and suffer, but that it may be thou who livest and sufferest in me, O my Saviour; and that thus, having some little part in thy sufferings, thou mayest fill me abundantly with the glory which they have purchased; in which thou livest with the Father, and the Holy Spirit, world without end. Amen.

CHAPTER XXIV.

A COMPARISON OF ANCIENT AND MODERN CHRISTIANS.

IN the infancy of the Christian church, we see no Christians but those who were thoroughly instructed in all matters necessary to salvation; but, in these days, we see on every side an ignorance so gross, that it agonizes all those who have a tender regard for the interests of the church. Then, no one entered the church, but after serious difficulties, and long cherished wishes; now, we find ourselves associated with it, without care or difficulty. Formerly, no one was admitted but after a most rigid examination; now, every one is admitted before he is capable of being examined. Formerly, no one was admitted but after repentance of his former life, and a renunciation of the world, the flesh, and the devil; now, they enter the church before they are in a state to do any of these things. In fact, formerly it was necessary to come out from the world, in order to be received into the church; whilst, in these days, we enter the church almost at the same time that we enter the world. Then there was distinctly recognised by those earlier proceedings, an essential difference between the world and the church. They were regarded as two things, in direct opposition, as two irreconcileable enemies; of which the one persecutes the other perpetually, and of which, that which seems the weakest, will one day triumph over the strongest; and between these two contending parties, it became necessary to abandon the one, in order to enter the other; to renounce the maxims of the one, in order to follow those of the other; each one must disencumber himself of the sentiments of the one, in order to put on the sentiments of the other; and finally, must be prepared to quit, to renounce, and to abjure the world where he had his former birth, and to devote himself entirely to the church in which he receives his second birth. And thus a wide distinction was habitually drawn between the one and the other. But now, we find ourselves almost at the same moment introduced into both; and, at the same time, we are born into the world, and born anew into the church.* So that, dawning reason now no longer perceives the broad line of distinction between these two opposing worlds, but matures and strengthens, at the same time, under the combined influence of both. The sacraments are partaken of, in conjunction with the pleasures of the world; and hence, instead of there being an essential distinction between the one and the other, they are now so mingled and confounded, that the distinction is almost entirely lost.

---

* It is quite evident by the tenor of the whole passage, that M. Pascal means here only a formal initiation by baptism, and not a spiritual birth—a real regeneration. At the same time, the error which his words appear to some degree to countenance, was held by the unenlightened part of the Romish Church; and it is still held by some members of the Church of England, who do not understand either her doctrines or her services; whilst some men among us, like M. Pascal, give an improper countenance to the error, by the adoption of the inexplicable notion of Baptismal Regeneration.

Hence it arises, that whilst then Christians were all well instructed; now, there are many in a fearful state of ignorance; then, those who had been initiated into Christianity by baptism, and who had renounced the vices of the world, to embrace the piety of the church, rarely declined again to the world which they had left; whilst now, we commonly see the vices of the world in the hearts of Christians. The church of the saints is all defiled with the intermingling of the wicked; and her children that she has conceived, and born from their infancy at her sides, are they who carry into her very heart, that is even to the participation of her holiest mysteries—her deadliest foes—the spirit of the world—the spirit of ambition, of revenge, of impurity, and of lust; and the love which she bears for her children, compels her to admit into her very bowels, the bitterest of her persecutors.

But we must not impute to the church the evils that have followed so fatal a change; for when she saw that the delay of baptism left a large proportion of infants still under the curse of original sin, she wished to deliver them from this perdition, by hastening the succour which she can give; and this good mother sees, with bitter regret, that the benefit which she thus holds out to infants, becomes the occasion of the ruin of adults.

The true meaning of the church is, that those whom she thus withdraws at so tender an age, from the contagion of the world, should subsequently become separate from its opinions. She anticipates the agency of reason, to prevent those vices into which corrupted reason might entice them; and that, before their natural mind could act, she might fill them with her better spirit, so that they might live in ignorance of the world, and in a state so much further removed from vice, in as much as they have never known it. This is evident in the baptismal service; for she does not confer baptism till the children have declared, by the lips of their parents, that they desire it—that they believe—that they renounce the world and the devil. And as the church wishes them to preserve these dispositions throughout life, she expressly enjoins upon them to keep them inviolate; and by an indispensible command, she requires the parents to instruct their children in all these things; for she does not wish that those whom, from their infancy, she has nourished in her bosom, should be less enlightened, and less zealous than those whom she formerly received as her own; she cannot be satisfied with a less degree of perfection in those whom she herself has trained, than in those whom she admits to her communion.

Yet the rule of the church is so perverted from its original intention, that it cannot be thought of without horror. Men think no more of the peculiar blessing which they have received, because they did not themselves ask it, because they do not even remember having received it. But since it is evident, that the church requires no less piety in those who have been brought up from infancy as the servants of faith, than in those who aspire to become such, it becomes such persons to set before them the example of the ancient Catechumens of the early church, to consider their ardour, their devotion, their dread of the world, their noble renunciation of it; and if *they* were not thought worthy to receive baptism, without these dispositions, those who do not find such dispositions in themselves, should at once submit to receive that instruction which they would have had, if they were now only about to seek an entrance into the communion of the church. It becomes them still further to humble themselves to such a penitence, as they may wish never again to throw aside; such that they may henceforth find less of disgust in the austere mortification of the senses, than of attraction in the criminal pleasures of sin.

To induce them to seek instruction, they must be made to understand the difference of the customs which have obtained in the church at different times. In the newly formed Christian church, the Catechumens, that is, those who offered for baptism, were instructed before the rite was conferred; and they were not admitted to it, till after full instruction in the mysteries of religion; till after penitence for their former life; till after a great measure of knowledge, of the grandeur and excellence of a profession of the Christian faith and obedience, on which they desire to enter for ever; till after some eminent marks of real conversion of heart, and an extreme desire for baptism. These facts being made known to the whole church, they then conferred upon them the sacrament of incorporation or initiation, by which they became members of the church.[*] But now, since baptism has been, for many very important reasons, permitted to infants before the dawn of reason, we find, through the negligence of parents, that nominal Christians grow old without any knowledge of our religion.

When teaching preceded baptism, all were instructed; but now, that baptism precedes instruction, that teaching which was then made necessary for the sacrament, is become merely voluntary, and is consequently neglected, and almost abolished. Reason then shewed the necessity

---

[*] This was the case with converted heathens; but if M. Pascal conceived it to be the case with the children of baptized believers, he is in error; and the whole tenor of the history of the church will prove him to be so.

of instruction; and when instruction went before baptism, the necessity of the one, compelled men necessarily to have recourse to the other. But in these days, when baptism precedes instruction, as men are made Christians, in the first instance, without instruction, so they believe that they may remain Christians without being instructed; and instead of its being the case, that the primitive Christians expressed the warmest gratitude for a grace which the church only granted after reiterated petitions—the Christians of these days, manifest nothing but ingratitude for this same blessing conferred upon them, before they were in a state to ask it. If the church so decidedly abhorred the occasional, though extremely rare instances of backsliding among the primitive Christians, how ought she to hold in abhorrence, the falling again and again of modern Christians, notwithstanding the far higher degree in which they stand indebted to the church, for having so speedily and liberally removed them from that state of curse, in which, by their natural birth, they were involved. She cannot see without bitter lamentation, this abuse of her richest blessings; and that the course which she has adopted for her childrens' safety, becomes the almost certain occasion of their ruin; for her spirit is not changed, though the primitive custom is.*

---

* These views of M. Pascal, evidently originate in the difficulty presented to a believing mind, by the formal and irreligious state of the Christian churches. The thought will occur to a considerate mind, lately awakened to feel the power of true religion, after a youth of nominal religion and carelessness, "Whence does this evil arise?" And this reference to the mode of admitting converts from heathenism, in earlier days, is one way of settling the point, to which young Christians frequently have recourse. Yet this is cutting the knot, instead of untying it. It is an error which originates in an unfounded and imaginary notion of the state of the Christian church at any time. A little patience and experience—a little practical knowledge of hu-

CHAPTER XXV.

ON THE CONVERSION OF A SINNER.

THE first thing which God imparts to a soul that he has really touched, is a degree of knowledge and perception, altogether extraordinary, by which the soul regards both itself, and other things in a totally novel manner.

This new light excites fear, and imparts to the soul a restlessness which thwarts the repose that it had formerly found in the wonted sources of indulgence.

The man can no longer relish, with tranquillity, the objects by which he had been previously charmed. A perpetual scrupulousness haunts him in his enjoyments; and this interior perception will not allow him any longer to find the wonted sweetness in those things to which he had yielded with all the melting fulness of the heart.

But he finds yet more bitterness in the exercises of piety, than in the vanities of the world. On one side, the vanity of the things that are seen, is felt more deeply than the hope of the things that are not seen; and, on the other, the reality of invisible things affects him more than the vanity of the things which are seen. And thus

---

the Christian system works, would give a very different view of the matter. It is, however, on this summary mode of settling the difficulty, to which the inexperienced mind resorts—that the Anabaptist Churches found their peculiar notions, and justify their separation; and it is in the ready application of this notion to meet the difficulty when it first arises, that they find their success. Pascal, after mature deliberation on the facts of the case, did not at all see the necessity of renouncing the custom of Infant Baptism. He could distinguish between an evil that casually accompanied, and an evil that originated in, that custom.

the presence of the one, and the absence of the other, excite his disgust, so that there arises within him a disorder and confusion which he can scarcely correct, but which is the result of ancient impressions long experienced, and new impressions now first communicated.

He considers perishable things as perishing, and even as already perished; and, in the certain conviction of the annihilation of all that he has loved, he trembles at the thought; whilst he sees, that every moment goes to rob him of the enjoyment of happiness, and that that which is dearest to him, is perpetually gliding away; and, that at length, a day will come, in which he will find himself bereft of all on which he had built his hope. So that he sees clearly, that as his heart is devoted only to things in themselves fragile and vain, his soul must, at the exit from this life, find itself solitary and destitute, since he has taken no care to unite himself to a real and self-subsistent good, which could support him in, and subsequently to, this present existence.

And hence he begins to consider as a nonentity, every thing which returns to nothingness,—the heavens, the earth, his body, his relations, his friends, his enemies, wealth or poverty, humiliation or prosperity, honour or ignominy, esteem or contempt, authority or insignificance, health or sickness, and even life itself. In fact, whatever is shorter in duration than his soul, is incapable of satisfying the desires of that soul, which earnestly seeks to establish itself on a basis of felicity as durable as itself.

He begins to regard with astonishment, the blindness in which he has been plunged; and, when he considers on the one hand, the length of time that he has lived without any such thoughts, and the great number of persons who live with equal thoughtlessness; and, on the other, how clear it is that the soul being immortal, cannot find happiness in the things that perish, and which must, at all events, be taken from him by death; then there comes upon him a holy anxiety and astonishment which gives rise to salutary sorrow.

For he considers that however great may be the number of those who grow old in the ways of the world, and whatever authority may be in the multitude of examples, of those who place their happiness in this world, it is nevertheless certain, that even if the things of this world had in them some substantial delight,—an assumption which is falsified by the fatal and continual experience of an infinite number of persons,—the loss of these things is certain, at the moment when death separates us from them.

So that, if the soul has amassed a treasure of temporal good, whether of gold, of science, or of reputation, it is inevitably necessary, that it must one day find itself denuded of all the objects of its felicity; and hence it appears, that though many objects have had in them that which ministered satisfaction, they had not that which would have satisfied him permanently; and that even if they procured him a happiness that was real, they could not procure a happiness that was lasting, because it must be terminated by the limits of human life.

Then by a holy humility, which God has exalted above pride, the man begins to rise above the common habits of men in general. He condemns their conduct; he detests their maxims; he laments their blindness; he devotes himself to the search for that which is truly good; he arrives at the conviction, that it must possess these two qualities,—the one, that it must be as durable as himself,—the other, that it must be more worthy of love than any thing else.

He sees that in the love which he has cherished towards the world, he has found in it, owing to his blindness, the second quality of these two, for he had discovered nothing more worthy of his love, but now as he sees not in it the former quality also, he knows that it is not the sovereign good. He seeks it then elsewhere; and knowing, by an illumination altogether pure, that it does not exist in the things which are within him, or around him, or before him, he begins to seek for it in those things which are above.

This elevation of soul is so lofty and transcendant, that it stops not at the heavens; they have not what would satisfy him; nor at the things above the heavens, nor at the angels, nor at the most perfect of created beings. It darts through universal creation, and cannot pause till it has reached the very throne of God; there the soul begins to find repose, and grasps that real good which is such, that there is nothing more truly worthy of love, and that it cannot be taken from him but by his own consent.

For though he does not yet taste those enjoyments by which God blesses the services of habitual piety, he learns, at least, that the creatures can never deserve his love more than the Creator; and his reason, aided by the light of grace, teaches him that there is nothing more worthy of love than God, and that He cannot be taken away except from those who reject him,—since to desire God, is to possess him; and to refuse him, is to lose him.

And thus he rejoices in having found a blessing which cannot be torn from him as long as he wishes to possess it, and which has nothing superior to itself.

And with these novel reflections, he enters upon the

view of the grandeur of his Creator, and upon acts of the deepest humiliation and reverence. He counts himself as less than nothing in that presence; and, being unable to form of himself an idea sufficiently humiliating, or to conceive of the sovereign Good a thought sufficiently exalted, he makes repeatedly fresh efforts, to lower himself to the last abysses of nothingness, whilst he surveys God still in interminably multiplying immensities; and, at last, exhausted by this mighty conception, he adores in silence, he looks on himself as a vile and useless creature, and by repeated acts of veneration, adores and blesses his God, and would for ever bless and adore.

Then he sees something of the grace by which God has manifested his infinite majesty to a worthless worm—he is ashamed and confounded at having preferred so many vanities to such a Divine Master; and, in the spirit of compunction and penitence, he looks up for his compassion to arrest that anger, the effect of which, seen through these immensities, seems to hang over him so awfully.

He sends up ardent prayers to God, to obtain this mercy, that as it has pleased Him to disclose himself to his soul, it would please Him also to lead it to himself, and prepare for him the means of reaching Him. For it is to God that he now aspires, and, at the same time, he only aspires to reach Him by those means which come from God himself, for he wishes God himself to be his way, his object, and his end. Then on the result of these prayers, he learns that he ought to act conformably to the new light which he has received.

He begins to know God, and to desire to go to him; but he is ignorant of the mode of reaching him. If, then, his desire is sincere and real, just as a person who wishes to go to a particular spot, but who has lost his way, and knows that he is in error, has recourse to those who are well acquainted with it, so he seeks advice from those who can teach him the way that leads to the God, from whom he has so long been alienated. And in thus seeking to know this way, he resolves to regulate his conduct for the remainder of his life by the truth, as far as he knows it; and seeing that his natural weakness, together with the habitual tendency which he now has to the sin in which he has lived, have incapacitated him for reaching the happiness of which he is in search, he implores from the mercy of God those gracious aids by which he may find him, devote himself to him, and adhere to him for ever. Heartily occupied by the loveliness of the Divine excellency,—old as eternity, in fact, but to him so new;—he feels that all he does ought to bear him towards this adorable object; he sees now clearly that he ought henceforth only to think of adoring God, as his creature, of gratitude to him for unnumbered obligations, of penitence as guilty, and prayer as necessitous; so that his entire occupation should be to contemplate, and love, and praise him throughout eternity.

CHAPTER XXVI.

REASONS FOR SOME OPINIONS OF THE PEOPLE.

I WRITE my thoughts here without order, but probably not in mere unmeaning confusion. It is, in fact, the true order, and will mark my object, even by the disorder itself.

We shall see that all the opinions of the multitude are

very sound: that the people are not so weak as they are reported; and, that consequently, the opinion which would destroy the opinion of the people, will be itself destroyed.

2. It is true in one sense, that all the world is in a state of delusion; for although the opinions of the people are sound, they are not so as held by them, because they conceive the truth to reside where it does not. There is truth in their opinions, but not where they suppose.

3. The people reverence men of high birth. Your half-informed men despise them, affirming, that birth is not a personal advantage, but a mere accident. Your really superior men honour them, not on the ground of the popular notion, but for loftier reasons. Certain zealots of narrow views, despise them, notwithstanding those reasons which secure to them the respect of superior men, because they judge by a new light, that their measure of piety imparts. But more advanced Christians give them honour, according to the dictates of light yet superior; and thus opinions, for and against, obtain in succession, according to the light possessed.

4. Civil wars are the greatest of evils. They are certain, if it is wished to recompense merit, for all would affirm that they deserved reward. The evil to be feared from a fool who succeeds by inheritance, is neither so great, nor so certain.

5. Why follow the majority? Is it because they have more reason? No. But because they have more force. Why follow ancient laws, and ancient opinions? Are

they wiser? No. But they stand apart from present interests; and thus take away the root of difference.

6. The empire founded on opinion and imagination, sometimes has the upper hand; and this dominion is mild and voluntary. The empire of force reigns always. Opinion is, as it were, the queen of the world; but force is its tyrant.

7. How wisely are men distinguished by their exterior, rather than their interior qualifications. Which of us two shall take the lead? Which shall yield precedence? The man of least talent? But I am as clever as he. Then we must fight it out for this. But he has four lacqueys, and I have but one. *There is a visible difference*; we have only to count them. It is my place then to give way; and I am a fool to contest the point. This arrangement keeps us in peace; which is of all blessings the greatest.

8. From the habit of seeing kings surrounded with guards, and drums, and officers, and with all these appendages which tend to create respect and terror, it happens, that the countenance of kings, even though seen sometimes without these adjuncts, still awakens in their subjects the same reverential feeling; because, even then, we do not mentally separate their person from the train with which we usually see them attended. The multitude who know not that this effect has its origin in custom, believe it to originate in native feeling; and hence arises such expressions as, The character of divinity is imprinted on his countenance, &c.

The power of kings is founded on the reason, and on

the folly of the people; but most chiefly on their folly. The greatest and most important thing in the world has weakness for its basis; and this basis is wonderfully secure, for there is nothing more certain, than that the people will be weak; whilst that which has its foundation in reason only, is very insecure, as the esteem for wisdom.

9. Our magistrates have well understood this mystery. Their crimson robes, their ermine, in which they wrap themselves, the palaces of justice, the fleur-de-lis—all this pomp and circumspection was necessary; and if physicians had not their cassock and their mule; and if theologians had not their square cap, and their flowing garments, they would never have duped the world, which could not withstand this authenticating demonstration. Soldiers are the only men who are not in some measure disguised; and that is, because their own share in the matter, is the most essential part of it. They gain their point by actual force,—the others by grimace.

On this account our kings have not had recourse to such disguises. They have not masked themselves in extraordinary habits, in order to appear impressive; but they have surrounded themselves with guards, and lancers, and whiskered faces, men who have hands and energies only for this service. The drums and trumpets which go before them, and the legions that surround them, make even brave men tremble. They not only wear a dress, but they are clothed with might. A man had need have an unprejudiced mind, to consider merely as another man, the Grand Signior surrounded by his glittering train of 40,000 Janissaries.

If magistrates were possessed of real justice, if physi-

232   REASONS FOR SOME OPINIONS

cians knew the true art of healing, there were no need of square caps. The majesty of science would be sufficiently venerable alone. But possessed as they mostly are, with only imaginary science, they must assume these vain adornments which impress the imagination of those among whom they labour, and, by that means, they obtain respect. We cannot look at an advocate in his gown and his wig, without a favourable impression of his abilities.

The Swiss are offended at being called gentlemen, and have to establish the proof of their low origin, in order to qualify them for stations of importance."

10. No one chooses for a pilot, the highest born passenger on board.

All the world sees that we labour with uncertainty before us, either by sea, in battle, &c. but all the world does not see the law of the chances, which shews that we do rightly. Montaigne saw that a narrow mind is an offence, and that custom rules every thing,—but he did not see the reason of this. Those who see only effects, and not their causes, are in relation to those who discover the causes, as those who have eyes only compared with those who have mind. For the effects are perceptible to the senses, but the reasons only to the understanding. And though, in fact, these effects are perceived by the understanding, yet such a mind, compared with that which discovers the causes, is as the bodily senses to the intellectual powers.

11. How is it that a lame man does not anger us, but

---

* At Basle they must renounce their nobility, in order to enter the senate.

a blundering mind does? Is it, that the cripple admits that we walk straight, but a crippled mind accuses us of limping? But for this, we should feel more of pity than of anger.

Epictetus asks also, Why we are not annoyed if any one tells us that we are unwell in the head, and yet are angry if they tell us that we reason falsely, or choose unwisely? The reason is, that we know certainly that nothing ails our heads, or that we are not crippled in the body. But we are not so certain that we have chosen correctly. So that having only assurance, inasmuch as we perceive the matter distinctly, whilst another sees it as clearly the contrary way, we are necessarily brought into doubt and suspense; and still more so, when a thousand others laugh at our decision; for we must prefer our own convictions to those of ever so many others, and yet that is a bold and difficult course. Now, we never feel this contradiction of our senses in a case of actual lameness.

12. Respect for others requires you to inconvenience yourself. This seems foolish; yet it is very proper. It says, " I would willingly inconvenience myself seriously, if it would serve you, seeing that I do so when it will not." Besides, the object of this respect is to distinguish the great. Now, if respect might show itself by lolling in an elbow chair, we should respect all the world, and then we should not distinguish the great; but being put to inconvenience, we distinguish them plainly enough.

13. A superior style of dress is not altogether vain. It shews how many persons labour for us. A man shews by his hair that he has a valet and perfumer, &c.; and

by his band, his linen and lace, &c. It is not then, a mere superficial matter, a mere harness, to have many hands employed in our service.

14. Strange indeed! they would have me not pay respect to that man dressed in embroidery, and followed by seven or eight lacqueys. Why he would horse-whip me if I did not. Now, this custom is a matter of compulsion; it does not exist between two horses, when one is better caparisoned than the other.

It is droll in Montaigne, that he does not see the difference between admiring what we see, and asking the reason of it.

15. The people have some wise notions: for example, the having chosen amusement and hunting, in preference to poetry. Your half-learned gentry laugh at them, and delight in pointing out their folly in this; but for reasons which they cannot perceive, the people are right. It is well also to distinguish men by externals, as by birth or property. The world strives to shew how unreasonable this is; but it is perfectly reasonable.

16. Rank is a great advantage, as it gives to a man of eighteen or twenty years of age, a degree of acceptance, publicity, and respect, which another can scarcely obtain by merit at fifty. There is a gain then, of thirty years without difficulty.

17. There are men, who, to shew us that we are wrong, in not esteeming them more highly, never fail to bring forward the names of those persons of quality who think well of them. I would answer them, " Shew us the merit

by which you have gained their esteem, and we will esteem you as they do."

18. If a man stands at the window to see those who pass, and I happen to pass by, can I say that he placed himself there to see me? No: for he did not think of me particularly. But if a man loves a woman for her beauty, Does he love *her?* No: for the small-pox which destroys her beauty without killing her, causes his love to cease. And if any one loves me for my judgment or my memory, Does he really love me? No: for I can lose these qualities without ceasing to be. Where then is this *me,* if it is neither in the body nor the soul? And how are we to love the body or the soul, except it be for those qualities which do not make up this *me,* because they are perishable? For can we love the soul of a person abstractedly, and some qualities that belong to it? That cannot be; and it would be unjust. Then they never love the person, but only the qualities; or, if they say that they love the person, they must say also, that the combination of qualities constitutes the person.

19. Those things about which we are most anxious, are very often a mere nothing; as, for instance, the concealment of our narrow circumstances. This evil of poverty is a mere nothing, that imagination has magnified to a mountain. Another turn of thought would induce us to tell it without difficulty.

20. Those who have the power of invention are but few. Those who have not are many, and consequently, the strongest party. And generally, we see that they refuse to the inventors the praise that they deserve, and that

they seek by their inventions. If they persist in seeking it, and treat contemptuously those who have not this talent, they will gain nothing but a few hard names, and they will be treated as visionaries. A man should take care, therefore, not to plume himself upon this advantage, great as it is; and he should be content to be esteemed by the few, who really can appreciate his merits.

CHAPTER XXVII.

DETACHED MORAL THOUGHTS.

THERE are plenty of good maxims in the world; we fail only in applying them. For instance, it is without doubt that we should expose life to defend the public good; and many do this: but scarcely any one does this for religion. It is necessary that there be inequality in the state of man; but that being granted, the door is opened, not only to the highest domination, but to the highest degree of tyranny. It is needful to allow some relaxation of mind; but this opens the door to the loosest dissipations. The limits should be marked; they are not laid down. The laws would prescribe them, but the human mind will not endure it.

2. The authority of reason is far more imperious than that of a master: for he who disobeys the one, is unhappy; but he who disobeys the other, is a fool.

3. Why would you kill me? Why? do you not live across the water? My friend, if you lived on this side, I should be an assassin; it would be unjust to kill you in

this way; but since you live on the other, I am brave, and the act is just.

4. Those who live irregularly, say to those who live discreetly, that it is they who swerve from the dictates of nature, and that they themselves live according to it; as those who are in a vessel believe that the people on shore are receding from them. Both parties use similar language. There should be a fixed point to decide the case. The port settles the question for those in the vessel, but where shall we find this fixed point in morals?*

5. As fashion makes pleasure, so does it justice. If men really knew what justice is, they would never have admitted this commonest of all maxims throughout the world, that each should follow the custom of his own country. Real equity would have subjugated all nations, by its native brilliancy; and legislators would not have taken in the stead of this invariable rule of right, the fancies and caprices of Persians and Germans, &c. It would have been set up in all the states of the earth, and at all times.

6. Justice is that which is by law established; and hence all our established laws are to be necessarily accounted just, because they are established.

7. The only universal rules are, the laws of the land in ordinary matters. In extraordinary matters, the majority carries it. Why is this? From the power that exists in it.

---

* The answer of M. Pascal would be, In the Holy Scriptures.

And hence, also, kings who possess an extrinsic force, do not follow even the majority of their ministers.

8. Undoubtedly an equality of rights is just; but not being able to compel men to be submissive to justice, legislators have made them obedient to force. Unable to fortify justice, they have justified force; so that justice and force uniting, there might be peace, for that is the sovereign good,—*summum jus, summa injuria.*

The power of the plurality is the best way; because it is a visible power; and it has force to command obedience. Yet this is the counsel only of inferior men.

If they could, they should have put power into the hands of justice; but since power will not let itself be used as men please, because it is a palpable quality, while justice is an intellectual quality, of which they may dispose as they please, they have placed justice in the hands of power, and now they call that justice which power requires to be observed.

9. It is just, that whatever is just should be observed. It is necessary that whatever is the strongest should be obeyed. Justice without power is inefficient: power without justice is tyranny. Justice without power is gainsayed, because there are always wicked men. Power without justice is soon questioned. Justice and power must be brought together, so that whatever is just may be powerful, and whatever is powerful may be just.

Justice may be disputed; but power speaks pretty plainly, and without dispute. So that it needs but to give power to justice; but seeing that it was not possible to make justice powerful, they have made the powerful just.

10. It is dangerous to tell the people that the laws are not just; for they only obey them because they believe them to be just. They must be told therefore at the same time, that they must obey them as laws; as they obey their superiors, not because they are just, but because they are their superiors. If you make them comprehend this, you prevent all sedition. This is the true definition of justice.

11. It were well for the people to obey laws and customs, because they are laws; and that they understood that this made them just. On this ground, they would never deviate from them: whilst on the other hand, if their justice is to rest on any other basis, it may easily be brought into question, and then the people are made liable to revolt.

12. When it is made a question, whether we should make war, and kill so many men, and doom so many Spaniards to die, it is one man only who decides, and he an interested party. It ought to be a third and an indifferent person.

13. Language such as this, is false and tyrannical: "I am well-looking; then men ought to fear me: I am strong; then men should love me." Tyranny is to seek to obtain that by one means, which should only be obtained by another. We owe different duties to different kinds of merit; a duty of love to that which is amiable; of fear, to that which is mighty; of teachableness, to the learned, &c. This duty should be done. It is unjust to withhold this. It is unjust to require more. And it savours equally of error and of tyranny to say,

"He has no might, then I will not esteem him. He has no talent, therefore I will not fear him." Tyranny consists in the desire of universal dominion, unwarranted by our real merit.

14. There are vices which have no hold upon us, but in connection with others; and which, when you cut down the trunk, fall like the branches.

15. When malice has reason on its side, it looks forth bravely, and displays that reason in all its lustre. When austerity and self-denial have not realized true happiness, and the soul returns to the dictates of nature, the re-action is fearfully extravagant.

16. To find recreation in amusements, is not happiness; for this joy springs from alien and extrinsic sources, and is therefore dependent upon, and subject to interruption by a thousand accidents, which may minister inevitable affliction.

17. The highest style of mind is accused of folly, as well as the lowest. Nothing is thoroughly approved but mediocrity. The majority has brought this about; and it instantly fixes its fangs on whatever gets beyond it either way. I will not resist their rule. I consent to be ranked among them; and if I object to be placed at the low extreme, it is not because it is low, but because it is the extreme; for I should in the same way refuse to be placed at the highest. To get really beyond mediocrity, is to pass the limits of human nature. The dignity of the human soul, lies in knowing how middle course; and so far from there being

leaving it, true greatness consists in never deviating from it.

18. No man obtains credit with the world for talent in poetry, who does not fairly hang out the sign of a poet; or for a talent in mathematics, if he has not put up the sign of a mathematician. But your truly honest men have recourse to no such expedients. They no more play themselves off for poets, than for embroiderers. They are neither called poets nor geometers; but they are at home in all these matters. Men do not make out specifically what they are. When they enter a room, they speak of the topic then in discussion. They do not discover a greater aptness for one subject than for another, except as circumstances call out their talents; for to such persons it is a matter of equal indifference, that it should not be said, "That man talks remarkably well," when conversational powers is not the point in question, or that this should be said of them when it is. It is poor praise, therefore, when a man is pointed out, on his entering a room, as a great poet, or that he should only be referred to, where the merit of some verses is to be considered. Man is full of wants; he only loves those who can satisfy them. "He is a good mathematician;" they say, "but then I must be bored incessantly with mathematics:" or, "That man thoroughly comprehends the art of war; but I do not wish to make war with any man." Give me, then, a polite man, with general talents, to meet and supply all my necessities.

19. When in health, we cannot at all judge how we would act in sickness; but when sickness comes, then we submit freely to the needful discipline. The disease it-

self is the cause of this. We feel then no longer the eager thirst for amusements and visiting, which originates in health, and which is quite incompatible with a state of sickness. Nature, then, gives inclinations and desires conformed to our present state. It is only the fears that originate with ourselves, and not with nature, that trouble us; for they associate with the state in which we then are, the feelings of a state in which we are not.

20. Injunctions to humility, are sources of humiliation to the humble; but of pride, to the proud. So also the language of Pyrrhonism and doubt, is matter of confirmation to those who believe. Few men speak humbly of humility, or chastely of chastity,—few of scepticism with real doubtfulness of mind. We are nothing but falsehood, duplicity, and contradiction. We hide and disguise ourselves from ourselves.

21. Concealed good actions are the most estimable of all. When I discover such in history, they delight me much. Yet even these cannot have been altogether hidden, because they have been so recorded; and even the degree in which they have come to light, detracts from their merit, for their finest trait is the wish to conceal them.

22. Your sayer of smart things, has a bad heart.

23. This *I* is hateful; and those who do not renounce it, who seek no further than to cover it, are always hateful also. Not at all, say you, for if we act obligingly to all men, they have no reason to hate us. That is true *If there were nothing hateful in that I, but the instant*

nience which it administers. But if I hate it, because it is essentially unjust, because it makes itself the centre of every thing, I shall hate it always. In fact, this *I* has two bad qualities. It is essentially unjust, because it will be the centre of all things; it is an annoyance to others, because it will serve itself by them; for each individual *I* is the enemy, and would be the tyrant of all the others. Now you may remove the annoyance, but not the radical injustice, and hence you cannot make it acceptable to those who abhor its injustice; you may make it pleasing to the unjust, who no longer discover their enemy, but you remain unjust yourself, and cannot be pleasing therefore but to similar persons.

24. I cannot admire the man who possesses one virtue in high perfection, if he does not, at the same time, possess the opposite virtue in an equal degree; as in the case of Epaminondas, who united the extremes of valour and of meekness; without this, it is not an elevated, but a fallen character. Greatness does not consist in being at one extreme, but in reaching both extremes at once, and occupying all the intermediate space. Perhaps this is in no case more than a sudden movement of the soul, from one extreme to the other, and, like a burning brand, whirled quickly round in a circle, it is never but in one point of its course at a time. Still this indicates the energy of the soul, if not its expansion.

25. If our condition were really happy, there were no need to divert us from thinking of it.

26. I have spent much time in the study of the abstract sciences; but the paucity of persons with whom you can

communicate on such subjects, disgusted me with them. When I began to study man, I saw that these abstract sciences are not suited to him, and that in diving into them, I wandered further from my real object, than those who knew them not, and I forgave them for not having attended to these things. I expected then, however, that I should find some companions in the study of man, since it was so specifically a duty. I was in error. There are fewer students of man, than of geometry.

27. When all things move similarly, nothing moves apparently—as on board a ship. When all things glide similarly to disorder, nothing seems to be going wrong. He who stops, considers the rapid recession of others, as immoveable point.

28. Philosophers boast of having arranged all moral duties in a certain classification. But why divide them into four, rather than into six divisions. Why make *four* sorts of virtues rather than ten. Why range them under the general heads of *abstine* and *sustine*, than any others. But then, say you, here they are all reduced to a single word. Well, but that is quite useless without explanation; and as soon as you begin to explain, and you develope the general precept which contains all the others, they issue in the same confusion that at first you wished to avoid, and thus, in reducing them to one, you hide and nullify them; and to be made known, they must still come forth in their native confusion. Nature has given each an independent subsistence; and though you may thus arrange the one within the other, they must subsist independently of each other. So that these divisions and technical terms have little use, but to assist the memory,

and to serve as guides to the several duties which they include.

29. To administer reproof with profit, and to shew another that he deceives himself, we should notice on what side he really has considered the thing—for on that side he generally has a right impression—and admit there the accuracy of his views. This will please him, for he then perceives that as far as he did see, he was not in error, but that he failed only in not observing the matter on all sides. Now, a man is not ashamed of not perceiving every thing; but he does not like to blunder. And perhaps this arises from the fact, that naturally the mind cannot be deceived on the side on which it looks at things, any more than the senses can give a false report.

30. A man's virtue should not be measured by his occasional exertions, but by his ordinary doings.

31. The great and the little are subject to the same accidents, vexations, and passions; but the one class are at the end of the spoke of the wheel, and the other near the centre; and consequently, they are differently agitated by the same impulses.

32. Though men have no interest in what they are saying, it will not do to infer from that absolutely, that they are not guilty of falsehood; for there are some who lie, simply for lying sake.

33. The example of chastity in Alexander, has not availed to the same degree to make men chaste, as his drunkenness has to make them intemperate. Men are

not ashamed not to be so virtuous as he; and it seems excusable not to be more vicious. A man thinks that he is not altogether sunk in the vices of the crowd, when he follows the vicious example of great men; but he forgets that in this respect they are associated with the multitude. He is linked with such men at the same point, at which they are linked with the people. However great they may be, they are associated at some point with the mass of mankind. They are not altogether suspended in mid air, and insulated from society. If they are greater than we, it is only that their heads are higher; but their feet are as low as ours. They are all on the same level—they tread the same earth; and, at this end, they are brought equally low with ourselves, with infants, and with the brutes that perish.

34. It is the contest that delights us; not the victory. We are pleased with the combat of animals, but not with the victor tearing the vanquished. What is sought for but the crisis of victory? and the instant it comes, it brings satiety. It is the same in play, and the same in the search for truth. We love to watch in arguments the conflict of opinions; but as for the discovered truth, we do not care to look at that. To see it with pleasure, we must see it gradually emerging from the disputation. It is the same with the passions; the struggle of two contending passions has great interest; but the dominion of one is mere brutality. We do not seek for things themselves, but for the search after them. So on the stage, scenes without anxiety, miseries without hope, and merely brutal indulgences, are accounted vapid and uninteresting.

35. Men are not taught to be honest, but they are taught every thing else; and yet they pique themselves on this, above all things. They boast then only of knowing the only thing which they do not learn.

36. How weak was Montaigne's plan for exhibiting himself! and that not incidently and contrary to his avowed maxims, as most men contrive to betray themselves; but in accordance with his rule, and as his first and principal design. For to speak fooleries accidentally, and as a matter of weakness, is every one's lot; but to do so designedly, and to speak such as he did, is beyond all bounds.

37. Pity for the unfortunate is no proof of virtue; on the contrary, it is found desirable to make this demonstration of humanity, and to acquire, at no expense, the reputation of tenderness. Pity therefore is little worth.

38. Would he who could boast the friendship of the Kings of England, and of Poland, and the Queen of Sweden, have believed that he might look through the world in vain for a home and a shelter?*

39. Things have various qualities, and the mind various inclinations; for nothing presents itself simply to the mind, neither does the mind apply itself simply to any subject. Hence, the same thing will at different times produce tears or laughter.

---

* The reference is to the cotemporary sovereigns, Charles I. of England, John Casimir of Poland, and Christina Queen of Sweden.

40. There are men of different classes, the powerful, the elegant, the kind, the pious, of which each one may reign in his own sphere, but not elsewhere. They come sometimes into collision, and contend who shall have the dominion; and most unwisely, for their mastery is in different matters. They do not understand one another. They err in seeking an universal dominion. But nothing can accomplish this, not even force. Force can do nothing in the realms of science; it has no power but over external actions.

41. *Ferox gens nullam esse vitam sine armis putat.* They prefer death to peace: others prefer death to war. Every variety of opinion may be preferred to that life—the love of which appears so strong and so natural.

42. How difficult is it to propose a matter to another man's judgment, without corrupting his judgment by the manner in which it is proposed. If we say, "I like this," or, "I think this obscure," we either entice the imagination that way, or produce irritation and opposition. It is more correct to say nothing, and then he will judge as the matter really is; that is, as it is then, and according as the other circumstances over which we have no control, may bias him; if even our very silence has not its effect according to the aspect of the whole, and the interpretation which the man's present humour may put upon it, or according to the conjecture he may form from the expression of my countenance, and the tone of my voice; so easy is it to bias the judgment from its natural and unfettered conclusion, or rather so few men are there of resolute and independant mind.

43. Montaigne is right. Custom should be followed because it is custom, and because it is found established, without inquiring whether it is reasonable or not; understanding of course those matters which are not contrary to natural or divine right. It is true that the people follow custom for this only reason, that they believe it to be just; without which, they would follow it no longer, for no one would be subjected to any thing but reason and justice. Custom without this would be accounted tyranny; but the dominion of reason and justice is no more tyrannous than that of pleasure.

44. The knowledge of external things will not console us in the days of affliction, for the ignorance of moral science: but attainments in moral science, will console us under the ignorance of external things.

45. Time deadens our afflictions and our strifes, because we change and become almost as it were other persons. Neither the offending nor the offended party remain the same. Like a people that have been irritated, and then revisited two generations after. They are yet the French nation, but not what they were.

46. What is the condition of man? Instability, dissatisfaction, distress. He who would thoroughly know the vanity of man, has only to consider the causes and the effects of love. The cause is a *je ne sais quoi*, an indefinable trifle; the effects are monstrous. Yet this indescribable something sets the whole earth—princes, armies, multitudes, in motion. If the nose of Cleopatra had been a little shorter, it would have changed the history of the world.

47. Caesar appears to me too old to have amused himself with the conquest of the world. Such sport might do for Alexander, an ardent youth, whom it was difficult to curb; but Caesar's day had gone by.

48. Fickleness has its rise in the experience of the fallaciousness of present pleasures, and in the ignorance of the vanity of absent pleasures.

49. Princes and kings must play themselves sometimes. They cannot be always upon their thrones. They become weary. Greatness to be realized, must be occasionally abandoned.

50. My humour depends but little on the weather. I have my cloud and my sunshine within me. Even prosperity or failure in my affairs affects me little. I sometimes rise spontaneously superior to misfortune; and from the mere joy of superiority, I get the better of it nobly. Whilst at other times, in the very tide of good fortune, I am heartless and fretful.

51. Sometimes in the very writing down my thought, it escapes me. But this teaches me my weakness, which I am ever forgetting. And this instructs me therefore as much as my forgotten thoughts would have done; for what I ought always to be learning, is my own nothingness.

52. It is a curious fact, that there are men in the world who, having renounced all the laws of God and man, have made laws for themselves, which they strictly obey; as *robbers*, &c.

53. "This is my dog," say the children; "that sunny seat is mine." There is the beginning and the exemplification of the usurpation of the whole earth.

54. You have a bad manner: excuse me if you please. Without the apology I should not have known that there was any harm done. Begging your pardon, the "excuse me," is all the mischief.

55. We scarcely ever think of Plato and Aristotle, but as grave and serious looking men, dressed in long robes. They were good honest fellows, who laughed with their friends as others do; and when they made their laws and their treatises on politics, it was to play and divert themselves. It was probably the least philosophical and serious part of their lives. The most philosophical was the living simply and tranquilly.

56. Man delights in malice; but it is not against the unfortunate, it is against the prosperous proud; and we deceive ourselves if we think otherwise. Martial's epigram on the blind, is utterly worthless, for it does not comfort them; it only adds another spark to the glory of the author: all that makes only for the author, is worthless. *Ambitiosa recidet ornamenta.* He should write to please men of a tender and humane spirit, and not your barbarous inhuman souls.

57. These compliments do not please me: "I have given you much trouble." "I fear to weary you." "I fear that this is too long." Things either hurry me away, or irritate me.

252　　　DETACHED MORAL THOUGHTS.

58. A true friend is such a blessing, even to great men, in order that he may speak well of them, and defend them in their absence, that they should leave no stone unturned to get one. But they should choose warily; for if they lavish all their efforts on a fool, whatever good he says of them will go for nothing; and in fact he will not speak well of them, if he feels his comparative weakness; for he has not any authority, and consequently he will slander for company's sake.

59. Do you wish men to speak well of you? Then never speak well of yourself.

60. Do not laugh at the men who seek respect through their duties and official stations; for we regard no man but for his acquired qualities. All men hate one another naturally. I hold it a fact, that if men knew exactly what one says of the other, there would not be four friends in the world. This appears from the quarrels to which occasional indiscreet reports give rise.

61. Death is more easy to endure without thinking about it, than the thoughts of death without the risk of it.

62. It is wonderful indeed, that a thing so visible as the utter vanity of this world, should be so little known, and that it should be so uncommon and surprising to hear any one condemn as folly, the search after its honours.

He who does not see the vanity of this world, is vain indeed. For, in fact, who does not see it, but those young persons who are hurried along in the bustle and din of its amusements, without a thought of the future?

But take away those diversions, and you will see them wither with *ennui*. They are then feeling their emptiness, without really knowing it: for surely it is a very wretched state, to sink into unbearable sadness, as soon as we cease to be diverted, and are left free to think.

63. Almost every thing is partly true and partly false; not so with essential truth. It is perfectly pure and true. This admixture in the world, dishonours and annihilates truth. There is nothing true, if we mean pure essential truth. We may say that homicide is *bad*, because that which is evil and false is well understood by us. But what can we say is good? Celibacy? I say no! for the world would terminate. Marriage? No; for continency is better. Not to kill? No; for disorders would increase, and the wicked would murder the good. To kill? No; for that destroys nature. We have nothing true or good, but what is only partially so, and mixed with evil and untruth.

64. Evil is easily discovered; there is an infinite variety. Good is almost *unique*. But some kinds of evil are almost as difficult to discover, as that which we call good; and often particular evil of this class passes for good. Nay, it needs even a certain greatness of soul to attain to this, as it does to attain to that which is good.

65. The ties which link the mutual respects of one to another, in general, are the bonds of necessity. And there must be different degrees of them, since all men seek to have dominion; and all cannot, though some can attain to it. But the bonds which secure our respect to this or that individual in particular, are the bonds of the imagination.

66. We are so unhappy, that we cannot take pleasure in any pursuit, but under the condition of experiencing distress, if it does not succeed, which may happen with a thousand things, and does happen every hour. He who shall find the secret of enjoying the good, without verging to the opposite evil, has hit the mark for happiness.

CHAPTER XXVIII.

THOUGHTS ON PHILOSOPHICAL AND LITERARY SUBJECTS.

THE more enlarged is our own mind, the greater number we discover of men of originality. Your commonplace people see no difference between one man and another.

2. A man may be possessed of sound sense, yet not be able to apply it equally to all subjects; for there are evidently men who are highly judicious in certain lines of thought, but who fail in others. The one class of men are adapted to draw conclusions from a few principles; the other, to draw conclusions in cases which involve a great variety of principles. For instance, the one understands well the phenomena of water; with reference to which, the principles are few, but the results of which are so extremely delicate, that none but a peculiarly acute intellect can trace them; and most probably, these men never would have been great geometricians, because geometry involves a great many principles; and that the nature of a mind may be such, that it can trace a few principles up to their extreme results; yet not adequately comprehend those things in which a multitude of principles are combined.

There are then two sorts of minds, the one fathoms rapidly and deeply the principles of things, and this is the spirit of accurate discrimination; the other comprehends a great many principles without confusing them, and this is the spirit of mathematics. The one is energy and clearness of mind; the other is expansion of mind. Now, the one may exist without the other. The mind may be powerful, but narrow; or, it may be expanded and feeble.

There is much difference between the geometrical mind, and the acute mind. The principles of the one are clear and palpable, but removed from common usages; so that, for want of the habit, it is difficult to bring the attention down to such things; but as far as the attention is given to them, the principles of those things are plainly seen, and would need a mind altogether in error, to reason falsely on such common-place matters; so that, it is almost impossible that the principles of such things should not be ascertained.

But in the case of the acute mind, the principles in which it is conversant are found in common usage, and before the eyes of all men. You have but to turn your head without effort, and they are before you. The only essential point is a right perception; for the principles are so interwoven and so numerous, that it is almost impossible but that some should be lost sight of. Now, the omission of one principle leads to error; hence it needs a very accurate perception to ascertain all the principles, and then a sound judgment not to reason falsely on known principles.

All the geometricians would be acute men, if they possessed this keenness of perception, for they cannot reason falsely on the principles which they perceive; and the men of acute mind would be geometricians, if they could but turn their attention to the less prominent principles of geometry.

The reason then why some men of acute intellect are not geometers is, that they cannot turn their attention to the principles of geometry; but the reason why geometers have not this acuteness is, that they do not perceive what is before their eyes, and that being accustomed to the plain and palpable principles of geometry, and never reasoning till they have well ascertained and handled their principles, they are lost in these matters of more acute perception, where the principles cannot be so easily ascertained. They are seen with difficulty,—they are felt rather than seen. It is scarcely possible to make them evident to those who do not feel them of themselves. They are so delicate and so multitudinous, that it requires a very keen and ready intellect to feel them; and that generally, without being at all able to demonstrate them in order, as in geometry; because these principles cannot be so gathered, and it were an endless labour to undertake it. The thing must be seen at once, at a glance, and not by a process of reasoning; at least, to a certain degree. And hence it is rarely the case, that geometers are acute men, or acute men geometers; because geometers will treat these nicer matters geometrically, and thus make themselves ridiculous; they will begin with definitions, and then go to principles—a mode that will not answer in this sort of reasoning. It is not that the mind does not take this method, but it does so silently, naturally, without the forms of art—for all men are capable of the expression of it; but this feeling of it is the talent of few.

And the acute mind, on the contrary, accustomed to *judge* at a glance, is so astonished when they present to it a series of propositions, where it understands but little, and when to enter into them, it is necessary to go' previously through a host of definitions and dry principles, that not having been accustomed thus to examine in detail, it turns away in disgust. There are, however, many weaker minds, which are neither acute nor geometrical.

Geometers, then, who are exclusively geometers, possess a sound judgment, provided only that the matter be properly explained to them by definitions and principles; otherwise they go wrong altogether, for they only judge rightly upon principles which are clearly laid down for them; and your acute men, who are exclusively so, have no patience to go down into first principles in matters of speculation and imagination, which they have never seen in use in the world.

3. It often happens, that to prove certain things, men adduce such examples, that they might actually take the things themselves to prove the examples; which does not fail of producing an effect; for as they believe always that the difficulty lies in the thing to be proved, the example, of course, appears more intelligible. Thus, when they wish to illustrate a general principle, they exhibit the rule of a particular case. But if they wish to illustrate a particular case, they begin with the general rule. They always find the thing to be proved obscure, but the medium of proof clear and intelligible; for when it is purposed to prove a point, the mind pre-occupies itself with the thought, that it is obscure and difficult. Whilst, on the contrary, it assumes that the mode by which it is to be proved will be clear, and consequently, under that impression, comprehends it easily.

4. All our reasonings are compelled to yield to feeling. A mere imagination, however, is both similar and contrary to feeling.—Similar, because it does not reason,—contrary, because it is false: so that it is difficult to distinguish between these contrarieties. One man says that my feeling is a mere fancy, and that his fancy is a real feeling; and I say the same of him. We need then a criterion: reason offers itself; but it may be biassed to either side, and hence there is no fixed rule.

5. They who judge of a work by rule, are, with respect to those who do not, as those who possess a watch, with respect to those who do not. One says, We have been here now two hours. Another says, It is but three quarters of an hour. I look at my watch, and say to one, You grow weary; and to the other, Time flies fast with you, for it is just an hour and a half; and I smile at those who tell me, that time lingers with me, and that I judge by imagination. They know not that I judge by my watch.

6. There are men who speak well, but who do not write well. The place, the circumstances, &c. excite them, and elicit from their mind, more than they would find in it without that extraordinary stimulus.

7. That which is good in Montaigne, can only be acquired with difficulty: that which is evil, (I except his morals,) might be corrected in a moment, if we consider that he tells too many stories, and speaks too much of himself.

8. It is a serious fault, to follow the exception instead

of the rule. We ought to be rigidly opposed to the exception. Yet since it is certain that there are exceptions to the rule, we should judge rigidly, but justly.

9. There are men who would have an author never speak of the things of which others have spoken; and if he does, they accuse him of saying nothing new. But if the subjects are not new, the disposition of them may be. When we play at tennis, both play with the same ball, but one may play it better than the other. They might just as well accuse us of using old words, as if the same thoughts differently arranged, would not form a different discourse; just as the same words differently arranged would express different thoughts.

10. We are more forcibly persuaded, in general, by the reasons which we ourselves search out, than by those which are the suggestion of the minds of others.

11. The mind makes progress naturally, and the will naturally clings to objects; so that in default of right objects, it will attach itself to wrong ones.

12. Those great efforts of mind to which the soul occasionally reaches, are such as it cannot habitually maintain. It reaches them by a sudden bound, but only to fall again.

13. Man is neither an angel nor a brute; and the mischief is, they who would play the angel, often play the brute.

14. Only discover a man's ruling passion, and you are

sure of pleasing him; and yet each one has in the very notion that he has formed of good, some phantasies which are opposed to his real interest; and this is a strange incongruity, which often disconcerts those who would gain his affection.

15. A horse does not seek to be admired by its companion. There is, to be sure, a sort of emulation in the course, but this leads to nothing; for in the stable, the clumsiest and worst made, will not on that account give up his corn to the others. It is not so among men. Their virtue is not satisfied with itself; and they are not satisfied, unless they obtain by it some advantage over others.

16. We injure the mind and the moral sentiments in the same way. The mind and the moral sentiments are formed by conversation. The good or the evil improve or injure them respectively. It is of importance then, to know how to choose well, so as to benefit, and not injure them. But we are unable to make this choice, unless the mind is already formed, and not injured. There, then, is a circle, from which happy are they who escape!

17. When among those things in nature, the knowledge of which is not absolutely necessary, there are some, the truth of which we do not know, it is perhaps not to be lamented, that frequently one common error obtains, which fixes most minds. As for example, the moon, to which we attribute the change of weather, and the fluctuations of disease, &c. For one of man's greatest evils is a restless curiosity after the things which he cannot know; and I know not whether it is not a less evil to be in error on such subjects, than to be indulging an idle curiosity.

18. If the lightning had fallen upon low places, the poets and other men who reason only from such analogies, would have failed of their best proofs.

19. Mind has its own order of proceeding, which is by principles and demonstrations: the heart has another. We do not prove that we ought to be loved, by setting forth systematically the causes of love; that would be ridiculous.

Jesus Christ and St Paul have rather followed this way of the heart, which is the way of charity, than that of the intellect; for their chief end was not merely to instruct, but to animate and warm. St Augustine does the same. This mode consists chiefly in a digression to each several point, which has a relation to the end, so as to aim at that end always.

20. There are men who put an artificial covering on all nature. There is no king with them, but an august monarch: no Paris, but the capital of the empire. There are places where we must call Paris, Paris; and others where we must call it, the capital of the empire.

21. When in a composition we find a word occurring more than once, and on an attempt to alter it, it is found so suitable that a change would weaken the sense; it should be left. To remove it, is the work of a blind envy, which cannot discern that this repetition is not, in this case, a fault; for there is no absolute general rule.

22. Those who make antitheses by forcing the sense, are like men who make false windows for the sake of symmetry. Their rule is not to speak justly, but to make accurate figures.

23. One language is with respect to another a cypher, in which words stand for words, and not letters for letters; and hence an unknown language cannot be decyphered.

24. There is a standard of taste and beauty which consists in a certain accordant relation between our nature—it may be weak or strong, but such as it is,—and the thing that pleases us. All that is formed by this standard delights us: houses, songs, writings, verse, prose, women, birds, rivers, trees, rooms, and dresses. All that is not formed by this standard, disgusts a man of good taste.

25. As we say, poetic beauty, so also we should say geometrical beauty, and medicinal beauty. Yet we do not say so, and the reason of this is, that we know distinctly the object of geometry, and the object of medicine; but we do not know so precisely in what consists that delight, which is the object of poetry. We do not rightly know what is that natural model which we ought to imitate; and, for want of this knowledge, we invent extravagant terms, as, *golden age, paragon of our days, fatal laurel, bright star, &c.* and we call this jargon poetical beauty. But he who should imagine to himself a lady dressed by such a model, would see a beautiful woman covered with mirrors and chains of brass, and could not refrain from laughing; because we understand better that which pleases in a woman, than that which pleases in poetry. But those who are not skilled in these matters, might admire her in this dress; and there are plenty of villages where they would take her for the queen; and hence there are some who call sonnets, made after such a model, *village queens.*

26. When a discourse paints a passion or an effect naturally, we find in ourselves the truth of what we hear,—and which was there without our knowing it;—and we feel induced to love him who causes us to discover it, for he does not shew us his good, but our own; and hence, this benefit conferred, makes us love him. Besides, that this community of intellectual enjoyment that we have with him, necessarily inclines the heart to love him.

27. There should be in eloquence that which is pleasing, and that which is real; but that which is pleasing, should itself be real.

28. When we meet with the natural style, we are surprized and delighted, for we expected to find an author, and we have found a man. Whilst those of good taste who look into a book, in the hope of finding a man, are altogether surprized to find an author: *plus poetice quam humane locutus est*. They confer the greatest honour on nature, who teach her that she can speak best on all subjects, even theology.

29. The last thing that we discover in writing a book, is to know what to put at the beginning.

30. In a discourse, it is wrong to divert the mind from one thing to another, except to prevent weariness; and that only in the time when it is really suitable, and not otherwise; for he who wishes to amuse inappropriately wearies,—men will turn away their attention altogether. So difficult is it to obtain any thing from man, but by pleasure,—the current coin for which we are willing to give every thing.

31. What a vanity is painting which attracts admiration, by the resemblances of things, that in the original, we do not at all admire!

32. The same sense is materially affected by the words that convey it. The sense receives its dignity from the words, instead of imparting it to them.

33. Those who are accustomed to judge by feeling, understand but little in matters of reasoning; for they, at once, penetrate the subject with one view, and are not accustomed to search for principles. Others, on the contrary, who are accustomed to reason from principles, comprehend little in matters of feeling; searching for principles, and not being able to discover them.

34. True eloquence despises eloquence. True morality despises morality; that is to say, the morality of the understanding, sets light by the morality of the fancy, which knows no rule.

35. All the false beauties that we condemn in Cicero, have their admirers in crowds.

36. To set light by philosophy, is the true philosophy.

37. Many persons understand a sermon, as they understand vespers.

38. Rivers are roads which move forward, and carry us to our destination.

39. Two faces which resemble each other, neither of

which is ludicrous alone, excite a smile from their resemblance, when seen together.

40. Astrologers and Alchymists have some sound principles, but they abuse them. Now, the abuse of truth ought to be as much punished as the invention of falsehood.

41. I cannot forgive Descartes. He would willingly, in all his philosophy, have done without God if he could; but he could not get on without letting him give the world a filip to set it a going; after that, he has nothing more to do with him.

CHAPTER XXIX.

ON EPICTETUS AND MONTAIGNE.

EPICTETUS is one of those philosophers of this world, who have best known the duties of man. He would have him before all things, to regard God as his chief object, to be persuaded that he governs all things with justice, to submit to him cordially, and to follow him willingly as infinitely wise, and he affirms that this disposition would stay all his complaints and miseries, and prepare him to endure patiently the most distressing events.

Never say, he enjoins, " I have lost that." Say rather, " I have restored it. My son is dead; I have surrendered him. My wife is dead; I have given her up." And so of every other good. " But he who deprived me of this good, is a wicked man." Why distress yourself about him, by whom He who lent the blessing, sent to seek it again? While the use of it is permitted to you, regard it as a good belonging to others, as a traveller does in an inn." " You should not wish," he continues, " that things should be as you desire, but you should wish that they may be as they are. Remember that you are here as an actor, and that you play that part which your master is pleased to appoint. If he gives you a short part, play short; if a long part, play long; remain on the stage as long as he pleases; appear on it rich or poor, according to his command. It is your duty to play well the part assigned; but to choose it, is the part of God. Set always before your eyes death and the evils which seem least bearable, and you would never think slightingly of any thing, nor desire any thing excessively." He shews, in many ways what man should do. He wishes him to be humble, to hide his good resolutions, especially in their commencement, and to fulfil them secretly, for that nothing so much injures them as exposure. He never wearies of repeating that all the study and the desire of men should be, to know and to do the will of God.

Such was the light of this great mind, who so well understood the duties of man; happy if he had as well known his weakness. But, after having so well understood what man ought to do, he loses himself in the presumption of that for which he thinks him equal. "God," he says, "has given to every man the means of acquitting himself of all his obligations; these means are always in his power. We should only seek happiness by the means that are in our power. Since God has given them for that end, we ought to ascertain what is our liberty. Wealth, life, respect, are not in our power, and do not lead to God; but the mind cannot be forced to believe that which it knows to be false; nor the will to love that which it knows will make it miserable. These two powers then are perfectly free; and by these only can we make ourselves perfect,—know God perfectly, love him, obey him, please him, vanquish all vices, attain all virtues, and thus, make ourselves the holy companions of God."

These proud notions lead Epictetus to other errors, such as, that the soul is a portion of the Divine essence; that pain and death are not evils; that we may kill ourselves when we are oppressed; that we may believe that God calls us, &c.

2. Montaigne, born in a Christian land, made a profession of the Roman Catholic religion; and so far there was nothing peculiar about him. But as he wished to seek a system of morals, founded on reason, independently of the illuminations of faith, he laid down his principles according to this supposition, and considered man as entirely destitute of a revelation. He places all things, therefore, in a state of doubt so general and universal, that man doubts even that he doubts; and this uncertainty returns restlessly upon itself in a circle perpetually, opposing equally those who affirm that every thing is uncertain, and those who affirm that nothing is; for he does not wish to give certainty in any thing. In this doubt which doubts itself, and in this ignorance which is ignorant of itself, consists the essence of his opinions. He cannot express it in positive terms; for, if he says, he doubts, he betrays himself by making it certain that he doubts; which being in form contrary to his intention, he is reduced to the necessity of explaining himself by a question; so that not wishing to say, I do not know; he asks, What do I know? And on this idea he

has framed his device, in which he has written this motto, "*Que sais je*," under the scales of a balance, each containing a contradictory proposition, and consequently, hanging in equilibrium. In fact, he is a pure Pyrrhonist. All his discourses, all his essays, proceed on this principle; and it is the only thing which he professes thoroughly to establish. He insensibly destroys all that passes for certain among men; not to establish the contrary with certainty; for to certainty he is chiefly hostile; but merely to make it appear that the evidence being equal on both sides, it is impossible to know where our confidence should be reposed.

In this spirit he derides every thing like assurance. He combats, for instance, those who have thought to establish a grand remedy against legal processes by the multitude and the professed justice of the laws, as if it were possible to annihilate the region of doubt in which litigation originates; as if we could throw a dam across the torrent of uncertainty, and restrain conjecture. He says, on this matter, that he would as soon commit his cause to the first passer by, as to the judges armed with law and precedent. He does not aim to change the order of the state; he does not pretend that his advice is better; he considers none good. He aims only to shew the vanity of the best received opinions, shewing that the annulling of all laws would sooner diminish the number of differences, than the multitude of laws which serve only to augment them; because the difficulties increase the more they are considered; the obscurities are multiplied by multiplied comments; and the surest way of understanding the sense of the passage is, not to examine it, but to determine on it at the first glance; for that the instant you look into it, all its clearness disappears. On this plan he judges at hap-hazard all human actions and historical facts, sometimes after one manner, sometimes after another, following freely the first impression, without controlling his thoughts by the rules of reason, which, according to him, are all false guides. Delighted with shewing, in his own example, the contrarieties of the same mind in this illimitable field, it is the same to him whether he grows warm or not in a dispute, having always the means by one example or another, of shewing the weakness of any opinion whatever; being so far elevated by the system of universal doubt, he strengthens himself equally by his triumph or his defeat.

It is from this position, fluctuating and variable as it is, that he combats with invincible firmness the heretics of his time, on the ground that they assumed to themselves the exclusive knowledge of the true sense of Scripture; and from thence also he thunders against the horrible impiety of those who dare to say, that there is no God. He attacks them, especially in the apology of Raimond de Sebonde, and finding them entirely stripped of the support of a revelation, and abandoned to their natural light, independent of faith, he demands of them on what authority they pretend to judge of this Sovereign Being, whose specific definition is Infinity—they who do not thoroughly know the smallest thing in nature. He asks them on what principles they rest, and presses them to disclose them. He examines all that they can produce; and he goes so deeply by that talent, in which he peculiarly excels, that he shews the vanity of those principles which pass for the clearest and the most established. He inquires if the soul knows any thing; if it knows itself; if it is a substance or an accident, body or spirit; what each of these things is, and if there are not some things which belong not to either of these orders; if the soul knows its own body; if it knows what matter is; how it can reason if it is matter, and how it can be united to a material frame, and feel its passions, if it is purely immaterial? When did its existence commence; with or before the body? Will it terminate with it or not? Does it never deceive itself? Does it know when it is in error? seeing that the very essence of error is not being aware of it. He asks also, If brutes reason, think, or speak? Who can say what is time or space; extension, motion, or unity; all being things by which we are surrounded, but utterly inexplicable? What are health, sickness, death, life, good or evil, justice or transgression: things of which we speak continually? If we have within us the principles of truth, and if those that we believe to be such, and that we call *axioms*, or *notions common to all men*, are really conformed to essential truth? Since we cannot know but by the light of faith, that an infinitely Good Being has really given us these principles, and formed us so as to comprehend truth: who could know without the light of faith, whether we may not be formed by accident; and that consequently, all our notions are uncertain; or, whether we may not be created by a false and wicked being, who has given us these false principles expressly to lead us astray? And thus, he shews that God and the truth are inseparable, and that if one is or is not, if one is certain or uncertain, the other is necessarily the same. Who knows that common sense which we generally regard as the judge of truth, has been appointed to this office by Him who made it? Who knows what is truth? and how can we be sure of possessing it without knowing it? Who knows, in fact, what *being* is, since it is impossible so to define it, but that there must be something more general; and since it requires, even in the explanation of it, to use the very idea of *Being*, saying it is such or such a thing? Since we know not what the soul, the body, time, space, motion, truth, and good are, and even what being is, nor how to explain the idea that we have formed of them; how can we know that the idea is the same in all men? We have no other mark than the uniformity of results, which is not always a sign of uniformity of principles; for they may be very different, and yet lead to the same conclusions; every one knowing that truth may be concluded from falsehood.

Then Montaigne examines very deeply the sciences:— Geometry, the uncertainty of which he points out in its axioms, and in its terms which it does not define, as *extension, motion, &c.*; physics and medicine, which he depresses in a variety of ways; history, politics, morals, jurisprudence, &c. So that, without revelation, we might believe according to him, that life is a dream, from which we do not wake till death, and during which, we have as few principles of truth as in natural sleep. In this way he attacks so fiercely and so cruelly reason when unaided by faith, that causing it to doubt whether it is rational or not, and whether the brutes are so or not, or more or less so than men, he brings it down from the excellence that is attributed to it, and places it as a matter of favour on a level with the brutes, without permitting it to rise above that level, till it shall be instructed by its Creator, as to that real rank which belongs to it, and of which it is ignorant; threatening, if it rebels, to place it beneath every thing else, which appears, at least, as easy as the reverse; and not allowing it power to act, except to recognize, with real humility, its feebleness, instead of elevating itself by a false and foolish vanity. We cannot behold but with joy, that in this writer, haughty reason has been so completely battered by its own weapons,—to see this deadly struggle between man and man, which, from the association with God, to which he had raised himself by the maxims of feeble reason, hurls him headlong to the level of the brutes: and we would cordially love the minister of this mighty vengeance, if, as an humble, believing disciple of the church, he had followed the rules of its morality, and taught man whom he had so beneficially humbled, no longer to irritate, by fresh crimes, Him who alone could redeem him from those already committed, and which evils God had already convinced him that man had not the power to discover. But, on the contrary, he acts like a heathen. Look at his moral system.

From this principle, that independent of faith, all is uncertainty; and from the consideration, how large a portion of time has been spent in seeking the true good, without any progress towards tranquillity; he concludes, that we should leave this care to others; resting, in the meantime, in a state of repose, and touching lightly on these subjects, lest we sink by pressure; that we should admit truth and the true good upon the first glance, without examining too closely, because they are so far from solid, that however little we grasp the hand, they escape between our fingers, and leave it empty. He follows, then, the report of the senses, and the prevailing notions, because to deny them, would be to do violence to himself, and he knows not in his ignorance of truth, if he would be the gainer by it. He avoids also pain and death, because his instinct shuns them, and yet for the same reason as before, he would not resist them. But he *does not* trust himself too much to these emotions of fear, and does not venture to conclude that pain and death are real evils; since we discover also emotions of pleasure which we condemn as evil, though nature affirms the contrary. "So that," says he, "I have nothing extravagant in my conduct. I do as others do: and all that they do under the foolish notion that they are seeking the true good, I do from another principle, which is that the probabilities on both sides being equal, example and my own convenience lead me." He adopts the manners of his country, because custom leads him; he mounts his horse and rides, because the horse allows it, but without regarding it as a matter of right; on the contrary, he does not know but that the horse has a right to ride him. He even does violence to himself, in order to avoid certain vices; he preserves matrimonial fidelity, on account of the annoyance resulting from irregularities, the real object of all his actions being convenience and tranquillity. He utterly rejects that stoical virtue, which is delineated with a sour countenance, and a frowning brow, with hair dishevelled, and her forehead wrinkled with care, and sitting in a painful attitude, in solitude and in silence on the top of a rock, an object fit only, as he says, to frighten youth, and doing nothing but seeking with unremitted toil for rest, where rest can never come; whilst, on the other hand, virtue, according to his notion, is ingenuous, open, pleasant, gay, and even sportive; she follows that which pleases her, and negligently trifles with the events of life, whether good or bad; she nestles luxuriously in the bosom of a quiet indolence, from whence she teaches those who seek so restlessly after happiness, that it is to be found no where but in the shrine where she reposes; and that, as he says, ignorance and indifference are the downy pillows for a well-made head.

3. On reading Montaigne, and comparing him with Epictetus, we cannot dissemble a conviction, that they were the two greatest defenders of the two most celebrated sects of the unbelieving world, and that they are the only persons among the varieties of men destitute of the light of true religion, who are in any degree rational and consistent. In fact, without revelation, what could we do but follow one or other of these systems? The first system is, There is a God, then he has created man; he has created him for himself; he has made him such as he ought to be, to be just, and to become happy. Then man may attain to the knowledge of truth; and it is within his range to elevate himself by wisdom, even to God himself who is the sovereign good. The other system is, Man cannot elevate himself to God; his native tendencies are contrary to God's law; his tendency is to seek happiness in visible things, and even in those which are most disgraceful. Every thing then appears uncertain, even the true good itself; and we are reduced to such a state, that we appear to have neither a fixed rule for morals, nor certainty in matters of science.

There is much pleasure in observing in these different lines of reasoning, in what respects men on either side have discovered any traces of that truth which they have endeavoured to seek. For if it is pleasant to observe in nature, the effort to shew forth God in the works of his hands, where some marks of him are seen, because those works are his image; how much more justifiable are the efforts of the human mind to arrive at truth, and the endeavour to ascertain in what respects they attain to it, and in what they go astray. This is the chief benefit to be derived from reading Montaigne's writings.

It would seem that the source of error in Epictetus,

and the Stoics on one side, and of Montaigne and the Epicureans on the other, is the not having known that the present state of man differs from that state in which he was created. The former, observing in man some remnant traces of his former greatness, and ignorant of his corruption, have treated human nature as in a healthy state, and without need of reparation—an error which has led to the most unbounded pride. The latter, sensible of man's present misery, and ignorant of his former dignity, have treated our nature as if it were necessarily impure and incurable, and have thus been led to despair of ever attaining the true good, and have sunk from thence to the lowest moral degradation. These two states, which ought to be taken cognizance of together, in order to ascertain the whole truth, being looked at separately, have led necessarily to one or other of these vices, either pride or immorality, in one of which, all unconverted men are infallibly plunged; since either from the power of corruption, they do not avoid irregular indulgence, or if they escape, it is only through pride; so that they are always in one way or other, the slaves of the spirit of wickedness, to whom, as St Augustin says, sacrifice is offered in many different ways.

And hence it follows, as the result of this imperfect light, that one class of men, knowing their powerlessness, and not their duty, sink down in sin; the other, knowing their duty, but not their weakness, lift themselves up with pride. One might suppose, that, by uniting these two classes, a perfect system of morals might be produced; but instead of peace, nothing would result from the meeting but conflict and destruction: for, since the one aimed to establish certainty, and the other universal doubt; the one, the dignity of man, and the other his weakness, they cannot possibly be reconciled; they cannot subsist alone because of their defects; nor together, because of the contrariety of their opinions.

4. But it was needful that they should come into collision, and destroy each other, in order to give place to the truth of revelation, which alone can harmonize by a principle truly Divine, such manifest contrarieties. Uniting all that is true, and setting aside all that is false, she indicates by a wisdom evidently "from above," that point at which those opposing principles unite, which, as stated in doctrines merely human, appear perfectly incompatible with each other. And here is the reason of it. The wise men of this world have placed these contrarieties in the same subject; the one side attributing strength to human nature; the other, weakness to this same nature; which things cannot be true together. Faith, however, teaches us to regard these two qualities as residing in different subjects, all the infirmity belonging to man, and all his might to divine assistance. There is the novel and surprising union which God only could teach us,—which God only could accomplish, and which is only an image and an effect of the ineffable union of the two natures in the one person of the God-man Mediator. In this way philosophy leads insensibly to theology. In fact it is difficult not to enter upon it whenever we treat of truth, because it is the centre of all truth, a fact which appears here unquestionably, because it so evidently unites in itself whatever there is of truth in these contrary opinions. Moreover, we can see no reason why either party should refuse to follow it. If they are filled with notions of human greatness, what is there in all that they have imagined, that does not yield to the gospel promises, which

are a purchase worthy of the inestimable price of the death of the Son of God. And if they take delight in the infirmity of human nature, no notion of theirs can equal that of the real weakness induced by sin, of which that same death is the remedy. Each party finds in the gospel, more even than it has wished; and what is wonderful, they find there the means of solid union—even they who could not of themselves approximate in an infinitely lower degree.

5. Christians in general have little need of these philosophical lectures. Yet Epictetus has an admirable talent for disturbing those who seek for repose in external things, and for compelling them to discover that they are really slaves and miserably blind, and that it is impossible to escape the error and the distress from which they endeavour to fly, unless they give themselves up unreservedly to God. Montaigne is equally successful in confounding the pride of those, who, without the aid of faith, boast themselves of a real righteousness; in correcting those who value their own opinion, and who believe that, independently of the existence and perfections of God, they shall find in the sciences infrangible truth. He exhibits to reason so convincingly the poverty of its light, and the multitude of its errors, that it is difficult afterwards to feel even the temptation to reject the mysteries of religion, on the ground that they may be contradicted; for the spirit is so humbled, that it does not even presume to judge if mysteries are possible, a point which ordinary men debate too readily. But Epictetus, in his reprehension of indifference, leads to pride, and may be most injurious to those who are not convinced of the corruption of all righteousness, but that

which is of faith. Montaigne, on the other hand, is positively evil in his influence on those whose bias is to impiety and vice. And hence, these authors should be read with great care and discretion, and with peculiar regard to the condition and morals of those who look into them. It seems, however, that the union of them can only have a beneficial influence, as the evil of the one corrects the evil of the other. It is true that they do not impart virtue, but they disturb men in their vices. For man finds himself assailed by contrarieties, one of which attacks his pride, and the other his carelessness, and ascertains that all his reason will not enable him either to obtain peace in the indulgence of his vices, or altogether to avoid them.

CHAPTER XXX.

ON THE CONDITION OF THE GREAT.

A MAN was thrown by a tempest on an unknown island, the inhabitants of which, were seeking their king, whom they had lost; and as he had accidentally some resemblance to him, both in face and figure, he was mistaken for him, and recognized as such by all the people. At first he knew not how to act; but he resolved, at length, to yield to his good fortune. He received, therefore, all the respect with which they honoured him, and allowed himself to be treated as their king.

But since he could not altogether forget his former condition, he thought even while he received their homage, that he was not the king whom this people sought, and that the kingdom did not really belong to him. His thoughts, consequently, were two-fold. One by which he played the king; the other which recognized his true condition, and that chance only had placed him in this extraordinary position. He hides this last thought, whilst he discloses the other. According to the former, he deals with the people; according to the latter, he deals with himself.

Think not, that by a less extraordinary chance, you possess your wealth, than that by which this man became a king. You have not in yourself any personal or natural right, more than he; and not only does your being the son of a duke, but your being in the world at all, depend upon a variety of contingencies. Your birth depended on a marriage, or rather on all the marriages of a long line of ancestry. But on what did these marriages depend? on an accidental meeting! on a morning's conversation! on a thousand unforeseen occurrences!

You hold, say you, your riches from your forefathers; but was it not the result of a thousand contingencies, that your forefathers acquired or preserved them? A thousand others as clever as they, have not been able to acquire wealth, or have lost it when they had. You conceive, that by some natural channel, this wealth descended from your ancestry to you: No such thing. This order is founded solely on the will of those who made the laws, and who might have had divers good reasons for so framing them; but none of which, most assuredly, was formed in the notion of your natural right in those possessions. If they had chosen to ordain, that this wealth, after having been possessed by the father during his life, should return at his death to the public treasury, you would have had no reason to complain.

Thus then, the whole title by which you possess your property, is not a title founded in nature, but in human appointment. Another train of thought in those who made the laws, would have made you poor; and it is only this favourable contingency, by which you are born in accordance with the whim of law, which has put you in possession of your present wealth.

I do not mean to say that your goods are not yours legitimately, and that others are at liberty to rob you of them; for God, our great master, has given to society the right of making laws for the division of property; and when these laws are once established, it is unjust to violate them. And here there is a slight distinction between you and the man of whom we have spoken, whose only right to the kingdom, was founded in an error of the people; for God would not sanction his possession, and, in fact, requires him to renounce it, whilst he authorizes yours. But the point in which the two cases completely coincide is this, that neither your right nor his is founded in any quality or merit whatever in you, or which renders you deserving of it. Your soul and your body are of themselves no more allied to the state of a duke, than to that of a labourer; there is no natural tie which binds you to the one condition, rather than to the other.

Then what follows from this? that you ought to have, as this man of whom we have spoken, a two-fold habit of thought; and that, if you act outwardly towards men, according to your rank in life, it becomes you, at the same time, to cherish a sentiment more concealed, but more true, that you are in no respect naturally above them; and if the more ostensible thought elevates you above men in general, this secret conviction should lower you, and reduce you to a perfect equality with all men; for *this* is your natural condition.

The people who admire you, are perhaps not aware of this secret. They believe that nobility is a real natural superiority; and they regard the great, as being of a different nature from others. You are not required to correct this error, if you do not wish it; but see that you do not insolently misuse this elevation, and, above all, do not mistake yourself, and imagine that there is in your nature something more elevated than in that of others.

What would you say of him who had been made king, through the mistake of the people, if he so far forgot his original condition, as to imagine that this kingdom was properly his, that he deserved it, and that it belonged to him as a matter of right. You would wonder at his folly. But is there less folly in men of rank, who live in such strange forgetfulness of their native condition?

How important is this advice! For all the arrogance, violence, and impatience of the great, springs but from this ignorance of what they really are. For it would be difficult for those who inwardly consider themselves on a level with all men, and who are thoroughly convinced that there is in them nothing that merits the little advantages which God has given them above others, to treat their fellow-creatures with insolence. To do this, they must forget themselves, and believe that there is in them some essential superiority to others. And in this consists the delusion which I am anxious to expose to you.

2. It is desirable that you should know what is really due to you, that you may not attempt to require of men that which is not your due, for that were a manifest injustice; and yet to act thus, is very common in men of your condition, because they are not aware of their real merit.

There is in the world two sorts of greatness; there is a greatness founded in nature, and a greatness founded in appointment. That which is constituted great, depends on the will of men, who have believed with reason, that they ought to honour certain situations in life, and pay them certain respects. Of this kind are titles and nobility. In one country, the nobles are reverenced; in another, the labourers. In this, the elder son; in that, the younger. Why is this? Because men would have it so. It was a matter of indifference before it was so constituted; since then, it has become a matter of right, for it is unjust to interfere with it.

Natural greatness is that which is independent of the caprices of men, because it consists in real and effective qualities of body and mind, which render the one or the other more estimable, as science, intellect, energy, virtue, health, or strength.

We owe a duty to each of these kinds of greatness; but as they differ in nature, we owe them also a very different kind of respect. To constituted greatness, we owe the appointed reverence; that is, certain outward ceremonies, which ought to be, at the same time, accompanied as we have shewn, with an internal recognition of the propriety of this arrangement; but which does not force upon us the idea of any real quality of greatness in those whom we so honour. We speak on our bended knee to kings. We must stand in the saloons of princes. It is folly and narrow-mindedness to refuse these observances.

But natural respect, which consists in esteem, we only owe to natural greatness; and we owe contempt and aversion to the opposite qualities to this greatness. It is not necessary that I should esteem you, because you are a duke; but it is that I bow to you. If you are both a duke and a virtuous man, then I will yield the reverence which I owe to both these qualities. I will not refuse you the obeisance which your ducal dignity demands; nor the esteem that your virtue merits. But if you were a duke without virtue, I would then also do you justice; for while I paid that outward respect which the laws of society have attached to your rank, I would not fail to cherish towards you that inward contempt, which your meanness of soul deserved.

This is the line that justice prescribes to such duties, and injustice consists in paying natural respect to artificial greatness, or in requiring external reverence to natural greatness. Mr. N. is a greater geometer than I, and, on this account, he would take precedence of me. I would tell him that he does not comprehend this matter rightly. Geometry is a natural superiority—it asks the preference of esteem; but men have not appointed to it any outward acknowledgment. I take precedence of him therefore; while, at the same time, I esteem him more than myself, for his geometrical talent.

In the same way, if as a duke, and a peer of the realm, you are not satisfied that I stand uncovered before you, and you require me to esteem you also, then I must beg you to shew me those qualities which deserve it. If you do this, then you gain your point, and I cannot refuse you with justice; but if you cannot do this, then you are unjust to ask it; and, most assuredly, you would not succeed, even if you were the mightiest potentate on earth.

3. I would have you, then, to know your true condition, for it is the thing, in all the world, of which you

men of rank are the most ignorant. What is it, according to your notion, to be a great lord? It is to have the command of many objects of human gratification, and to be able thus to satisfy the wants and the desires of many. It is the wants and the wishes of men which collect them round you, and render them subservient; without that, they would not look to you exclusively; but they hope, by their attentions and adulation, to obtain from you some part of those good things which they seek, and which they see that you have to bestow.

God is surrounded by people full of the need of charity, who ask of him those blessings of charity that are his to give. Hence He is appropriately called, "The king of charity."

You are in the same way surrounded with a little crowd of people, over whom you reign in your way. These people are full of sensual wants. They ask of you sensual blessings. They then are bound to you by covetousness. You are then properly the king of covetousness. Your dominion may be of small extent; but as to the kind of royalty, you are on a level with the greatest kings of the earth. They are like you, monarchs of animal wants. This it is which invests them with power, namely, the possession of things after which men greedily crave.

But in thus recognizing your real and natural condition, use the means which are consistent with it, and do not pretend to reign by any other way than by that which actually constitutes you a king. It is not your natural energy and power which subjects the people round you. Do not pretend then to rule them by force, nor to treat them harshly. Satisfy their just desires; relieve their wants; find your pleasure in beneficence; help them as much as you can ; and act in your true character as the king of animal necessities.

What I have said to you, does not go far into the subject of duty; and if therefore you rest there, you will not fail to lose yourself, though you will then, at least, sink as a virtuous man should do. There are men who destroy their own souls by avarice, by brutality, by dissipation, by violence, by passion, by blasphemy. The path which I point out to you, is undoubtedly more virtuous than these. But in any way, it is unpardonable folly to lose one's self; and therefore, I say, you must not rest at that point. You should despise sensuality and its dominion, and aspire to that kingdom of charity, where all its subjects breath nothing but charity, and desire no other blessings. Others will direct you better than I can in this way; it will be sufficient for me to have turned you aside from those low and sensualizing ways, along which, I see so many persons of rank hurried, from the want of a due acquaintance with their own real condition.

THE END.

the United States
004B/86